SCHOLASTIC

KID'S ALMANAC

facts, figures, and stats

A GEORGIAN BAY BOOK

Written by
Elaine Pascoe, Deborah Kops, and Jenifer Morse

Illustrated by
Bob Italiano and David C. Bell

SCHOLASTIC REFERENCE

CREATED AND PRODUCED BY GEORGIAN BAY ASSOCIATES, LLC

Georgian Bay Staff
Bruce Glassman, Executive Editor
Calico Harington, Design and Production
Jenifer Corr Morse, Assistant Editor
Kathleen Rocheleau, Indexer

Scholastic Reference Staff
Kenneth Wright, Editorial Director
Mary Varilla Jones, Editor
Elysa L. Jacobs, Assistant Editor
Nancy Sabato, Art Director
Tatiana Sperhacke, Designer

Library of Congress Cataloging-in-Publication Data available.

ISBN 0-439-56078-0

10 9 8 7 6 5 4 3 2 1   04 05 06 07 08
Printed in the U.S.A.
Revised edition, June 2004

CONTENTS

AEROSPACE

Flight Food

Before each space shuttle mission, astronauts taste the available menu items and select which foods to take with them into space. When selecting their meals, astronauts can choose from approximately 100 different food items and 50 beverages. The first astronaut to eat in space was John Glenn in 1962. He squeezed applesauce out of a tube!

Space Sleepers

Sleeping in space can be quite a challenge. Some astronauts prefer to float freely in the space shuttle. Others zip themselves into sleeping bags to stay put. There are even little pillows that strap onto the astronauts' heads!

Super Space Sight

If you could see as well as the wide field and planetary camera on the Hubble Space Telescope, you would be able to read the fine print on a newspaper 1 mile (1.6 km) away!

Give Me a Boost

Astronauts are really "flying" as they cruise around in space. The two solid rocket boosters on the space shuttle generate a combined thrust of 5.3 million pounds (2.4 million kg). That's equivalent to the engine power of 400,000 subcompact cars! At liftoff, these rocket boosters consume 11,000 pounds (4,989 kg) of fuel per second. That's two million times the rate at which fuel is burned by the average family car.

Cost Cutter

The space shuttles are black and white with orange fuel tanks because these are the natural colors of the materials used to manufacture them. Adding paint would mean adding weight to the shuttle, and that would cost more money for fuel.

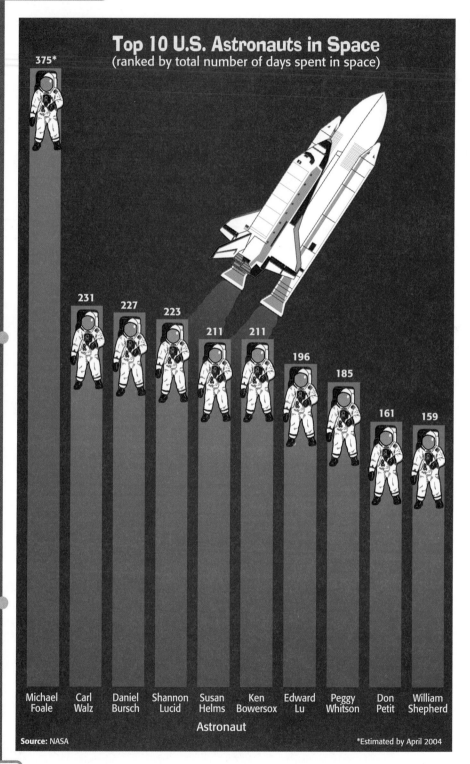

Top 10 U.S. Astronauts in Space
(ranked by total number of days spent in space)

375* Michael Foale
231 Carl Walz
227 Daniel Bursch
223 Shannon Lucid
211 Susan Helms
211 Ken Bowersox
196 Edward Lu
185 Peggy Whitson
161 Don Petit
159 William Shepherd

Astronaut

Source: NASA

*Estimated by April 2004

Scheduled U.S. Shuttle Missions, 2000–2003

	Flight	Orbiter	Launch date
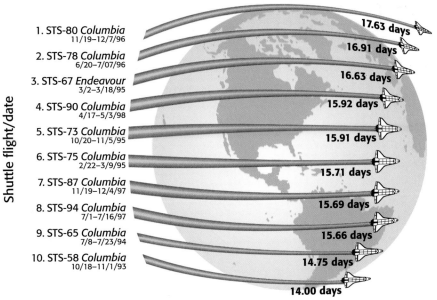	STS-106	*Atlantis*	September 8, 2000
	STS-92	*Discovery*	October 24, 2000
	STS-97	*Endeavour*	December 11, 2000
	STS-98	*Atlantis*	February 7, 2001
	STS-102	*Discovery*	March 8, 2001
	STS-100	*Endeavour*	May 1, 2001
	STS-104	*Atlantis*	July 12, 2001
	STS-105	*Discovery*	August 10, 2001
	STS-108	*Endeavour*	December 5, 2001
	STS-109	*Columbia*	March 1, 2002
	STS-110	*Atlantis*	April 8, 2002
	STS-111	*Endeavour*	June 5, 2002
	STS-112	*Atlantis*	October 7, 2002
	STS-113	*Endeavour*	November 23, 2002
	STS-107	*Columbia*	January 16, 2003
	STS-114	*Atlantis*	TBD*
	STS-115	*Endeavour*	TBD*
	STS-116	*Atlantis*	TBD*
	STS-117	*Endeavour*	TBD*
	STS-118	*TBD*	TBD*
	STS-119	*Atlantis*	TBD*
	STS-120	*Endeavour*	TBD*

Key

- Atlantis
- Discovery
- Columbia*
- Endeavour

*After the loss of the *Columbia* during STS-107, NASA has yet to determine the exact launch dates of future missions.

Source: NASA

Top 10 Longest Space Shuttle Missions

(ranked by number of days in orbit)

Shuttle flight/date

1. STS-80 *Columbia*
   11/19–12/7/96 — **17.63 days**
2. STS-78 *Columbia*
   6/20–7/07/96 — **16.91 days**
3. STS-67 *Endeavour*
   3/2–3/18/95 — **16.63 days**
4. STS-90 *Columbia*
   4/17–5/3/98 — **15.92 days**
5. STS-73 *Columbia*
   10/20–11/5/95 — **15.91 days**
6. STS-75 *Columbia*
   2/22–3/9/95 — **15.71 days**
7. STS-87 *Columbia*
   11/19–12/4/97 — **15.69 days**
8. STS-94 *Columbia*
   7/1–7/16/97 — **15.66 days**
9. STS-65 *Columbia*
   7/8–7/23/94 — **14.75 days**
10. STS-58 *Columbia*
    10/18–11/1/93 — **14.00 days**

Source: NASA

Top 10 Longest Flights Ever Recorded
(ranked by miles [kilometers] traveled in the air)

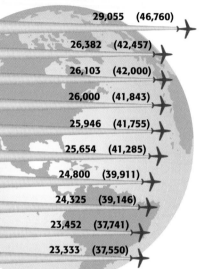

Pilot(s)/craft

1. B. Jones Piccard
Switzerland to Egypt, Mar. 1–21, 1999 — 29,055 (46,760)

2. Boeing 747
San Francisco, CA, to San Francisco, Oct. 28–31, 1977 — 26,382 (42,457)

3. Two U.S. Army airplanes
Seattle, WA, to Seattle, 1924 — 26,103 (42,000)

4. Linda Finch
Oakland, CA, to Oakland, Mar. 17–May 28, 1997 — 26,000 (41,843)

5. Max Conrad (solo)
Miami, FL, to Miami, Feb. 28–Mar. 8, 1961 — 25,946 (41,755)

6. H. R. Ekins
Lakehurst, NJ, to Lakehurst, Oct. 1–19, 1936 — 25,654 (41,285)

7. Trevor K. Bougham
Darwin, Australia, to Darwin, Aug. 5–10, 1972 — 24,800 (39,911)

8. Three U.S. Air Force B-52 Stratofortresses
Merced, CA, to Merced, Jan. 15–18, 1957 — 24,325 (39,146)

9. USAF B-50 *Lucky Lady II*
Fort Worth, TX, to Fort Worth, Mar. 2, 1949 — 23,452 (37,741)

10. A. Godfrey, R. Merrill, F. Austin, K. Keller
New York, NY, to New York, Jun. 4–7, 1966 — 23,333 (37,550)

0   4,000   8,000   12,000   16,000   20,000   24,000   28,000

Miles traveled

Source: Civil Aviation and Aeronautics Association

Top Countries to Put People in Space
(ranked by number of individuals sent into orbit)

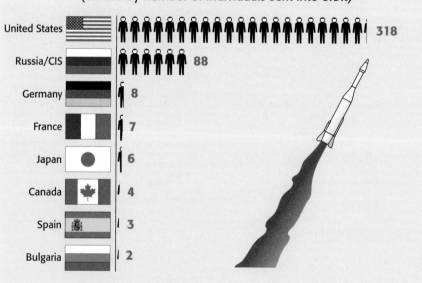

Country	Individuals
United States	318
Russia/CIS	88
Germany	8
France	7
Japan	6
Canada	4
Spain	3
Bulgaria	2

Source: Congressional Research Service

Important U.S. Planetary Missions

Spacecraft	Launch date	Mission	Highlights
Mariner 2	Aug. 27, 1962	Venus	Passed within 22,000 mi. (35,400 km) of Venus 12/14/62; contact lost 1/3/63 at 54 million mi. (87 million km)
Mariner 5	June 14, 1967	Venus	In solar orbit; closest Venus flyby 10/19/67
Mariner 6	Feb. 24, 1969	Mars	Came within 2,000 mi. (3,218 km) of Mars 7/31/69; sent back data, photos
Mariner 7	Mar. 27, 1969	Mars	Came within 2,000 mi. (3,218 km) of Mars 8/5/69
Mariner 9	May 30, 1971	Mars	First craft to orbit Mars 11/13/71; sent back more than 7,000 photos
Mariner 10	Nov. 3, 1973	Venus, Mercury	Passed Venus 2/5/74; arrived Mercury 3/29/74. First time gravity of one planet (Venus) used to whip spacecraft toward another (Mercury)
Viking 1	Aug. 20, 1975	Mars	Landed on Mars 7/20/76; did scientific research, sent photos; functioned $6\frac{1}{2}$ years
Viking 2	Sep. 9, 1975	Mars	Landed on Mars 9/3/76; functioned $3\frac{1}{2}$ years
Voyager 1	Sep. 5, 1977	Jupiter, Saturn	Encountered Jupiter 3/5/79, provided evidence of Jupiter ring; passed near Saturn 11/12/80
Voyager 2	Aug. 20, 1977	Jupiter, Saturn, Uranus, Neptune	Encountered Jupiter 7/9/79; Saturn 8/5/81; Uranus 1/24/86; Neptune 8/25/87
Pioneer Venus 1	May 20, 1978	Venus	Entered Venus orbit 12/4/78; spent 14 years studying planet; ceased operating 10/19/92
Magellan	May 4, 1989	Venus	Orbited and mapped Venus; monitored geological activity on surface; first planetary spacecraft to lower its orbit by using planet's atmosphere (aerobraking) 5/25/93–8/3/93; ceased operating 10/12/94
Titan IV	June 14, 1989	Orbit Earth	First of 41 such rockets whose primary purpose is defense
Galileo	Oct. 18, 1989	Jupiter	Used Earth's gravity to propel it toward Jupiter; encountered Venus Feb. 1991; launched robot to Jupiter 7/13/95
Mars Pathfinder	Dec. 4, 1996	Mars	The rover Sojourner measured planet's climate and soil composition. Sent back thousands of surface photographs
Cassini	Oct. 15, 1997	Saturn	Four-year mission to study planet's atmosphere, rings, and moons
Spirit and Opportunity	Summer 2003	Mars	Twin rovers studied and identified rocks and soil for clues about past water activities
Phoenix	May 2007	Mars	The mission will study the history of water to look for climate change as well as check for any habitable areas on the planet

Source: NASA

Speed of Sound Timeline

(Mach 1 = speed of sound)

1947 Chuck Yeager pilots Bell X-1, first aircraft to fly faster than the speed of sound. Aircraft reached Mach 1.015.

1953 F100 Super Sabre becomes first jet-powered aircraft to exceed the speed of sound in level flight. Aircraft reached Mach 1.17.

1967 The world's fastest aircraft, the X-15, reaches Mach 6.72, powered by rockets.

1976 The spy jet aircraft SR-71 *Blackbird* reaches Mach 3.3, which is the record for jet aircraft.

1969 Powered by four turbojets, the Concorde offers commercial flights at Mach 2.2.

2003 A hypersonic engine capable of Mach 5 is ground tested and cleared for flight tests in 2006.

Source: NASA; Smithsonian Institution/Air and Space Museum

Top 10 Longest Spacewalks

(Ranked by total time walking in hours and minutes)

	Astronauts	NASA mission number	Date	Length
1.	J. Voss, S. Helms	STS-102	Mar 11, 2001	8:56
2.	T. Akers, R. Hieb, P. Thuot	STS-49	May 13, 1992	8:29
3.	J. Grunsfeld, S. Smith	STS-103	Dec 22, 1999	8:15
4.	C. Foale, C. Nicollier	STS-103	Dec 23, 1999	8:10
5.	J. Grunsfeld, S. Smith	STS-103	Dec 24, 1999	8:08
6.	D. Barry, T. Jernigan	STS-96	May 29, 1999	7:55
7.	J. Hoffman, F. Musgrave	STS-61	Dec 4, 1993	7:54
8.	T. Akers, K. Thornton	STS-49	May 14, 1992	7:44
9.	T. Doi, W. Scott	STS-87	Nov 24, 1997	7:43
10.	C. Hadfield, S. Parazynski	STS-100	Apr 24, 2001	7:40

Source: NASA

Flying Firsts Timeline

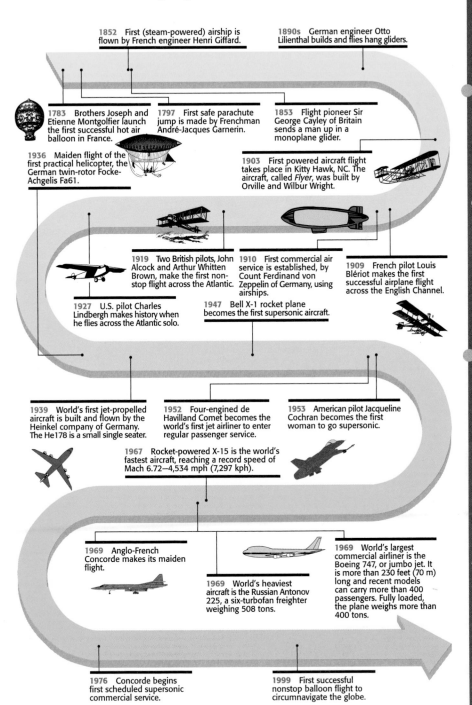

1852 First (steam-powered) airship is flown by French engineer Henri Giffard.

1890s German engineer Otto Lilienthal builds and flies hang gliders.

1783 Brothers Joseph and Etienne Montgolfier launch the first successful hot air balloon in France.

1797 First safe parachute jump is made by Frenchman André-Jacques Garnerin.

1853 Flight pioneer Sir George Cayley of Britain sends a man up in a monoplane glider.

1936 Maiden flight of the first practical helicopter, the German twin-rotor Focke-Achgelis Fa61.

1903 First powered aircraft flight takes place in Kitty Hawk, NC. The aircraft, called *Flyer*, was built by Orville and Wilbur Wright.

1919 Two British pilots, John Alcock and Arthur Whitten Brown, make the first non-stop flight across the Atlantic.

1910 First commercial air service is established, by Count Ferdinand von Zeppelin of Germany, using airships.

1909 French pilot Louis Blériot makes the first successful airplane flight across the English Channel.

1927 U.S. pilot Charles Lindbergh makes history when he flies across the Atlantic solo.

1947 Bell X-1 rocket plane becomes the first supersonic aircraft.

1939 World's first jet-propelled aircraft is built and flown by the Heinkel company of Germany. The He178 is a small single seater.

1952 Four-engined de Havilland Comet becomes the world's first jet airliner to enter regular passenger service.

1953 American pilot Jacqueline Cochran becomes the first woman to go supersonic.

1967 Rocket-powered X-15 is the world's fastest aircraft, reaching a record speed of Mach 6.72—4,534 mph (7,297 kph).

1969 Anglo-French Concorde makes its maiden flight.

1969 World's heaviest aircraft is the Russian Antonov 225, a six-turbofan freighter weighing 508 tons.

1969 World's largest commercial airliner is the Boeing 747, or jumbo jet. It is more than 230 feet (70 m) long and recent models can carry more than 400 passengers. Fully loaded, the plane weighs more than 400 tons.

1976 Concorde begins first scheduled supersonic commercial service.

1999 First successful nonstop balloon flight to circumnavigate the globe.

ANIMALS

A Need to Feed

Some animals have an unsavory food requirement—blood! A leech is a worm that can drink three to four times its own body weight in blood. After one feeding, it will not eat again for a few months. Female mosquitoes also feed on blood. They use the protein from blood to lay eggs.

Say What?

Different animals have interesting ways of communicating with one another. A pair of giraffes may rub their necks together when they like each other. A gorilla may stick out its tongue when it is angry. A chimpanzee might greet another chimpanzee with something similar to a handshake. To show affection, elephants sometimes wrap their trunks together with other members of the herd.

Animals Around the World

Household pets differ from country to country. In China and Hong Kong, cats are thought to bring good luck. The Japanese keep birds and crickets as pets. In Italy, many people also find cats charming and companionable. The Inuit Eskimo of northern Canada adopt bear cubs, foxes, birds, and baby seals. Half of all the households in England have a pet, usually a cat or a bird.

The Pet Population

There are approximately 68 million owned dogs in the United States. Four in ten—or 40 million—U.S. households own at least one dog. There are approximately 73 million owned cats in the United States. Three in ten—or 34.7 million—U.S. households own at least one cat. One-half of cat-owning households (49%) own one cat; the remaining own two or more.

Double Vision

In 1997, Dolly the sheep became the first cloned (or humanly reproduced) animal. Since then, scientists have cloned rhesus monkeys in Oregon, piglets in Virginia, a bull in Japan, an endangered wild sheep in Italy, and a cat in Texas.

Biological Kingdom of Animals

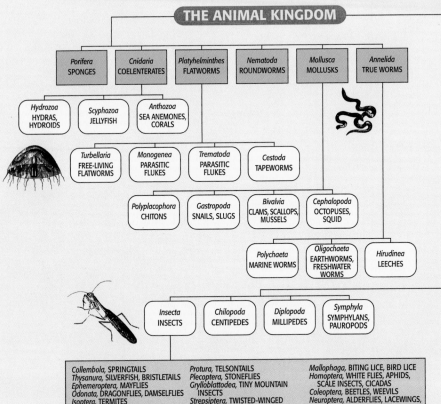

THE ANIMAL KINGDOM

| Porifera SPONGES | Cnidaria COELENTERATES | Platyhelminthes FLATWORMS | Nematoda ROUNDWORMS | Mollusca MOLLUSKS | Annelida TRUE WORMS |

Cnidaria:
- Hydrozoa — HYDRAS, HYDROIDS
- Scyphozoa — JELLYFISH
- Anthozoa — SEA ANEMONES, CORALS

Platyhelminthes:
- Turbellaria — FREE-LIVING FLATWORMS
- Monogenea — PARASITIC FLUKES
- Trematoda — PARASITIC FLUKES
- Cestoda — TAPEWORMS

Mollusca:
- Polyplacophora — CHITONS
- Gastropoda — SNAILS, SLUGS
- Bivalvia — CLAMS, SCALLOPS, MUSSELS
- Cephalopoda — OCTOPUSES, SQUID

Annelida:
- Polychaeta — MARINE WORMS
- Oligochaeta — EARTHWORMS, FRESHWATER WORMS
- Hirudinea — LEECHES

Arthropoda:
- Insecta — INSECTS
- Chilopoda — CENTIPEDES
- Diplopoda — MILLIPEDES
- Symphyla — SYMPHYLANS, PAUROPODS

Insecta

Collembola, SPRINGTAILS
Thysanura, SILVERFISH, BRISTLETAILS
Ephemeroptera, MAYFLIES
Odonata, DRAGONFLIES, DAMSELFLIES
Isoptera, TERMITES
Orthoptera, LOCUSTS, CRICKETS, GRASSHOPPERS
Dictyptera, COCKROACHES, MANTIDS
Dermaptera, EARWIGS
Phasmida, STOCK INSECTS, LEAF INSECTS
Psocoptera, BOOK LICE, BARK LICE
Diplura, SIMPLE INSECTS

Protura, TELSONTAILS
Plecoptera, STONEFLIES
Grylloblattodea, TINY MOUNTAIN INSECTS
Strepsiptera, TWISTED-WINGED STYLOPIDS
Trichoptera, CADDIS FLIES
Embioptera, WEBSPINNERS
Thysanoptera, THRIPS
Mecoptera, SCORPION FLIES
Zoraptera, RARE TROPICAL INSECTS
Hemiptera, TRUE BUGS
Anoplura, SUCKING LICE

Mallophaga, BITING LICE, BIRD LICE
Homoptera, WHITE FLIES, APHIDS, SCALE INSECTS, CICADAS
Coleoptera, BEETLES, WEEVILS
Neuroptera, ALDERFLIES, LACEWINGS, ANT LIONS, SNAKE FLIES, DOBSONFLIES
Hymenoptera, ANTS, BEES, WASPS
Siphonaptera, FLEAS
Diptera, TRUE FLIES, MOSQUITOS, GNATS
Lepidoptera, BUTTERFLIES, MOTHS

Mammalia

Insectivora, INSECTIVORES (e.g., shrews, moles, hedgehogs)
Chiroptera, BATS
Dermoptera, FLYING LEMURS
Edentata, ANTEATERS, SLOTHS, ARMADILLOS
Pholidota, PANGOLINS
Primates, PROSIMIANS (e.g., lemurs, tarsiers, monkeys, apes, humans)
Rodentia, RODENTS (e.g., squirrels,

rats, beavers, mice, porcupines)
Lagomorpha, RABBITS, HARES, PIKAS
Cetacea, WHALES, DOLPHINS, PORPOISES
Carnivora, CARNIVORES (e.g., cats, dogs, weasels, bears, hyenas)
Pinnipedia, SEALS, SEA LIONS, WALRUSES
Tubulidentata, AARDVARKS
Hyracoidea, HYDRAXES

Proboscidea, ELEPHANTS
Sirenia, SEA COWS (e.g., manatees, dugongs)
Perissodactyla, ODD-TOED HOOFED ANIMALS (e.g., horses, rhinoceroses, tapirs)
Artiodactyla, EVEN-TOED HOOFED ANIMALS (e.g., hogs, cattle, camels, hippopotamuses)

Source: University of Michigan, 2002

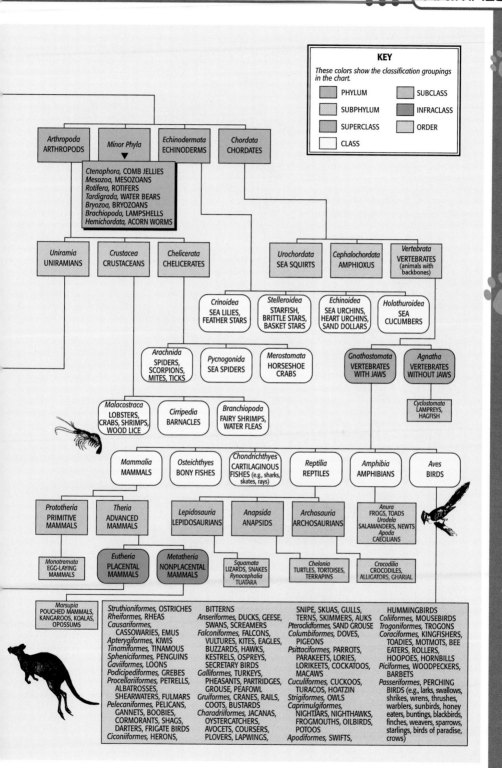

KEY

These colors show the classification groupings in the chart.

- PHYLUM
- SUBPHYLUM
- SUPERCLASS
- CLASS
- SUBCLASS
- INFRACLASS
- ORDER

Arthropoda ARTHROPODS — **Minor Phyla** ▼ — **Echinodermata** ECHINODERMS — **Chordata** CHORDATES

Ctenophora, COMB JELLIES
Mesozoa, MESOZOANS
Rotifera, ROTIFERS
Tardigrada, WATER BEARS
Bryozoa, BRYOZOANS
Brachiopoda, LAMPSHELLS
Hemichordata, ACORN WORMS

Uniramia UNIRAMIANS — **Crustacea** CRUSTACEANS — **Chelicerata** CHELICERATES — **Urochordata** SEA SQUIRTS — **Cephalochordata** AMPHIOXUS — **Vertebrata** VERTEBRATES (animals with backbones)

Crinoidea SEA LILIES, FEATHER STARS — **Stelleroidea** STARFISH, BRITTLE STARS, BASKET STARS — **Echinoidea** SEA URCHINS, HEART URCHINS, SAND DOLLARS — **Holothuroidea** SEA CUCUMBERS

Arachnida SPIDERS, SCORPIONS, MITES, TICKS — **Pycnogonida** SEA SPIDERS — **Merostomata** HORSESHOE CRABS — **Gnathostomata** VERTEBRATES WITH JAWS — **Agnatha** VERTEBRATES WITHOUT JAWS

Malacostraca LOBSTERS, CRABS, SHRIMPS, WOOD LICE — **Cirripedia** BARNACLES — **Branchiopoda** FAIRY SHRIMPS, WATER FLEAS — *Cyclostomata* LAMPREYS, HAGFISH

Mammalia MAMMALS — **Osteichthyes** BONY FISHES — **Chondrichthyes** CARTILAGINOUS FISHES (e.g., sharks, skates, rays) — **Reptilia** REPTILES — **Amphibia** AMPHIBIANS — **Aves** BIRDS

Prototheria PRIMITIVE MAMMALS — **Theria** ADVANCED MAMMALS — **Lepidosauria** LEPIDOSAURIANS — **Anapsida** ANAPSIDS — **Archosauria** ARCHOSAURIANS — *Anura* FROGS, TOADS *Urodela* SALAMANDERS, NEWTS *Apoda* CAECILIANS

Monotremata EGG-LAYING MAMMALS — **Eutheria** PLACENTAL MAMMALS — **Metatheria** NONPLACENTAL MAMMALS — *Squamata* LIZARDS, SNAKES *Rynocephalia* TUATARA — *Chelonia* TURTLES, TORTOISES, TERRAPINS — *Crocodilia* CROCODILES, ALLIGATORS, GHARIAL

Marsupia POUCHED MAMMALS, KANGAROOS, KOALAS, OPOSSUMS

Struthioniformes, OSTRICHES
Rheiformes, RHEAS
Causariformes, CASSOWARIES, EMUS
Apterygiformes, KIWIS
Tinamiformes, TINAMOUS
Sphenisciformes, PENGUINS
Gaviiformes, LOONS
Podicipediformes, GREBES
Procellariiformes, PETRELLS, ALBATROSSES, SHEARWATERS, FULMARS
Pelecaniformes, PELICANS, GANNETS, BOOBIES, CORMORANTS, SHAGS, DARTERS, FRIGATE BIRDS
Ciconiiformes, HERONS,

BITTERNS
Anseriformes, DUCKS, GEESE, SWANS, SCREAMERS
Falconiformes, FALCONS, VULTURES, KITES, EAGLES, BUZZARDS, HAWKS, KESTRELS, OSPREYS, SECRETARY BIRDS
Galliformes, TURKEYS, PHEASANTS, PARTRIDGES, GROUSE, PEAFOWL
Gruiformes, CRANES, RAILS, COOTS, BUSTARDS
Charadriiformes, JACANAS, OYSTERCATCHERS, AVOCETS, COURSERS, PLOVERS, LAPWINGS,

SNIPE, SKUAS, GULLS, TERNS, SKIMMERS, AUKS
Pteroclidiformes, SAND GROUSE
Columbiformes, DOVES, PIGEONS
Psittaciformes, PARROTS, PARAKEETS, LORIES, LORIKEETS, COCKATOOS, MACAWS
Cuculiformes, CUCKOOS, TURACOS, HOATZIN
Strigiformes, OWLS
Caprimulgiformes, NIGHTJARS, NIGHTHAWKS, FROGMOUTHS, OILBIRDS, POTOOS
Apodiformes, SWIFTS,

HUMMINGBIRDS
Coliiformes, MOUSEBIRDS
Trogoniformes, TROGONS
Coraciiformes, KINGFISHERS, TOADIES, MOTMOTS, BEE EATERS, ROLLERS, HOOPOES, HORNBILLS
Piciformes, WOODPECKERS, BARBETS
Passeriformes, PERCHING BIRDS (e.g., larks, swallows, shrikes, wrens, thrushes, warblers, sunbirds, honey eaters, buntings, blackbirds, finches, weavers, sparrows, starlings, birds of paradise, crows)

15

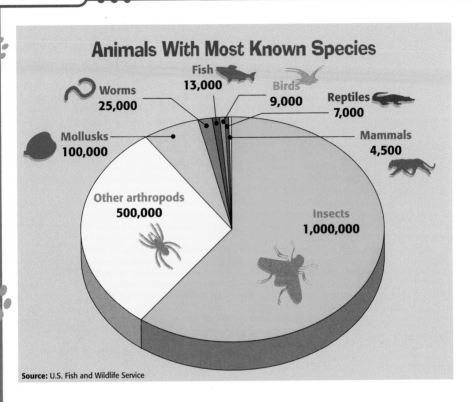

Animals With Most Known Species

Worms
25,000

Fish
13,000

Birds
9,000

Reptiles
7,000

Mollusks
100,000

Mammals
4,500

Other arthropods
500,000

Insects
1,000,000

Source: U.S. Fish and Wildlife Service

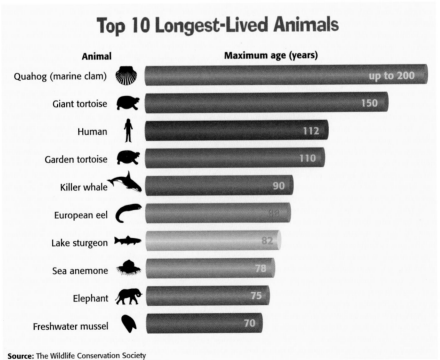

Top 10 Longest-Lived Animals

Animal	Maximum age (years)
Quahog (marine clam)	up to 200
Giant tortoise	150
Human	112
Garden tortoise	110
Killer whale	90
European eel	88
Lake sturgeon	82
Sea anemone	78
Elephant	75
Freshwater mussel	70

Source: The Wildlife Conservation Society

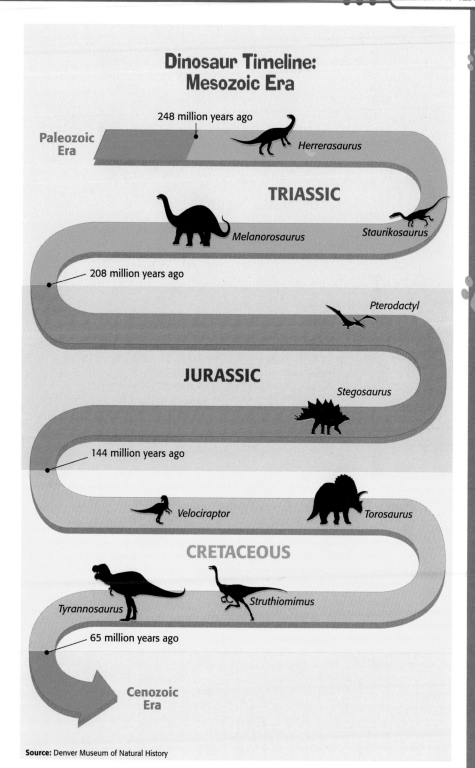

Dinosaur Timeline: Mesozoic Era

Paleozoic Era

248 million years ago

Herrerasaurus

TRIASSIC

Melanorosaurus

Staurikosaurus

208 million years ago

Pterodactyl

JURASSIC

Stegosaurus

144 million years ago

Velociraptor

Torosaurus

CRETACEOUS

Tyrannosaurus

Struthiomimus

65 million years ago

Cenozoic Era

Source: Denver Museum of Natural History

Packs and Prides: Animal Multiples

ants: colony
bears: sleuth, sloth
bees: grist, hive swarm
birds: flight, volery
cattle: drove

cats: clutter, clowder
chicks: brood, clutch
clams: bed
cranes: sedge, seige
crows: murder
doves: dule
ducks: brace, team
elephants: herd
elks: gang

finches: charm
fish: school, shoal,
drought

foxes: leash, skulk
geese: flock, gaggle,
skein
gnats: cloud, horde
goats: trip
gorillas: band

hares: down, husk
hawks: cast
hens: brood
hogs: drift
horses: pair, team
hounds: cry, mute, pack
kangaroos: troop

kittens: kindle, litter
larks: exaltation

lions: pride

locusts: plague
magpies: tidings
mules: span

nightingales: watch
oxen: yoke
oysters: bed
parrots: company
partridges: covey
peacocks: muster,
ostentation
pheasants: nest,
bouquet
pigs: litter

ponies: string
quail: bevy, covey
rabbits: nest
seals: pod
sheep: drove, flock
sparrows: host
storks: mustering

swans: bevy, wedge
swine: sounder
toads: knot
turkeys: rafter

turtles: bale
vipers: nest
whales: gam, pod
wolves: pack, route
woodcocks: fall

Source: The Wildlife Conservation Society

Top 10 Most Common Insects

Approximate number of known species

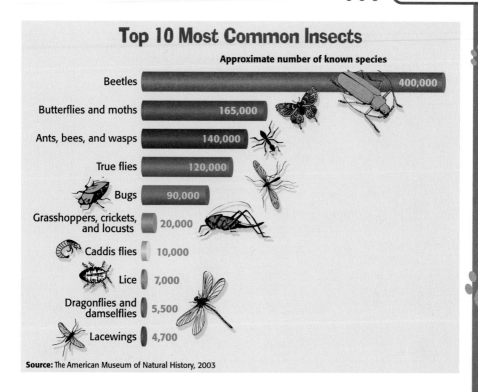

Beetles	400,000
Butterflies and moths	165,000
Ants, bees, and wasps	140,000
True flies	120,000
Bugs	90,000
Grasshoppers, crickets, and locusts	20,000
Caddis flies	10,000
Lice	7,000
Dragonflies and damselflies	5,500
Lacewings	4,700

Source: The American Museum of Natural History, 2003

Most Popular Official State Insects

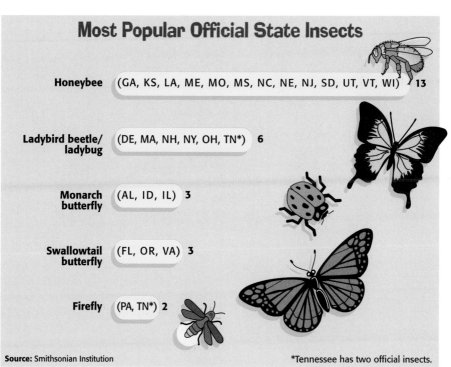

Honeybee	(GA, KS, LA, ME, MO, MS, NC, NE, NJ, SD, UT, VT, WI)	13
Ladybird beetle/ ladybug	(DE, MA, NH, NY, OH, TN*)	6
Monarch butterfly	(AL, ID, IL)	3
Swallowtail butterfly	(FL, OR, VA)	3
Firefly	(PA, TN*)	2

Source: Smithsonian Institution

*Tennessee has two official insects.

Top 10 Heaviest Land Mammals

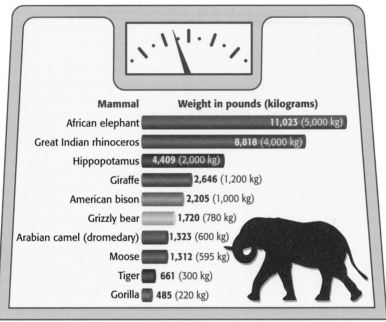

Mammal	Weight in pounds (kilograms)
African elephant	11,023 (5,000 kg)
Great Indian rhinoceros	8,818 (4,000 kg)
Hippopotamus	4,409 (2,000 kg)
Giraffe	2,646 (1,200 kg)
American bison	2,205 (1,000 kg)
Grizzly bear	1,720 (780 kg)
Arabian camel (dromedary)	1,323 (600 kg)
Moose	1,312 (595 kg)
Tiger	661 (300 kg)
Gorilla	485 (220 kg)

Source: The Wildlife Conservation Society

Top 10 Heaviest Marine Mammals

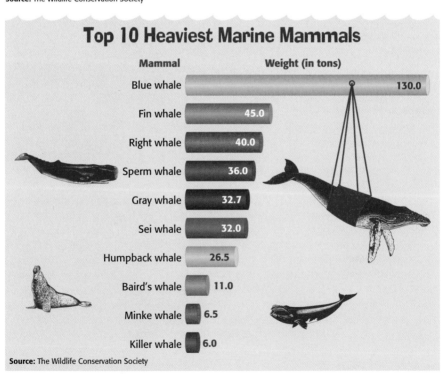

Mammal	Weight (in tons)
Blue whale	130.0
Fin whale	45.0
Right whale	40.0
Sperm whale	36.0
Gray whale	32.7
Sei whale	32.0
Humpback whale	26.5
Baird's whale	11.0
Minke whale	6.5
Killer whale	6.0

Source: The Wildlife Conservation Society

Top 10 Smallest Mammals

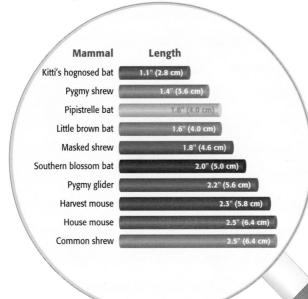

Mammal	Length
Kitti's hognosed bat	1.1" (2.8 cm)
Pygmy shrew	1.4" (3.6 cm)
Pipistrelle bat	1.6" (4.0 cm)
Little brown bat	1.6" (4.0 cm)
Masked shrew	1.8" (4.6 cm)
Southern blossom bat	2.0" (5.0 cm)
Pygmy glider	2.2" (5.6 cm)
Harvest mouse	2.3" (5.8 cm)
House mouse	2.5" (6.4 cm)
Common shrew	2.5" (6.4 cm)

Source: The Wildlife Conservation Society

The World's Fastest Mammals

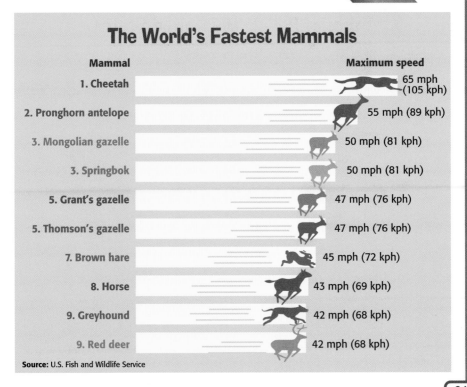

Mammal	Maximum speed
1. Cheetah	65 mph (105 kph)
2. Pronghorn antelope	55 mph (89 kph)
3. Mongolian gazelle	50 mph (81 kph)
3. Springbok	50 mph (81 kph)
5. Grant's gazelle	47 mph (76 kph)
5. Thomson's gazelle	47 mph (76 kph)
7. Brown hare	45 mph (72 kph)
8. Horse	43 mph (69 kph)
9. Greyhound	42 mph (68 kph)
9. Red deer	42 mph (68 kph)

Source: U.S. Fish and Wildlife Service

Names of Male, Female, and Young Animals

Animal	Male ♂	Female ♀	Young
Bear	Boar	Sow	Cub
Cat	Tom	Queen	Kitten
Cattle	Bull	Cow	Calf
Chicken	Rooster	Hen	Chick
Deer	Buck	Doe	Fawn
Dog	Dog	Bitch	Pup
Donkey	Jack	Jenny	Foal
Duck	Drake	Duck	Duckling
Elephant	Bull	Cow	Calf
Fox	Dog	Vixen	Cub
Goose	Gander	Goose	Gosling
Horse	Stallion	Mare	Foal
Lion	Lion	Lioness	Cub
Rabbit	Buck	Doe	Bunny
Sheep	Ram	Ewe	Lamb
Swan	Cob	Pen	Cygnet
Swine	Boar	Sow	Piglet
Tiger	Tiger	Tigress	Cub
Whale	Bull	Cow	Calf
Wolf	Dog	Bitch	Pup

Source: The Wildlife Conservation Society

Types of Pets in the United States

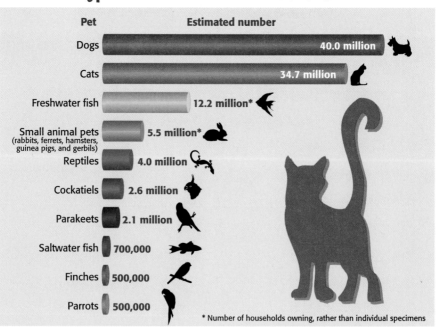

Pet	Estimated number
Dogs	40.0 million
Cats	34.7 million
Freshwater fish	12.2 million*
Small animal pets (rabbits, ferrets, hamsters, guinea pigs, and gerbils)	5.5 million*
Reptiles	4.0 million
Cockatiels	2.6 million
Parakeets	2.1 million
Saltwater fish	700,000
Finches	500,000
Parrots	500,000

* Number of households owning, rather than individual specimens

Source: American Pet Products Manufacturers Assoc., 2002

Top 10 Registered U.S. Dog Breeds

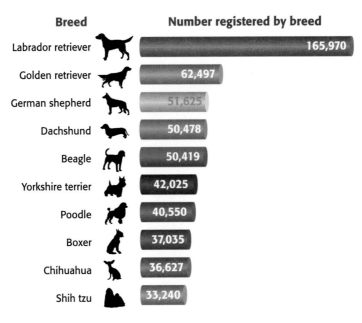

Breed	Number registered by breed
Labrador retriever	165,970
Golden retriever	62,497
German shepherd	51,625
Dachshund	50,478
Beagle	50,419
Yorkshire terrier	42,025
Poodle	40,550
Boxer	37,035
Chihuahua	36,627
Shih tzu	33,240

Source: American Kennel Club, 2001

Top 10 Registered U.S. Cat Breeds

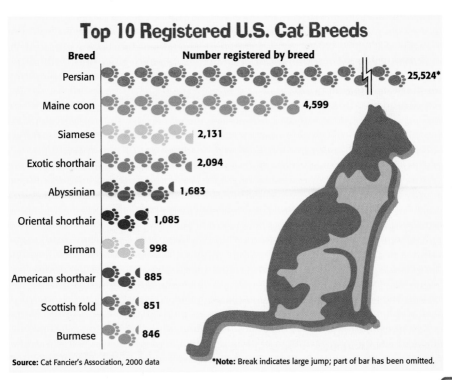

Breed	Number registered by breed
Persian	25,524*
Maine coon	4,599
Siamese	2,131
Exotic shorthair	2,094
Abyssinian	1,683
Oriental shorthair	1,085
Birman	998
American shorthair	885
Scottish fold	851
Burmese	846

Source: Cat Fancier's Association, 2000 data

*__Note:__ Break indicates large jump; part of bar has been omitted.

ARTS AND MUSIC

Sculpture Sales

The most valuable sculpture in the world is *The Three Graces* by Antonio Canova. In 1994, the sculpture was purchased jointly by the Victoria and Albert Museum in England and the National Gallery of Scotland for $11.5 million. The sculpture moves between the two institutions every seven years.

Gigantic Gallery

The State Hermitage Museum in St. Petersburg, Russia, is the largest art gallery in the world. It has 322 galleries and holds almost 3 million works of art.

The Load-Down on Downloads

The biggest problem facing the music industry these days is unauthorized file sharing and commerical piracy. In 2003, this problem cost the global music industry an estimated $2 billion dollars in revenue. Eminem was the most popular artist with illegal file-sharers and downloaders. In one recent analysis, his songs were downloaded more than 8.6 million times in one day!

Singles Sensation

LeAnn Rimes holds the record for the single that stayed the longest on the U.S. charts. Her 1997 hit "How Do I Live" remained on the charts for 69 weeks.

Top 5 Longest-Running Broadway Shows of All Time

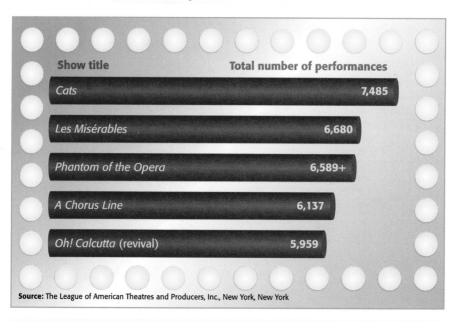

Show title	Total number of performances
Cats	7,485
Les Misérables	6,680
Phantom of the Opera	6,589+
A Chorus Line	6,137
Oh! Calcutta (revival)	5,959

Source: The League of American Theatres and Producers, Inc., New York, New York

Top 10 Best-Selling Books of All Time

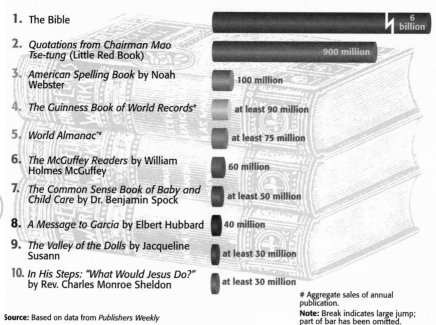

1. The Bible — 6 billion
2. *Quotations from Chairman Mao Tse-tung* (Little Red Book) — 900 million
3. *American Spelling Book* by Noah Webster — 100 million
4. *The Guinness Book of World Records*# — at least 90 million
5. *World Almanac*# — at least 75 million
6. *The McGuffey Readers* by William Holmes McGuffey — 60 million
7. *The Common Sense Book of Baby and Child Care* by Dr. Benjamin Spock — at least 50 million
8. *A Message to Garcia* by Elbert Hubbard — 40 million
9. *The Valley of the Dolls* by Jacqueline Susann — at least 30 million
10. *In His Steps: "What Would Jesus Do?"* by Rev. Charles Monroe Sheldon — at least 30 million

Aggregate sales of annual publication.
Note: Break indicates large jump; part of bar has been omitted.

Source: Based on data from *Publishers Weekly*

Typical Orchestra Seating Plan

In the usual orchestral seating plan, instruments of the four "families"—woodwinds, brass, percussion, and strings—are positioned in groups. This arrangement offers the best blending of tones of individual instruments and helps the musicians play together in their groups.

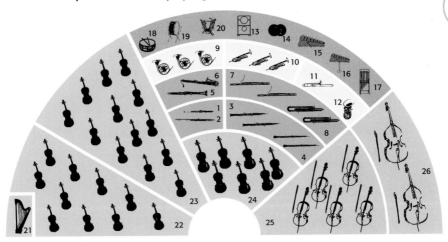

Woodwind
1 Piccolos
2 Flutes
3 Oboes
4 English horns
5 Clarinets
6 Bass clarinets
7 Bassoons
8 Contrabassoons

Percussion
13 Tam-tams
14 Cymbals
15 Xylophones
16 Glockenspiels
17 Tubular bells
18 Side drums
19 Bass drums
20 Timpanis

Brass
9 French horns
10 Trumpets
11 Trombones
12 Tubas

Strings
21 Harps
22 1st violins
23 2nd violins
24 Violas
25 Cellos
26 Double basses

Note: Numbers of instruments illustrated in the above diagram do not reflect actual numbers of instruments, which vary by orchestra.

Most Expensive Paintings Ever Sold at Auction

Portrait of Dr. Gachet
Vincent van Gogh
(Dutch; 1853–1880),
Christie's, New York,
May 15, 1990
$82.5 Million

The Massacre of the Innocents
Peter Paul Rubens
(Flemish; 1577–1640),
Sotheby's, London,
July 19, 2002
$77 Million

Au Moulin de la Galette
Pierre-Auguste Renoir
(French; 1841–1919),
Sotheby's, New York,
May 17, 1990
$71 Million

Portrait de l'Artiste sans Barbe
Vincent van Gogh,
Christie's, New York,
Nov. 19, 1998
$65 Million

Rideau, Cruchon et Compotier
Paul Cézanne
(French; 1839–1906),
Sotheby's, New York,
May 10, 1999
$55 Million

Les Noces de Pierrette
Pablo Picasso
(Spanish; 1881–1973),
Binoche et Godeau,
Paris, Nov. 30, 1990
$51 Million

Source: Based on data from Sotheby's, New York, and Christie's, New York

Artists With the Most Number One Singles

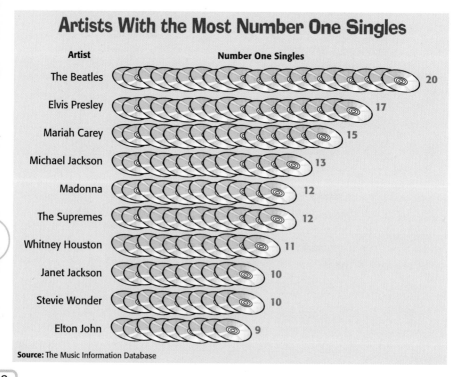

Artist	Number One Singles
The Beatles	20
Elvis Presley	17
Mariah Carey	15
Michael Jackson	13
Madonna	12
The Supremes	12
Whitney Houston	11
Janet Jackson	10
Stevie Wonder	10
Elton John	9

Source: The Music Information Database

The Best-Selling Albums of All Time

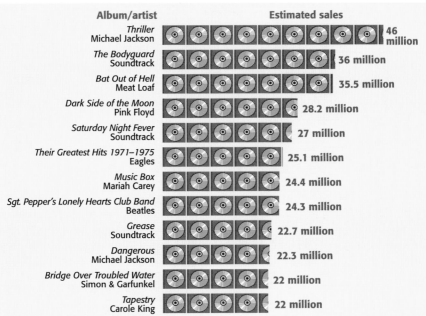

Album/artist	Estimated sales
Thriller — Michael Jackson	46 million
The Bodyguard — Soundtrack	36 million
Bat Out of Hell — Meat Loaf	35.5 million
Dark Side of the Moon — Pink Floyd	28.2 million
Saturday Night Fever — Soundtrack	27 million
Their Greatest Hits 1971–1975 — Eagles	25.1 million
Music Box — Mariah Carey	24.4 million
Sgt. Pepper's Lonely Hearts Club Band — Beatles	24.3 million
Grease — Soundtrack	22.7 million
Dangerous — Michael Jackson	22.3 million
Bridge Over Troubled Water — Simon & Garfunkel	22 million
Tapestry — Carole King	22 million

Source: Based on data from *Billboard*, 2002

Top 10 Groups With the Most Platinum Albums* in the U.S.

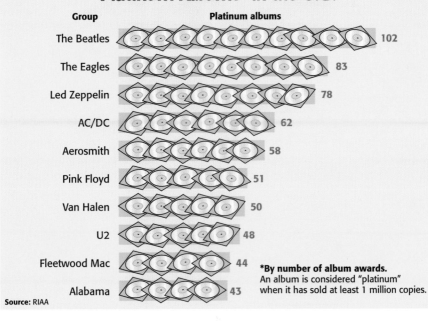

Group	Platinum albums
The Beatles	102
The Eagles	83
Led Zeppelin	78
AC/DC	62
Aerosmith	58
Pink Floyd	51
Van Halen	50
U2	48
Fleetwood Mac	44
Alabama	43

Source: RIAA

*By number of album awards.
An album is considered "platinum" when it has sold at least 1 million copies.

ASTRONOMY

That Rocks

There are an estimated 30,000 asteroids, or pieces of rocky debris, in the solar system. The largest asteroid is called Ceres and it measures 485 miles (780.5 km) in diameter. That's 88 times the height of Mt. Everest!

One Smoking Hot Star

The sun is thought to be 4.6 billion years old and has a diameter of 864,989 miles (1,392,000 km). It is a medium-sized star known as a yellow dwarf and the temperature in its core is estimated to be more than 27,000,000 degrees Fahrenheit (15,000,000 degrees Celsius).

It's Comet Sense

Although very low in mass, comets are among the largest objects in the solar system. The nucleus, or center of the head, of a comet may be up to 10,000 miles (16,093 km) in diameter. Its coma (head) may measure between 10,000 to 50,000 miles (16,093 to 80,465 km) in diameter. And its tail can be as long as 28 million miles (45.1 million km)—long enough to wrap around the Earth 3,533 times!

A Weighty Issue

Every planet has a different gravitational field. For instance, Mercury has a gravitation field that is .38 to that of Earth's. So, a 90-pound (41 kg) person would weigh just 34 pounds (15.4 kg) on Mercury. On the other hand, Neptune has a gravitation field that is 1.2 times that of Earth's. This same person would then weigh 108 pounds (48.9 kg) on Neptune.

Star Power

The sun is 93 million miles (150 million km) from Earth, yet it is 270,000 times closer than the next nearest star.

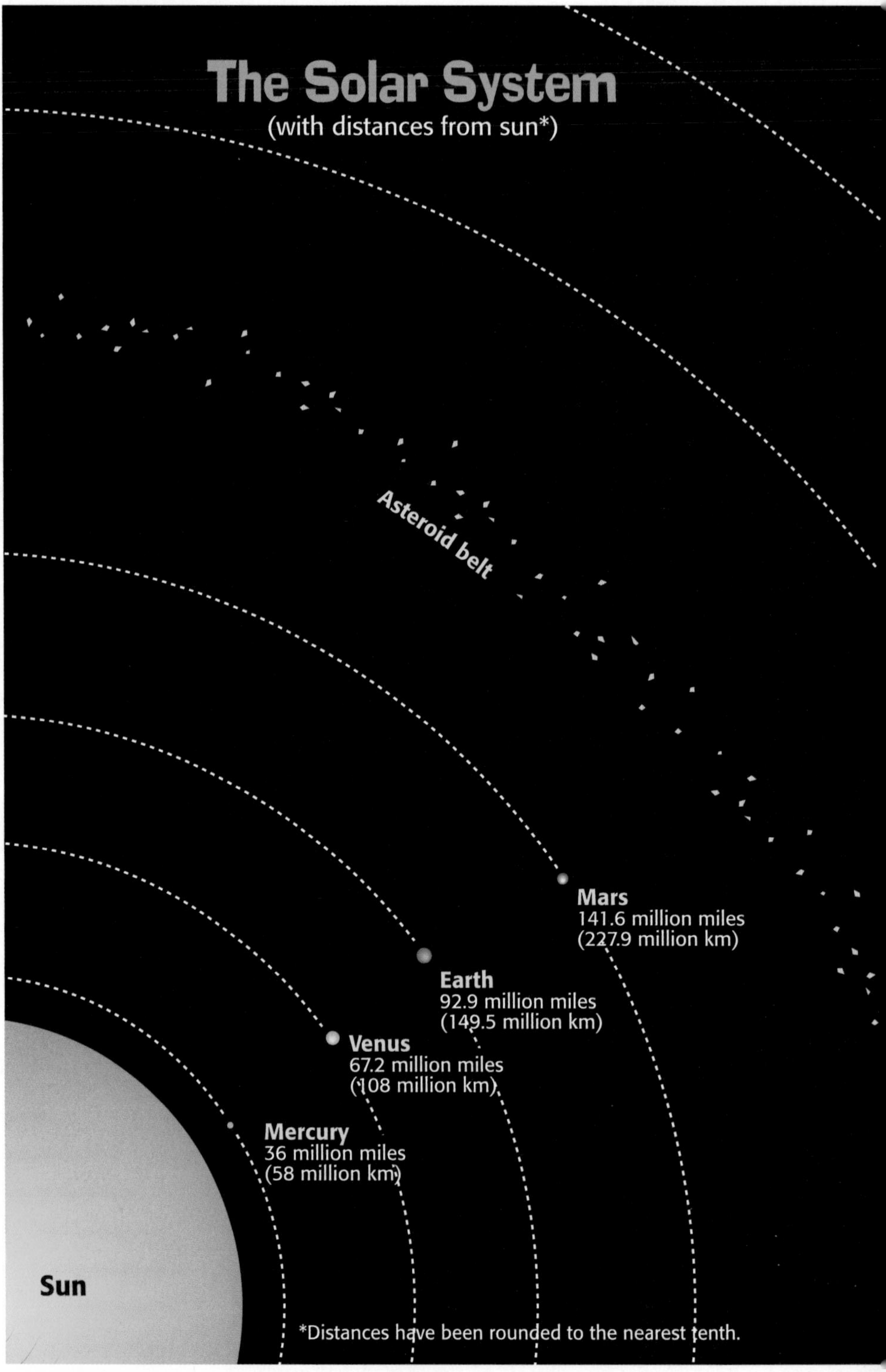

The Solar System
(with distances from sun*)

Asteroid belt

Mars
141.6 million miles
(227.9 million km)

Earth
92.9 million miles
(149.5 million km)

Venus
67.2 million miles
(108 million km)

Mercury
36 million miles
(58 million km)

Sun

*Distances have been rounded to the nearest tenth.

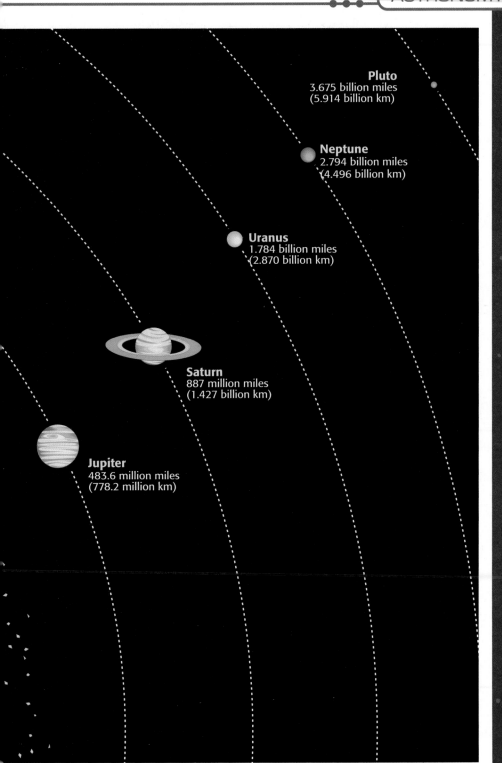

Pluto
3.675 billion miles
(5.914 billion km)

Neptune
2.794 billion miles
(4.496 billion km)

Uranus
1.784 billion miles
(2.870 billion km)

Saturn
887 million miles
(1.427 billion km)

Jupiter
483.6 million miles
(778.2 million km)

Basic Facts About the Planets in Our Solar System

	Average distance from sun	Rotation period (hours)	Period of revolution (in Earth days)	Diameter relative to Earth	Average surface temperature	Planetary satellites (moons)
Mercury	35,900,000 miles (57.8 mil. km)	1,407.6 hours	88 days	38.2%	332°F (166°C)	0
Venus	67,200,000 miles (108.1 mil. km)	–5,832.2* hours	224.7 days	94.9%	854°F (456°C)	0
Earth	92,960,000 miles (150 mil. km)	23.9 hours	365.26 days	100%	59°F (15°C)	1
Mars	141,600,000 miles (227.9 mil. km)	24.6 hours	687 days	53.2%	–67°F (–55°C)	2
Jupiter	483,600,000 miles (778.2 mil. km)	9.8 hours	4,332.6 days	1,121%	–162°F (–108°C)	61
Saturn	886,700,000 miles (1.43 bil. km)	10.2 hours	10,759.2 days	941%	–208°F (–133°C)	31
Uranus	1,783,000,000 miles (2.87 bil. km)	17.2 hours	30,685.4 days	410%	–344°F (–207°C)	21
Neptune	2,794,000,000 miles (4.5 bil. km)	16.1 hours	60,268 days	388%	–365°F (–220°C)	11
Pluto	3,666,100,000 miles (5.9 bil. km)	–153* hours	90,950 days	18%	–355°F (–215°C)	1

Source: NASA   *Retrograde rotation; rotates backward, or in the opposite direction from most other planetary bodies.

Basic Facts About the Sun

Position in solar system	center
Mean distance from Earth	92,955,600 mi. (150 mil. km)
Distance from center of Milky Way galaxy	27,710 light-years
Period of rotation	27 days on average
Equatorial diameter	864,930 mi. (1.4 mil. km)
Diameter relative to Earth	109 times larger
Temperature at core	27,000,000°F (15,000,000°C)
Temperature at surface	8,700°F (4,811°C)
Main components	hydrogen and helium
Expected life of hydrogen fuel supply	6.4 billion years

Source: NASA

Top 10 Largest Bodies in the Solar System
(ranked by size in diameter)

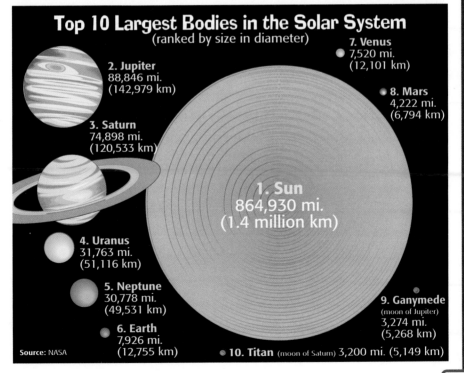

2. Jupiter
88,846 mi.
(142,979 km)

3. Saturn
74,898 mi.
(120,533 km)

4. Uranus
31,763 mi.
(51,116 km)

5. Neptune
30,778 mi.
(49,531 km)

6. Earth
7,926 mi.
(12,755 km)

7. Venus
7,520 mi.
(12,101 km)

8. Mars
4,222 mi.
(6,794 km)

1. Sun
864,930 mi.
(1.4 million km)

9. Ganymede
(moon of Jupiter)
3,274 mi.
(5,268 km)

10. Titan (moon of Saturn) 3,200 mi. (5,149 km)

Source: NASA

Astronomy Terms and Definitions

Light-year (distance traveled by light in one year)	5,880 billion miles (9,462 billion km)
Velocity of light (speed of light)	186,281.7 miles/sec. (299,782 km/sec.)
Mean distance, Earth to moon	238,860 miles (384,397 km)
Equatorial radius of Earth (distance around middle of Earth)	3,963.34 miles (6,378 km)
Polar radius of Earth (distance around top to bottom)	3,949.99 miles (6,357 km)
Earth's mean radius (how far around, averaged)	3,958.89 miles (6,371 km)
Earth's mean velocity in orbit (how fast it travels)	18.5 miles/sec. (29.8 km/sec.)

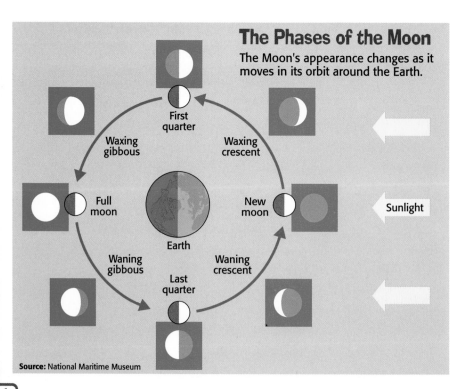

The Phases of the Moon

The Moon's appearance changes as it moves in its orbit around the Earth.

First quarter

Waxing gibbous

Waxing crescent

Full moon

New moon

Sunlight

Earth

Waning gibbous

Waning crescent

Last quarter

Source: National Maritime Museum

Fast Facts About The Moon

Age	4.5 billion years
Location	Solar system
Avg. distance from Earth	238,900 miles (384,400 km)
Diameter	2,160 miles (3,476 km)
Period of revolution	27 Earth days
Interesting features	The Moon has no atmosphere or magnetic field. Most rocks on the surface of the Moon seem to be between 4.5 and 3 billion years old. Thus the Moon provides evidence about the early history of our solar system.

Source: NASA

Top 10 Closest Comet Approaches to Earth
(ranked by distance in miles/kilometers)

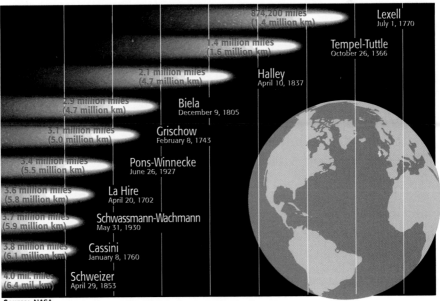

874,200 miles (1.4 million km) — Lexell, July 1, 1770

1.4 million miles (1.6 million km) — Tempel-Tuttle, October 26, 1366

2.1 million miles (4.7 million km) — Halley, April 10, 1837

2.9 million miles (4.7 million km) — Biela, December 9, 1805

3.1 million miles (5.0 million km) — Grischow, February 8, 1743

3.4 million miles (5.5 million km) — Pons-Winnecke, June 26, 1927

3.6 million miles (5.8 million km) — La Hire, April 20, 1702

3.7 million miles (5.9 million km) — Schwassmann-Wachmann, May 31, 1930

3.8 million miles (6.1 million km) — Cassini, January 8, 1760

4.0 mil. miles (6.4 mil. km) — Schweizer, April 29, 1853

Source: NASA

Major Constellations

Here is a table of selected major constellations
and their English names.

Latin	English	Latin	English
Andromeda	Andromeda	Lepus	Hare
Aquarius	Water Bearer	Libra	Scales
Aquila	Eagle	Lupus	Wolf
Aries	Ram	Lynx	Lynx
Camelopardalis	Giraffe	Lyra	Harp
Cancer	Crab	Microscopium	Microscope
Canes Venatici	Hunting Dogs	Monoceros	Unicorn
Canis Major	Big Dog	Musca	Fly
Canis Minor	Little Dog	Orion	Orion
Capricornus	Goat	Pavo	Peacock
Cassiopeia	Cassiopeia	Pegasus	Pegasus
Centaurus	Centaur	Phoenix	Phoenix
Cetus	Whale	Pictor	Painter
Chameleon	Chameleon	Pisces	Fish
Circinus	Compass	Piscis Austrinus	Southern Fish
Columba	Dove	Sagitta	Arrow
Corona Australis	Southern Crown	Sagittarius	Archer
Corona Borealis	Northern Crown	Scorpius	Scorpion
Corvus	Crow	Sculptor	Sculptor
Crater	Cup	Scutum	Shield
Crux	Southern Cross	Serpens	Serpent
Cygnus	Swan	Sextans	Sextant
Delphinus	Dolphin	Taurus	Bull
Dorado	Goldfish	Telescopium	Telescope
Draco	Dragon	Triangulum	Triangle
Equuleus	Little Horse	Triangulum Australe	Southern Triangle
Gemini	Twins	Tucana	Toucan
Grus	Crane	Ursa Major	Big Bear
Hercules	Hercules	Ursa Minor	Little Bear
Horologium	Clock	Virgo	Virgin
Lacerta	Lizard	Volans	Flying Fish
Leo	Lion	Vulpecula	Little Fox
Leo Minor	Little Lion		

Top 10 Closest Stars to Earth

(ranked by distance in light-years*, excluding the sun)

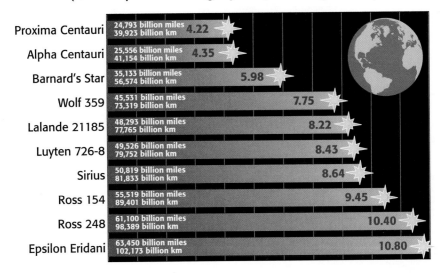

Star	Distance (miles/km)	Light-years
Proxima Centauri	24,793 billion miles / 39,923 billion km	4.22
Alpha Centauri	25,556 billion miles / 41,154 billion km	4.35
Barnard's Star	35,133 billion miles / 56,574 billion km	5.98
Wolf 359	45,531 billion miles / 73,319 billion km	7.75
Lalande 21185	48,293 billion miles / 77,765 billion km	8.22
Luyten 726-8	49,526 billion miles / 79,752 billion km	8.43
Sirius	50,819 billion miles / 81,833 billion km	8.64
Ross 154	55,519 billion miles / 89,401 billion km	9.45
Ross 248	61,100 billion miles / 98,389 billion km	10.40
Epsilon Eridani	63,450 billion miles / 102,173 billion km	10.80

*Note: One light-year = 5,880 billion miles/9,462 billion kilometers, which is the distance light travels in one year.

Source: NASA

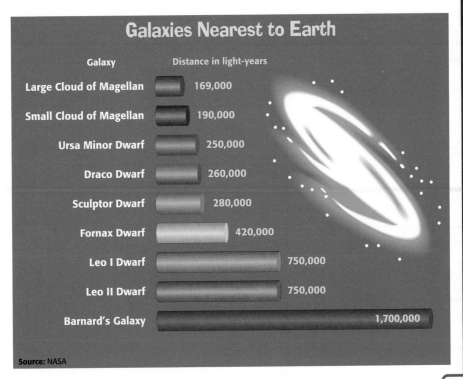

Galaxies Nearest to Earth

Galaxy	Distance in light-years
Large Cloud of Magellan	169,000
Small Cloud of Magellan	190,000
Ursa Minor Dwarf	250,000
Draco Dwarf	260,000
Sculptor Dwarf	280,000
Fornax Dwarf	420,000
Leo I Dwarf	750,000
Leo II Dwarf	750,000
Barnard's Galaxy	1,700,000

Source: NASA

BUILDINGS, BRIDGES, DAMS, AND TUNNELS

A Bendable Bridge?

At 4,260 feet (1,299 m), the Verrazano-Narrows Bridge is the longest bridge in the United States. The height of the roadway varies by season, however, because the steel cables contract in the cold weather and expand in the heat. So the roadway is 12 feet (3.6 m) lower in the summer.

The Tallest Tower

The CN Tower in Toronto, Canada, measures 1,815 feet (553 m)—or 181 stories—making it the world's tallest tower. Six elevators speed visitors up the tower at a rate of 20 feet (6 m) per second. The total weight of the tower is 130,000 tons (117,910 tn). And at 1,465 feet (447 m), the Sky Pod is the world's highest observation deck.

The Presidential Palace

The White House is truly an architectural marvel. It has 35 bathrooms, 412 doors, 147 windows, 28 fireplaces, 8 staircases, and 3 elevators. It requires 570 gallons (2,158 l) of paint to cover its outside surface. For fun, the White House offers a tennis court, a jogging track, a swimming pool, a movie theater, a billiard room, and a bowling lane.

A Super Skyscraper

At 1,454 feet (443 m), the Sears Tower in Chicago, Illinois, is the tallest building in the United States. It took 3 years to build at a cost of $150 million. The building contains enough steel to build 50,000 cars and enough telephone wiring to wrap around the world 1.75 times!

Maritime Markers

Lighthouses have played an important part in the maritime history of the United States. The first lighthouse was built in Boston, Massachusetts, in 1716, but is no longer in service. The oldest lighthouse still in service was built in Sandy Hook, New Jersey, in 1764. Although not as old, a lighthouse in Cape Hatteras, North Carolina, is the country's tallest at 191 feet (58 m).

Milestones in Modern Architecture Timeline

1884 First modern metal-frame skyscraper, Chicago's 10-story Home Insurance Building, is designed by U.S. architect William Jenney (1832–1907). It features a metal skeleton of cast-iron columns and nonsupporting curtain walls, which become characteristic of modern design.

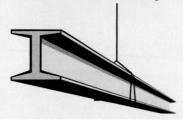

1900 U.S. architect Frank Lloyd Wright (1867–1959) becomes famous for designing houses in Prairie style, characterized by low, horizontal lines and use of natural earth colors. Wright believes buildings should complement settings.

1919 Walter Gropius (1883–1969) founds Bauhaus, a German school of design, to combine arts and architecture with modern industrial technology. Bauhaus styles are notable for geometric lines and use of steel, glass, and concrete.

1928 Noted American architect (Richard) Buckminster Fuller (1895–1983) designs self-contained "4-D" technological house. Fuller becomes known for his "Dymaxion" principle of trying to get the most from the least amount of material and energy.

1937 Ludwig Mies van der Rohe (1886–1969) emigrates to United States and becomes leader in glass-and-steel architecture. He pioneers rectangular lines in design, including cubelike brick structures, uncovered steel columns, and large areas of tinted glass.

1951 Finnish-born American architect Eero Saarinen (1910–1961) becomes known for innovative designs for various buildings in the United States. His sweeping style features soaring roof lines, extensive use of glass, and curved lines.

1998

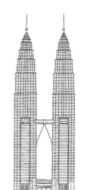

The Petronas Towers in Kuala Lumpur, Malaysia, are built and become the world's tallest buildings at a height of 1,483 feet (452 m). In 2003, the Towers lose their title to the Taipei 101 tower in Taiwan. Taipei 101 measures 1,674 feet (508 m) tall.

Construction Timeline of Important Earthworks, Dams, and Canals

1718 Elaborate system of earthen levees is built along Mississippi River at New Orleans, Louisiana, to control floodwaters.

1825 United States opens New York's Erie Canal, linking Great Lakes with New York City by way of Hudson River. It leads to increased development of western New York State.

1869 Suez Canal, 100 miles (161km) long, is completed, built by French engineer Ferdinand de Lesseps (1805–1894) to connect Mediterranean and Red seas. It is enlarged in 1980 to enable passage of supertankers.

1902 Aswan Dam is built on Nile River in Egypt. Considered one of the finest dams of all time, it has a record-setting length of 6,400 feet (1,951 m).

1904–1914 Panama Canal, dug across Isthmus of Panama, connects Atlantic and Pacific oceans. It is built by U.S. military engineers on land leased from Republic of Panama. Canal Zone is returned to Panama in 1979.

1941 Grand Coulee Dam, built for electric generation and irrigation, is completed on Columbia River in Washington State. At 550 feet (168 m) high and 4,173 feet (1,272 m) long, it is world's largest concrete structure.

1944 World's longest tunnel, Delaware Aqueduct, is completed. It is 105 miles (169 km) long and supplies water to New York City.

1959 United States and Canada complete construction of St. Lawrence Seaway. It provides access to Lake Ontario for oceangoing traffic by way of St. Lawrence River.

1970 Aswan High Dam, on Nile River in Egypt, is completed. Dam is 364 feet (111 m) high and 12,565 feet (3,830 m) long.

1985 Construction on world's longest railroad tunnel is completed in Japan. Almost 33.5 miles (54 km) long, Seikan tunnel connects islands of Hokkaido and Honshū.

2000 Laerdal Tunnel—the world's longest road tunnel—opens in Norway. This 15.2-mile (24.5-km) tunnel connects Oslo to the port of Bergen.

The Seven Wonders of the Modern World

Wonder/Location	Description
Channel Tunnel England and France 	The 31-mile (50-km) Channel Tunnel (Chunnel) is actually three concrete tubes, each 5 ft. (2 m) thick, which plunge into the earth at Coquelles, France, and burrow through the English Channel. They reemerge at Folkstone, England, behind the white cliffs of Dover. Through two of the tubes rush the broadest trains ever built—double-decker mega-trains 14 ft. (4 m) across—that travel close to 100 mph (161 kph).
CN Tower Toronto	The world's tallest free-standing structure soars 1,815 ft. (553 m) above the sidewalks of Toronto, Canada, three times the height of its better-known cousin, the Seattle Space Needle. Designed with the aid of a wind tunnel, the CN Tower can withstand 260-mph (418-kph) gusts.
Empire State Building New York City	At 1,250 ft. (381 m), the Empire State Building is the best-known skyscraper in the world and was by far the tallest building in the world for more than 40 years. Construction was completed in only one year and 45 days, without requiring overtime. Ironworkers set a breathtaking pace, riveting the 58,000-ton (53,000-tn) frame together in 23 weeks.
Golden Gate Bridge San Francisco 	The world's tallest suspension bridge, it hangs from two 746-ft. (227-m)-high towers. Its cables—each a yard (meter) thick—are the biggest ever to support a bridge. In fact, the Golden Gate Bridge contains enough cable to encircle the earth three times.
Itaipu Dam Brazil/Paraguay	Five miles (8 km) wide and requiring enough concrete to build five Hoover Dams, the main dam, as high as a 65-story building, is composed of hollow concrete segments, while the flanking wings are earth and rock fill. Some 160 tons (145 tn) of water per second pour onto each turbine, generating 12,600 megawatts—enough energy to power most of California.
Netherlands North Sea Protection Works Netherlands 	Unique in the world, this is a vast and complex system of dams, floodgates, storm surge barriers, and other engineered works. This vital system protects the country against devastating floods. The North Sea Protection Works also includes a 19-mile (31-km)-long enclosure dam which is 100 yards (91 m) thick at the waterline, and the Delta Project, which controls the treacherous area where the mouths of the Meuse and Rhine rivers become a delta.
Panama Canal Panama 	One of civil engineering's greatest triumphs, the Panama Canal employed 42,000 workers who dredged, blasted, and excavated from Colón to Balboa. They moved enough earth and rubble to bury the island of Manhattan to a depth of 12 ft. (4 m)—or enough to open a 16-ft. (5-m)-wide tunnel to the center of the Earth.

Source: International Engineering Society

The Seven Wonders of the Ancient World

Wonder/Location	Description
Colossus of Rhodes harbor of Rhodes, in Aegean Sea, off coast of Turkey	Huge bronze statue of sun god Helios, erected in harbor by people of Rhodes at end of year-long siege; took 12 years to build; about 105 feet (35 m) tall; destroyed by an earthquake in 224 B.C.
Hanging Gardens of Babylon ancient city of Babylon (now near Baghdad, Iraq)	Series of landscaped terraces along banks of the Euphrates River, connected by marble stairways and planted with many trees, flowers, and shrubs. Probably built by King Nebuchadnezzar II for his wife.
Mausoleum of Halicarnassus ancient city of Halicarnassus, now Turkish town of Bodrum	A monumental, expansive marble tomb built by the widow of Mausolus, king of Anatolia, in 353 B.C.
Pharos (lighthouse) Pharos Island off coast of Alexandria, Egypt	Built around 270 B.C., it was the world's first important lighthouse. It stood in the harbor for 1,000 years until it was destroyed by an earthquake; also a prototype for all others built by Roman Empire.
Pyramids of Egypt Giza, Egypt	The oldest pyramid, Cheops, was built with more than two million limestone blocks and stands more than 480 feet (146 m) high. The only one of the ancient wonders still in existence. 
Statue of Zeus Olympia, Greece	A huge, ornate statue of the god on his throne that was almost 60 feet (18 m) tall.
Temple of Artemis ancient Greek city of Ephesus, now in Turkey near Selçuk	Built in the sixth century B.C. to honor goddess Artemis; one of the largest Greek temples ever built; famous for its artistic decoration and use of marble.

Source: International Engineering Society

World's Top 10 Tallest Dams

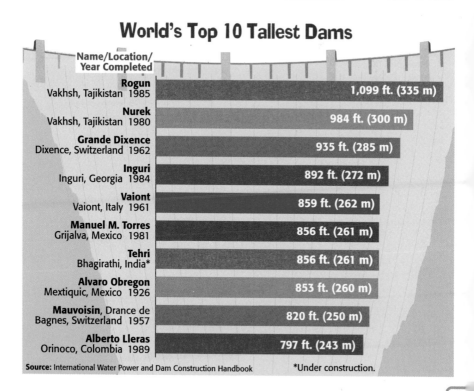

Name/Location/Year Completed	Height
Rogun Vakhsh, Tajikistan 1985	1,099 ft. (335 m)
Nurek Vakhsh, Tajikistan 1980	984 ft. (300 m)
Grande Dixence Dixence, Switzerland 1962	935 ft. (285 m)
Inguri Inguri, Georgia 1984	892 ft. (272 m)
Vaiont Vaiont, Italy 1961	859 ft. (262 m)
Manuel M. Torres Grijalva, Mexico 1981	856 ft. (261 m)
Tehri Bhagirathi, India*	856 ft. (261 m)
Alvaro Obregon Mextiquic, Mexico 1926	853 ft. (260 m)
Mauvoisin, Drance de Bagnes, Switzerland 1957	820 ft. (250 m)
Alberto Lleras Orinoco, Colombia 1989	797 ft. (243 m)

Source: International Water Power and Dam Construction Handbook   *Under construction.

Top 10 Longest Suspension Bridges in the U.S.

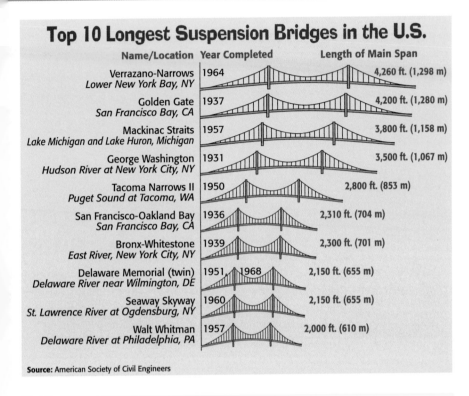

Name/Location	Year Completed	Length of Main Span
Verrazano-Narrows *Lower New York Bay, NY*	1964	4,260 ft. (1,298 m)
Golden Gate *San Francisco Bay, CA*	1937	4,200 ft. (1,280 m)
Mackinac Straits *Lake Michigan and Lake Huron, Michigan*	1957	3,800 ft. (1,158 m)
George Washington *Hudson River at New York City, NY*	1931	3,500 ft. (1,067 m)
Tacoma Narrows II *Puget Sound at Tacoma, WA*	1950	2,800 ft. (853 m)
San Francisco-Oakland Bay *San Francisco Bay, CA*	1936	2,310 ft. (704 m)
Bronx-Whitestone *East River, New York City, NY*	1939	2,300 ft. (701 m)
Delaware Memorial (twin) *Delaware River near Wilmington, DE*	1951, 1968	2,150 ft. (655 m)
Seaway Skyway *St. Lawrence River at Ogdensburg, NY*	1960	2,150 ft. (655 m)
Walt Whitman *Delaware River at Philadelphia, PA*	1957	2,000 ft. (610 m)

Source: American Society of Civil Engineers

World's Top 10 Longest Road Tunnels

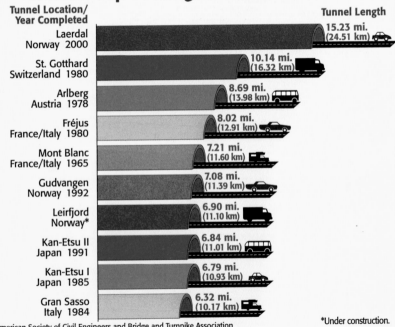

Tunnel Location/Year Completed	Tunnel Length
Laerdal Norway 2000	15.23 mi. (24.51 km)
St. Gotthard Switzerland 1980	10.14 mi. (16.32 km)
Arlberg Austria 1978	8.69 mi. (13.98 km)
Fréjus France/Italy 1980	8.02 mi. (12.91 km)
Mont Blanc France/Italy 1965	7.21 mi. (11.60 km)
Gudvangen Norway 1992	7.08 mi. (11.39 km)
Leirfjord Norway*	6.90 mi. (11.10 km)
Kan-Etsu II Japan 1991	6.84 mi. (11.01 km)
Kan-Etsu I Japan 1985	6.79 mi. (10.93 km)
Gran Sasso Italy 1984	6.32 mi. (10.17 km)

*Under construction.

Source: American Society of Civil Engineers and Bridge and Turnpike Association

World's Top 10 Cities with the Most Skyscrapers*

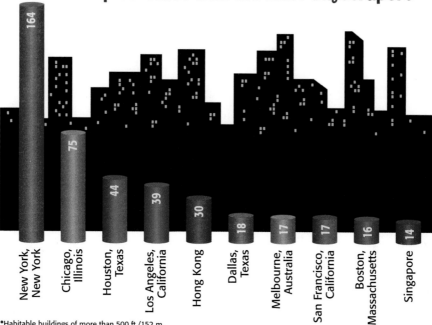

New York, New York	164
Chicago, Illinois	75
Houston, Texas	44
Los Angeles, California	39
Hong Kong	30
Dallas, Texas	18
Melbourne, Australia	17
San Francisco, California	17
Boston, Massachusetts	16
Singapore	14

*Habitable buildings of more than 500 ft./152 m.
Source: Based on data from Council on High Buildings and Urban Habitat, 2003

The Top 10 Tallest Buildings in the World

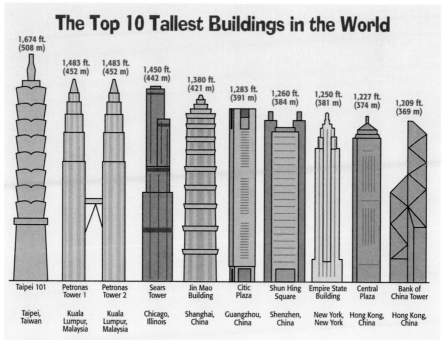

Building	Location	Height
Taipei 101	Taipei, Taiwan	1,674 ft. (508 m)
Petronas Tower 1	Kuala Lumpur, Malaysia	1,483 ft. (452 m)
Petronas Tower 2	Kuala Lumpur, Malaysia	1,483 ft. (452 m)
Sears Tower	Chicago, Illinois	1,450 ft. (442 m)
Jin Mao Building	Shanghai, China	1,380 ft. (421 m)
Citic Plaza	Guangzhou, China	1,283 ft. (391 m)
Shun Hing Square	Shenzhen, China	1,260 ft. (384 m)
Empire State Building	New York, New York	1,250 ft. (381 m)
Central Plaza	Hong Kong, China	1,227 ft. (374 m)
Bank of China Tower	Hong Kong, China	1,209 ft. (369 m)

Source: Council on High Buildings and Urban Habitat, Lehigh University, 2003

BUSINESS AND MONEY

Martha Money

The only woman ever to appear on U.S. paper money was Martha Washington. She was on the $1 silver certificate issued from 1886 to 1891.

Cashing In

The largest paper denomination ever printed was the $100,000 gold certificate in 1934. They were only used by Federal Reserve banks and were not available to the public.

Supreme Sandwich Shops

Restaurant franchises are big business for U.S. investors. There are more than 12,600 Subway restaurants around the world. It costs between $63,400 to $175,000 to open a store, in addition to $10,000 in franchise fees.

Internet Investments

The popularity of online stock trading has skyrocketed in the last few years, growing from 1.5 million accounts in 1997 to 19.7 million in 2002. Each day approximately 2.5 million trades take place.

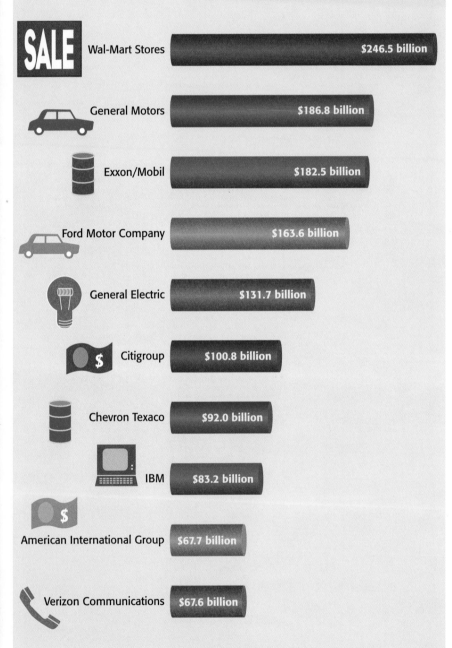

Top 10 Largest Corporations in the United States
(by annual sales)

SALE Wal-Mart Stores	$246.5 billion
General Motors	$186.8 billion
Exxon/Mobil	$182.5 billion
Ford Motor Company	$163.6 billion
General Electric	$131.7 billion
Citigroup	$100.8 billion
Chevron Texaco	$92.0 billion
IBM	$83.2 billion
American International Group	$67.7 billion
Verizon Communications	$67.6 billion

Source: Based on data from www.fortune.com/*Fortune* magazine, 2002

Glossary of Stock Market Terms

Bear market A market in which stock prices are declining. Opposite of *bull market*.

Big board A popular term for the New York Stock Exchange.

Blue chip Common stock in a company known nationally for the quality of its products or services and for its ability to make money and pay dividends in good times and bad.

Broker One who executes orders as an agent for others and receives a commission, as distinct from dealer.

Bull market A market in which stock prices are rising. Opposite of *bear market*.

Common stock Securities that represent an ownership interest in a corporation. If the company has also issued preferred stock, both common and preferred have ownership rights, but the preferred normally has prior claim on dividends and, in the event of liquidation, on assets.

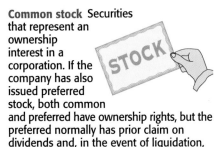

Stock dividend A dividend paid in securities rather than cash.

Ticker The instrument that prints prices and volume of security transactions in cities and towns throughout the United States within minutes after each trade on the floor.

The World's Richest Women

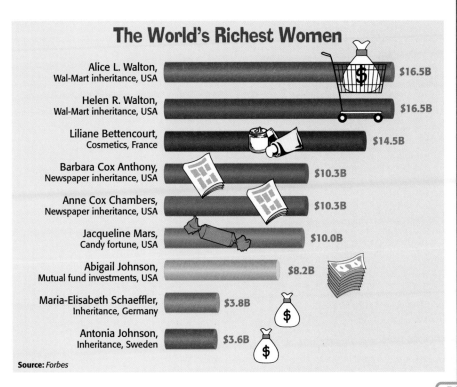

Name	Source	Net Worth
Alice L. Walton,	Wal-Mart inheritance, USA	$16.5B
Helen R. Walton,	Wal-Mart inheritance, USA	$16.5B
Liliane Bettencourt,	Cosmetics, France	$14.5B
Barbara Cox Anthony,	Newspaper inheritance, USA	$10.3B
Anne Cox Chambers,	Newspaper inheritance, USA	$10.3B
Jacqueline Mars,	Candy fortune, USA	$10.0B
Abigail Johnson,	Mutual fund investments, USA	$8.2B
Maria-Elisabeth Schaeffler,	Inheritance, Germany	$3.8B
Antonia Johnson,	Inheritance, Sweden	$3.6B

Source: *Forbes*

World's Richest People

Name/Source of wealth	Net worth

Bill Gates
Computer software,
USA
 $40.7 billion

Warren Buffett
Stock market,
USA
 $30.5 billion

Karl and Theo Albrecht
Supermarkets,
Germany
 $25.6 billion

Paul Allen
Computer software,
USA
 $20.1 billion

**Prince Alwaleed
Bin Talal Alsaud**
Investments,
Saudi Arabia
 $17.7 billion

Lawrence Ellison
Computer software,
USA
 $16.6 billion

Walton Family
Wal-Mart inheritance,
USA
 $16.6 billion

Liliane Bettencourt
Cosmetics,
France
 $14.5 billion

Kenneth Thomson
Publishing,
Canada
 $14.0 billion

Ingvar Kamprad
Furniture,
Sweden
$13.0 billion

Source: Based on data from www.forbes.com/*Forbes* magazine, 2003

Top 10 Biggest U.S. Advertisers

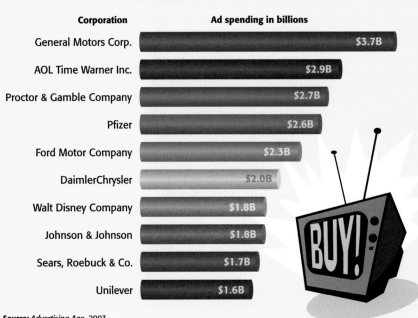

Corporation	Ad spending in billions
General Motors Corp.	$3.7B
AOL Time Warner Inc.	$2.9B
Proctor & Gamble Company	$2.7B
Pfizer	$2.6B
Ford Motor Company	$2.3B
DaimlerChrysler	$2.0B
Walt Disney Company	$1.8B
Johnson & Johnson	$1.8B
Sears, Roebuck & Co.	$1.7B
Unilever	$1.6B

Source: *Advertising Age,* 2003

Top 10 Internet Retailers

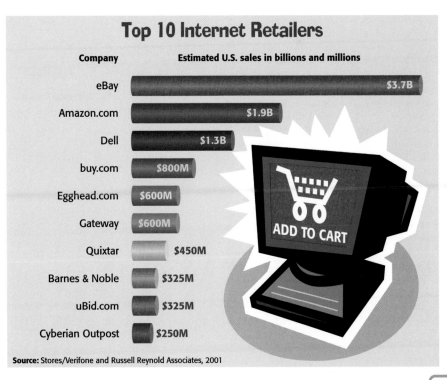

Company	Estimated U.S. sales in billions and millions
eBay	$3.7B
Amazon.com	$1.9B
Dell	$1.3B
buy.com	$800M
Egghead.com	$600M
Gateway	$600M
Quixtar	$450M
Barnes & Noble	$325M
uBid.com	$325M
Cyberian Outpost	$250M

Source: Stores/Verifone and Russell Reynold Associates, 2001

Countries With the Most Stores

Country	Number of Stores
China	19,306,800
India	10,537,080
Brazil	1,595,062
Japan	1,240,237
Mexico	1,087,993
Spain	780,247
Vietnam	727,268
South Korea	704,032
Italy	697,853
United States	685,367

Source: Euromonitor

Top 10 U.S. Franchises, by Number of U.S. Retail Outlets

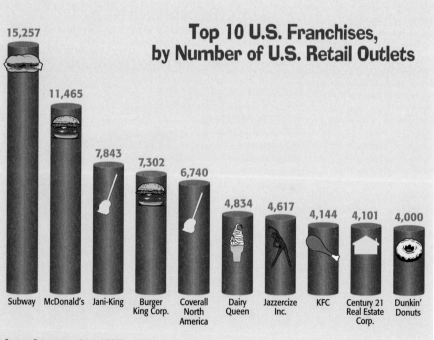

Subway	McDonald's	Jani-King	Burger King Corp.	Coverall North America	Dairy Queen	Jazzercize Inc.	KFC	Century 21 Real Estate Corp.	Dunkin' Donuts
15,257	11,465	7,843	7,302	6,740	4,834	4,617	4,144	4,101	4,000

Source: *Entrepreneur,* January 2003

Who Is on Our Bills?

Bill	Portrait
$1	George Washington
$2	Thomas Jefferson
$5	Abraham Lincoln
$10	Alexander Hamilton
$20	Andrew Jackson
$50	Ulysses S. Grant
$100	Benjamin Franklin
$500	William McKinley
$1,000	Grover Cleveland
$5,000	James Madison
$10,000	Salmon P. Chase
$100,000	Woodrow Wilson

Anatomy of a Personal Check

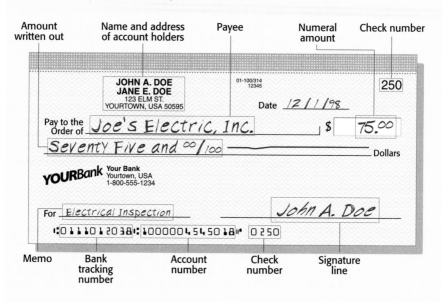

Amount written out | Name and address of account holders | Payee | Numeral amount | Check number

JOHN A. DOE
JANE E. DOE
123 ELM ST.
YOURTOWN, USA 50595

01-100/314
12345

250

Date 12/1/98

Pay to the Order of Joe's Electric, Inc. $ 75.00

Seventy Five and 00/100 ———————————————— Dollars

YOURBank Your Bank
Yourtown, USA
1-800-555-1234

For Electrical Inspection

John A. Doe

⑆011101203⑈:100000454550118⑈ 0250

Memo | Bank tracking number | Account number | Check number | Signature line

Anatomy of a Personal Check Register

Check number | Date of transaction | Payee | Starting balance

PLEASE BE SURE TO **DEDUCT** CHARGES THAT AFFECT YOUR ACCOUNT

ITEM NO. OR TRANS. CODE	DATE	TRANSACTION DESCRIPTION	SUBTRACTIONS AMOUNT OF PAYMENT OR WITHDRAWAL (-)	✓ T	(-) FEE IF ANY	ADDITIONS AMOUNT OF DEPOSIT OR INTEREST (+)	BALANCE	
							100	00
250	12/1	Joe's Electric, Inc.	75 00				-75	00
							25	00
	12/4	Paycheck Deposit				300 25	+300	25
							325	25

Who Is on Our Coins?

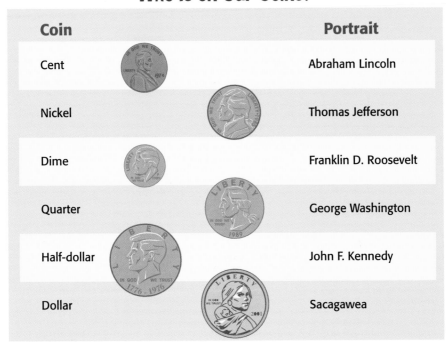

Coin		Portrait
Cent		Abraham Lincoln
Nickel		Thomas Jefferson
Dime		Franklin D. Roosevelt
Quarter		George Washington
Half-dollar		John F. Kennedy
Dollar		Sacagawea

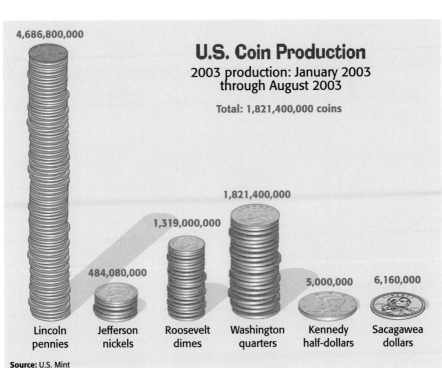

U.S. Coin Production

2003 production: January 2003 through August 2003

Total: 1,821,400,000 coins

4,686,800,000	Lincoln pennies	
484,080,000	Jefferson nickels	
1,319,000,000	Roosevelt dimes	
1,821,400,000	Washington quarters	
5,000,000	Kennedy half-dollars	
6,160,000	Sacagawea dollars	

Source: U.S. Mint

State Quarters

	Release Date	State	Statehood Date
1999	January 4, 1999	Delaware	December 7, 1787
	March 8, 1999	Pennsylvania	December 12, 1787
	May 17, 1999	New Jersey	December 18, 1787
	July 19, 1999	Georgia	January 2, 1788
	October 12, 1999	Connecticut	January 9, 1788
2000	January 3, 2000	Massachusetts	February 6, 1788
	March 13, 2000	Maryland	April 28, 1788
	May 22, 2000	South Carolina	May 23, 1788
	August 7, 2000	New Hampshire	June 21, 1788
	October 16, 2000	Virginia	June 25, 1788
2001	January 2, 2001	New York	July 26, 1788
	March 12, 2001	North Carolina	November 21, 1789
	May 21, 2001	Rhode Island	May 29, 1790
	August 6, 2001	Vermont	March 4, 1791
	October 15, 2001	Kentucky	June 1, 1792
2002	January 2, 2002	Tennessee	June 1, 1796
	March 11, 2002	Ohio	March 1, 1803
	May 20, 2002	Louisiana	April 30, 1812
	August 2, 2002	Indiana	December 11, 1816
	October 15, 2002	Mississippi	December 10, 1817
2003	January 2, 2003	Illinois	December 3, 1818
	March 17, 2003	Alabama	December 14, 1819
	June 2, 2003	Maine	March 15, 1820
	August 4, 2003	Missouri	August 10, 1821
		Arkansas	June 15, 1836
2004	January 26, 2004	Michigan	January 26, 1837
		Florida	March 3, 1845
		Texas	December 29, 1845
		Iowa	December 28, 1846
		Wisconsin	May 29, 1848
2005		California	September 9, 1850
		Minnesota	May 11, 1858
		Oregon	February 14, 1859
		Kansas	January 29, 1861
		West Virginia	June 20, 1863
2006		Nevada	October 31, 1864
		Nebraska	March 1, 1867
		Colorado	August 1, 1876
		North Dakota	November 2, 1889
		South Dakota	November 2, 1889
2007		Montana	November 8, 1889
		Washington	November 11, 1889
		Idaho	July 3, 1890
		Wyoming	July 10, 1890
		Utah	January 4, 1896
2008		Oklahoma	November 16, 1907
		New Mexico	January 6, 1912
		Arizona	February 14, 1912
		Alaska	January 3, 1959
		Hawaii	August 21, 1959

Source: U.S. Mint

Lifespans of U.S. Dollars

Bills in more frequent circulation, such as the one-dollar and five-dollar bills, wear out faster than those less passed bills, such as the one hundred–dollar bill.

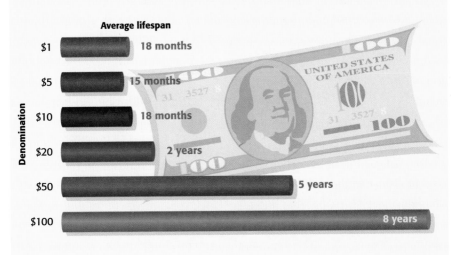

Average lifespan

Denomination

- $1 — 18 months
- $5 — 15 months
- $10 — 18 months
- $20 — 2 years
- $50 — 5 years
- $100 — 8 years

Source: Federal Reserve

Top 10 Biggest U.S. Employers

(by number of employees)

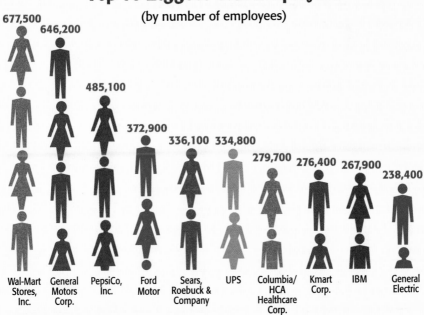

- Wal-Mart Stores, Inc. — 677,500
- General Motors Corp. — 646,200
- PepsiCo, Inc. — 485,100
- Ford Motor — 372,900
- Sears, Roebuck & Company — 336,100
- UPS — 334,800
- Columbia/HCA Healthcare Corp. — 279,700
- Kmart Corp. — 276,400
- IBM — 267,900
- General Electric — 238,400

Source: Based on data from www.fortune.com/*Fortune* magazine, 2001

CALENDARS AND HOLIDAYS

Monthly Meanings

The names for the months of the year come from Latin words. The translations for several of the calendar months may be confusing. For instance, September (the ninth month) translates to "seven" and October (the tenth month) translates to "eight." This is because the earliest Latin calendar only had 10 months; September was originally the seventh month and October was the eighth.

Zoning Out

A day is calculated by how long it takes Earth to rotate once on its axis, which occurs every 24 hours. Earth is also divided into 24 time zones so everyone in the world can be on a similar schedule. It takes the sun an hour to cross each zone. These time zones are marked by imaginary lines called meridians, which run north and south on the globe.

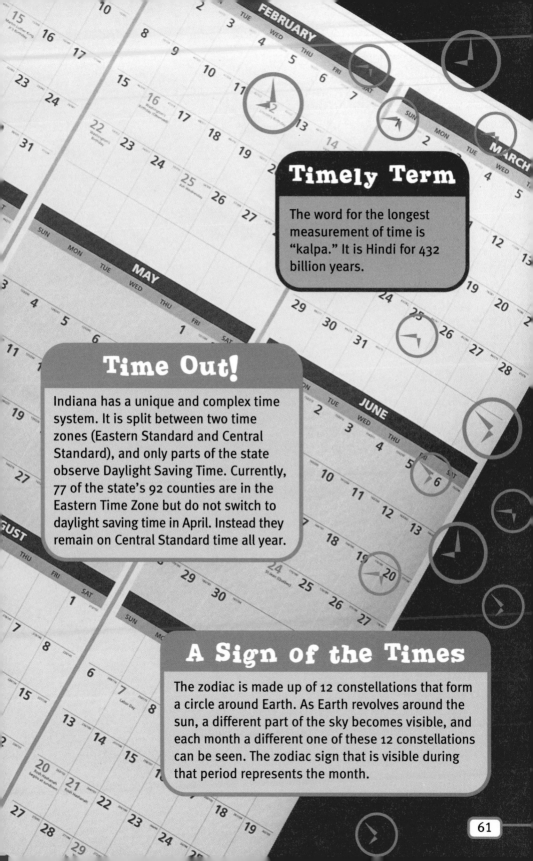

Timely Term

The word for the longest measurement of time is "kalpa." It is Hindi for 432 billion years.

Time Out!

Indiana has a unique and complex time system. It is split between two time zones (Eastern Standard and Central Standard), and only parts of the state observe Daylight Saving Time. Currently, 77 of the state's 92 counties are in the Eastern Time Zone but do not switch to daylight saving time in April. Instead they remain on Central Standard time all year.

A Sign of the Times

The zodiac is made up of 12 constellations that form a circle around Earth. As Earth revolves around the sun, a different part of the sky becomes visible, and each month a different one of these 12 constellations can be seen. The zodiac sign that is visible during that period represents the month.

Chinese Years, 1900–2019

Rat	Ox	Tiger	Hare (Rabbit)	Dragon	Snake
1900	1901	1902	1903	1904	1905
1912	1913	1914	1915	1916	1917
1924	1925	1926	1927	1928	1929
1936	1937	1938	1939	1940	1941
1948	1949	1950	1951	1952	1953
1960	1961	1962	1963	1964	1965
1972	1973	1974	1975	1976	1977
1984	1985	1986	1987	1988	1989
1996	1997	1998	1999	2000	2001
2008	2009	2010	2011	2012	2013

Horse	Sheep (Goat)	Monkey	Rooster	Dog	Pig
1906	1907	1908	1909	1910	1911
1918	1919	1920	1921	1922	1923
1930	1931	1932	1933	1934	1935
1942	1943	1944	1945	1946	1947
1954	1955	1956	1957	1958	1959
1966	1967	1968	1969	1970	1971
1978	1979	1980	1981	1982	1983
1990	1991	1992	1993	1994	1995
2002	2003	2004	2005	2006	2007
2014	2015	2016	2017	2018	2019

Months of the Year

Gregorian	Hebrew	Hindu	Muslim
January	Shevat	Magha	Muharram
February	Adar	Phalguna	Safar
March	Nisan	Caitra	Rabi I
April	Iyar	Vaisakha	Rabi II
May	Sivan	Jyaistha	Jumada I
June	Tammuz	Asadha	Jumada II
July	Av	Sravana	Rajab
August	Elul	Bhadrapada	Sha'ban
September	Tishrei	Asvina	Ramadan
October	Heshvan	Karttika	Shawwal
November	Kislev	Margasirsa	Dhu'l-Qa'dah
December	Tevet	Pausa	Dhu'l-Hijja

Birthstones

January	garnet	deep red
February	amethyst	light purple
March	aquamarine	light blue
April	diamond	colorless
May	emerald	green
June	pearl	white
July	ruby	red
August	peridot	light greenish-yellow
September	sapphire	dark blue
October	opal	iridescent
November	topaz	brownish-yellow
December	turquoise	blue-green

Periods of Time

annual	yearly
biannual	twice a year
bicentennial	marking a period of 200 years
biennial	marking a period of two years
bimonthly	every two months; twice a month
biweekly	every two weeks; twice a week
centennial	marking a period of 100 years
decennial	marking a period of 10 years
diurnal	daily; of a day
duodecennial	marking a period of 12 years
millennial	marking a period of 1,000 years
novennial	marking a period of nine years
octennial	marking a period of eight years
perennial	occurring year after year
quadrennial	marking a period of four years
quadricentennial	marking a period of 400 years
quincentennial	marking a period of 500 years
quindecennial	marking a period of 15 years
quinquennial	marking a period of five years
semiannual	every six months
semicentennial	marking a period of 50 years
semidiurnal	twice a day
semiweekly	twice a week
septennial	marking a period of seven years
sesquicentennial	marking a period of 150 years
sexennial	marking a period of six years
thrice weekly	three times a week
tricennial	marking a period of 30 years
triennial	marking a period of three years
trimonthly	every three months
triweekly	every three weeks; three times a week
undecennial	marking a period of 11 years
vicennial	marking a period of 20 years

Wedding Anniversary Gift Chart

Anniversary	Traditional	Modern	Anniversary	Traditional	Modern
1st	paper	clocks	13th	lace	textiles
2nd	cotton	china	14th	ivory	gold jewelry
3rd	leather	crystal	15th	crystal	watches
4th	fruit/flowers	appliances	20th	china	platinum
5th	wood	silverware	25th	silver	silver
6th	iron	wood	30th	pearl	diamond
7th	wool	desk set	35th	coral	jade
8th	bronze	linen	40th	ruby	ruby
9th	pottery	leather	45th	sapphire	sapphire
10th	tin	diamond jewelry	50th	gold	gold
11th	steel	fashion jewelry	55th	emerald	emerald
12th	silk/linen	pearls	60th	diamond	diamond

Solar Eclipse Calendar for the 21ST Century

During the 21st century, Halley's Comet will return (2061–2062), and there will be eight solar eclipses visible in the continental United States. The first comes after a long gap; the last one to be seen was on Feb. 26, 1979, in the northwestern United States.

Date	Latitudes Where Visible
Aug. 21, 2017	Oregon to South Carolina
April 8, 2024	Mexico to Texas and up through Maine
Aug. 23, 2044	Montana to North Dakota
Aug. 12, 2045	N. California to Florida
Mar. 30, 2052	Florida to Georgia
May 11, 2078	Louisiana to North Carolina
May 1, 2079	New Jersey to the lower edge of New England
Sept. 14, 2099	North Dakota to Virginia

Perpetual Calendar, 1775–2050

A perpetual calendar lets you find the day of the week for any date in any year. The number next to each year corresponds to one of the 14 calendars.

Year	No.	Year	No.	Year	No.	Year	No.	Year	No.	Year	No.
1775	1	1821	2	1868	11	1914	5	1961	1	2007	2
1776	9	1822	3	1869	6	1915	6	1962	2	2008	10
1777	4	1823	4	1870	7	1916	14	1963	3	2009	5
1778	5	1824	12	1871	1	1917	2	1964	11	2010	6
1779	6	1825	7	1872	9	1918	3	1965	6	2011	7
1780	14	1826	1	1873	4	1919	4	1966	7	2012	8
1781	2	1827	2	1874	5	1920	12	1967	1	2013	3
1782	3	1828	10	1875	6	1921	7	1968	9	2014	4
1783	4	1829	5	1876	14	1922	1	1969	4	2015	5
1784	12	1830	6	1877	2	1923	2	1970	5	2016	13
1785	7	1831	7	1878	3	1924	10	1971	6	2017	1
1786	1	1832	8	1879	4	1925	5	1972	14	2018	2
1787	2	1833	3	1880	12	1926	6	1973	2	2019	3
1788	10	1834	4	1881	7	1927	7	1974	3	2020	11
1789	5	1835	5	1882	1	1928	8	1975	4	2021	6
1790	6	1836	13	1883	2	1929	3	1976	12	2022	7
1791	7	1837	1	1884	10	1930	4	1977	7	2023	1
1792	8	1838	2	1885	5	1931	5	1978	1	2024	9
1793	3	1839	3	1886	6	1932	13	1979	2	2025	4
1794	4	1840	11	1887	7	1933	1	1980	10	2026	5
1795	5	1841	6	1888	8	1934	2	1981	5	2027	6
1796	13	1842	7	1889	3	1935	3	1982	6	2028	14
1797	1	1843	1	1890	4	1936	11	1983	7	2029	2
1798	2	1844	9	1891	5	1937	6	1984	8	2030	3
1799	3	1845	4	1892	13	1938	7	1985	3	2031	4
		1846	5	1893	1	1939	1	1986	4	2032	12
1800	4	1847	6	1894	2	1940	9	1987	5	2033	7
1801	5	1848	14	1895	3	1941	4	1988	13	2034	1
1802	6	1849	2	1896	11	1942	5	1989	1	2035	2
1803	7	1850	3	1897	6	1943	6	1990	2	2036	10
1804	8	1851	4	1898	7	1944	14	1991	3	2037	5
1805	3	1852	12	1899	1	1945	2	1992	11	2038	6
1806	4	1853	7			1946	3	1993	6	2039	7
1807	5	1854	1	1900	2	1947	4	1994	7	2040	8
1808	13	1855	2	1901	3	1948	12	1995	1	2041	3
1809	1	1856	10	1902	4	1949	7	1996	9	2042	4
1810	2	1857	5	1903	5	1950	1	1997	4	2043	5
1811	3	1858	6	1904	13	1951	2	1998	5	2044	13
1812	11	1859	7	1905	1	1952	10	1999	6	2045	1
1813	6	1860	8	1906	2	1953	5			2046	2
1814	7	1861	3	1907	3	1954	6	2000	14	2047	3
1815	1	1862	4	1908	11	1955	7	2001	2	2048	11
1816	9	1863	5	1909	6	1956	8	2002	3	2049	6
1817	4	1864	13	1910	7	1957	3	2003	4	2050	7
1818	5	1865	1	1911	1	1958	4	2004	12		
1819	6	1866	2	1912	9	1959	5	2005	7		
1820	14	1867	3	1913	4	1960	13	2006	1		

1

JANUARY
```
 S  M  T  W  T  F  S
 1  2  3  4  5  6  7
 8  9 10 11 12 13 14
15 16 17 18 19 20 21
22 23 24 25 26 27 28
29 30 31
```
FEBRUARY
```
 S  M  T  W  T  F  S
             1  2  3  4
 5  6  7  8  9 10 11
12 13 14 15 16 17 18
19 20 21 22 23 24 25
26 27 28
```
MARCH
```
 S  M  T  W  T  F  S
             1  2  3  4
 5  6  7  8  9 10 11
12 13 14 15 16 17 18
19 20 21 22 23 24 25
26 27 28 29 30 31
```
APRIL
```
 S  M  T  W  T  F  S
                      1
 2  3  4  5  6  7  8
 9 10 11 12 13 14 15
16 17 18 19 20 21 22
23 24 25 26 27 28 29
30
```
MAY
```
    1  2  3  4  5  6
 7  8  9 10 11 12 13
14 15 16 17 18 19 20
21 22 23 24 25 26 27
28 29 30 31
```
JUNE
```
             1  2  3
 4  5  6  7  8  9 10
11 12 13 14 15 16 17
18 19 20 21 22 23 24
25 26 27 28 29 30
```
JULY
```
                      1
 2  3  4  5  6  7  8
 9 10 11 12 13 14 15
16 17 18 19 20 21 22
23 24 25 26 27 28 29
30 31
```
AUGUST
```
       1  2  3  4  5
 6  7  8  9 10 11 12
13 14 15 16 17 18 19
20 21 22 23 24 25 26
27 28 29 30 31
```
SEPTEMBER
```
                   1  2
 3  4  5  6  7  8  9
10 11 12 13 14 15 16
17 18 19 20 21 22 23
24 25 26 27 28 29 30
```
OCTOBER
```
 1  2  3  4  5  6  7
 8  9 10 11 12 13 14
15 16 17 18 19 20 21
22 23 24 25 26 27 28
29 30 31
```
NOVEMBER
```
          1  2  3  4
 5  6  7  8  9 10 11
12 13 14 15 16 17 18
19 20 21 22 23 24 25
26 27 28 29 30
```
DECEMBER
```
                   1  2
 3  4  5  6  7  8  9
10 11 12 13 14 15 16
17 18 19 20 21 22 23
24 25 26 27 28 29 30
31
```

2

JANUARY
```
 S  M  T  W  T  F  S
    1  2  3  4  5  6
 7  8  9 10 11 12 13
14 15 16 17 18 19 20
21 22 23 24 25 26 27
28 29 30 31
```
FEBRUARY
```
 S  M  T  W  T  F  S
                1  2  3
 4  5  6  7  8  9 10
11 12 13 14 15 16 17
18 19 20 21 22 23 24
25 26 27 28
```
MARCH
```
 S  M  T  W  T  F  S
                1  2  3
 4  5  6  7  8  9 10
11 12 13 14 15 16 17
18 19 20 21 22 23 24
25 26 27 28 29 30 31
```
APRIL
```
 S  M  T  W  T  F  S
 1  2  3  4  5  6  7
 8  9 10 11 12 13 14
15 16 17 18 19 20 21
22 23 24 25 26 27 28
29 30
```
MAY
```
       1  2  3  4  5
 6  7  8  9 10 11 12
13 14 15 16 17 18 19
20 21 22 23 24 25 26
27 28 29 30 31
```
JUNE
```
                   1  2
 3  4  5  6  7  8  9
10 11 12 13 14 15 16
17 18 19 20 21 22 23
24 25 26 27 28 29 30
```
JULY
```
 1  2  3  4  5  6  7
 8  9 10 11 12 13 14
15 16 17 18 19 20 21
22 23 24 25 26 27 28
29 30 31
```
AUGUST
```
          1  2  3  4
 5  6  7  8  9 10 11
12 13 14 15 16 17 18
19 20 21 22 23 24 25
26 27 28 29 30 31
```
SEPTEMBER
```
                      1
 2  3  4  5  6  7  8
 9 10 11 12 13 14 15
16 17 18 19 20 21 22
23 24 25 26 27 28 29
30
```
OCTOBER
```
    1  2  3  4  5  6
 7  8  9 10 11 12 13
14 15 16 17 18 19 20
21 22 23 24 25 26 27
28 29 30 31
```
NOVEMBER
```
                1  2  3
 4  5  6  7  8  9 10
11 12 13 14 15 16 17
18 19 20 21 22 23 24
25 26 27 28 29 30
```
DECEMBER
```
                      1
 2  3  4  5  6  7  8
 9 10 11 12 13 14 15
16 17 18 19 20 21 22
23 24 25 26 27 28 29
30 31
```

3

JANUARY
S	M	T	W	T	F	S
		1	2	3	4	5
6	7	8	9	10	11	12
13	14	15	16	17	18	19
20	21	22	23	24	25	26
27	28	29	30	31		

FEBRUARY
S	M	T	W	T	F	S
					1	2
3	4	5	6	7	8	9
10	11	12	13	14	15	16
17	18	19	20	21	22	23
24	25	26	27	28		

MARCH
S	M	T	W	T	F	S
					1	2
3	4	5	6	7	8	9
10	11	12	13	14	15	16
17	18	19	20	21	22	23
24	25	26	27	28	29	30
31						

APRIL
S	M	T	W	T	F	S
	1	2	3	4	5	6
7	8	9	10	11	12	13
14	15	16	17	18	19	20
21	22	23	24	25	26	27
28	29	30				

MAY
S	M	T	W	T	F	S
			1	2	3	4
5	6	7	8	9	10	11
12	13	14	15	16	17	18
19	20	21	22	23	24	25
26	27	28	29	30	31	

JUNE
S	M	T	W	T	F	S
						1
2	3	4	5	6	7	8
9	10	11	12	13	14	15
16	17	18	19	20	21	22
23	24	25	26	27	28	29
30						

JULY
S	M	T	W	T	F	S
	1	2	3	4	5	6
7	8	9	10	11	12	13
14	15	16	17	18	19	20
21	22	23	24	25	26	27
28	29	30	31			

AUGUST
S	M	T	W	T	F	S
				1	2	3
4	5	6	7	8	9	10
11	12	13	14	15	16	17
18	19	20	21	22	23	24
25	26	27	28	29	30	31

SEPTEMBER
S	M	T	W	T	F	S
1	2	3	4	5	6	7
8	9	10	11	12	13	14
15	16	17	18	19	20	21
22	23	24	25	26	27	28
29	30					

OCTOBER
S	M	T	W	T	F	S
		1	2	3	4	5
6	7	8	9	10	11	12
13	14	15	16	17	18	19
20	21	22	23	24	25	26
27	28	29	30	31		

NOVEMBER
S	M	T	W	T	F	S
					1	2
3	4	5	6	7	8	9
10	11	12	13	14	15	16
17	18	19	20	21	22	23
24	25	26	27	28	29	30

DECEMBER
S	M	T	W	T	F	S
1	2	3	4	5	6	7
8	9	10	11	12	13	14
15	16	17	18	19	20	21
22	23	24	25	26	27	28
29	30	31				

4

JANUARY
S	M	T	W	T	F	S
			1	2	3	4
5	6	7	8	9	10	11
12	13	14	15	16	17	18
19	20	21	22	23	24	25
26	27	28	29	30	31	

FEBRUARY
S	M	T	W	T	F	S
						1
2	3	4	5	6	7	8
9	10	11	12	13	14	15
16	17	18	19	20	21	22
23	24	25	26	27	28	

MARCH
S	M	T	W	T	F	S
						1
2	3	4	5	6	7	8
9	10	11	12	13	14	15
16	17	18	19	20	21	22
23	24	25	26	27	28	29
30	31					

APRIL
S	M	T	W	T	F	S
		1	2	3	4	5
6	7	8	9	10	11	12
13	14	15	16	17	18	19
20	21	22	23	24	25	26
27	28	29	30			

MAY
S	M	T	W	T	F	S
				1	2	3
4	5	6	7	8	9	10
11	12	13	14	15	16	17
18	19	20	21	22	23	24
25	26	27	28	29	30	31

JUNE
S	M	T	W	T	F	S
1	2	3	4	5	6	7
8	9	10	11	12	13	14
15	16	17	18	19	20	21
22	23	24	25	26	27	28
29	30					

JULY
S	M	T	W	T	F	S
		1	2	3	4	5
6	7	8	9	10	11	12
13	14	15	16	17	18	19
20	21	22	23	24	25	26
27	28	29	30	31		

AUGUST
S	M	T	W	T	F	S
					1	2
3	4	5	6	7	8	9
10	11	12	13	14	15	16
17	18	19	20	21	22	23
24	25	26	27	28	29	30
31						

SEPTEMBER
S	M	T	W	T	F	S
	1	2	3	4	5	6
7	8	9	10	11	12	13
14	15	16	17	18	19	20
21	22	23	24	25	26	27
28	29	30				

OCTOBER
S	M	T	W	T	F	S
			1	2	3	4
5	6	7	8	9	10	11
12	13	14	15	16	17	18
19	20	21	22	23	24	25
26	27	28	29	30	31	

NOVEMBER
S	M	T	W	T	F	S
						1
2	3	4	5	6	7	8
9	10	11	12	13	14	15
16	17	18	19	20	21	22
23	24	25	26	27	28	29
30						

DECEMBER
S	M	T	W	T	F	S
	1	2	3	4	5	6
7	8	9	10	11	12	13
14	15	16	17	18	19	20
21	22	23	24	25	26	27
28	29	30	31			

5

JANUARY
S	M	T	W	T	F	S
				1	2	3
4	5	6	7	8	9	10
11	12	13	14	15	16	17
18	19	20	21	22	23	24
25	26	27	28	29	30	31

FEBRUARY
S	M	T	W	T	F	S
1	2	3	4	5	6	7
8	9	10	11	12	13	14
15	16	17	18	19	20	21
22	23	24	25	26	27	28

MARCH
S	M	T	W	T	F	S
1	2	3	4	5	6	7
8	9	10	11	12	13	14
15	16	17	18	19	20	21
22	23	24	25	26	27	28
29	30	31				

APRIL
S	M	T	W	T	F	S
			1	2	3	4
5	6	7	8	9	10	11
12	13	14	15	16	17	18
19	20	21	22	23	24	25
26	27	28	29	30		

MAY
S	M	T	W	T	F	S
					1	2
3	4	5	6	7	8	9
10	11	12	13	14	15	16
17	18	19	20	21	22	23
24	25	26	27	28	29	30
31						

JUNE
S	M	T	W	T	F	S
	1	2	3	4	5	6
7	8	9	10	11	12	13
14	15	16	17	18	19	20
21	22	23	24	25	26	27
28	29	30				

JULY
S	M	T	W	T	F	S
			1	2	3	4
5	6	7	8	9	10	11
12	13	14	15	16	17	18
19	20	21	22	23	24	25
26	27	28	29	30	31	

AUGUST
S	M	T	W	T	F	S
						1
2	3	4	5	6	7	8
9	10	11	12	13	14	15
16	17	18	19	20	21	22
23	24	25	26	27	28	29
30	31					

SEPTEMBER
S	M	T	W	T	F	S
		1	2	3	4	5
6	7	8	9	10	11	12
13	14	15	16	17	18	19
20	21	22	23	24	25	26
27	28	29	30			

OCTOBER
S	M	T	W	T	F	S
				1	2	3
4	5	6	7	8	9	10
11	12	13	14	15	16	17
18	19	20	21	22	23	24
25	26	27	28	29	30	31

NOVEMBER
S	M	T	W	T	F	S
1	2	3	4	5	6	7
8	9	10	11	12	13	14
15	16	17	18	19	20	21
22	23	24	25	26	27	28
29	30					

DECEMBER
S	M	T	W	T	F	S
		1	2	3	4	5
6	7	8	9	10	11	12
13	14	15	16	17	18	19
20	21	22	23	24	25	26
27	28	29	30	31		

6

JANUARY
S	M	T	W	T	F	S
					1	2
3	4	5	6	7	8	9
10	11	12	13	14	15	16
17	18	19	20	21	22	23
24	25	26	27	28	29	30
31						

FEBRUARY
S	M	T	W	T	F	S
	1	2	3	4	5	6
7	8	9	10	11	12	13
14	15	16	17	18	19	20
21	22	23	24	25	26	27
28						

MARCH
S	M	T	W	T	F	S
	1	2	3	4	5	6
7	8	9	10	11	12	13
14	15	16	17	18	19	20
21	22	23	24	25	26	27
28	29	30	31			

APRIL
S	M	T	W	T	F	S
				1	2	3
4	5	6	7	8	9	10
11	12	13	14	15	16	17
18	19	20	21	22	23	24
25	26	27	28	29	30	

MAY
S	M	T	W	T	F	S
						1
2	3	4	5	6	7	8
9	10	11	12	13	14	15
16	17	18	19	20	21	22
23	24	25	26	27	28	29
30	31					

JUNE
S	M	T	W	T	F	S
		1	2	3	4	5
6	7	8	9	10	11	12
13	14	15	16	17	18	19
20	21	22	23	24	25	26
27	28	29	30			

JULY
S	M	T	W	T	F	S
				1	2	3
4	5	6	7	8	9	10
11	12	13	14	15	16	17
18	19	20	21	22	23	24
25	26	27	28	29	30	31

AUGUST
S	M	T	W	T	F	S
1	2	3	4	5	6	7
8	9	10	11	12	13	14
15	16	17	18	19	20	21
22	23	24	25	26	27	28
29	30	31				

SEPTEMBER
S	M	T	W	T	F	S
			1	2	3	4
5	6	7	8	9	10	11
12	13	14	15	16	17	18
19	20	21	22	23	24	25
26	27	28	29	30		

OCTOBER
S	M	T	W	T	F	S
					1	2
3	4	5	6	7	8	9
10	11	12	13	14	15	16
17	18	19	20	21	22	23
24	25	26	27	28	29	30
31						

NOVEMBER
S	M	T	W	T	F	S
	1	2	3	4	5	6
7	8	9	10	11	12	13
14	15	16	17	18	19	20
21	22	23	24	25	26	27
28	29	30				

DECEMBER
S	M	T	W	T	F	S
			1	2	3	4
5	6	7	8	9	10	11
12	13	14	15	16	17	18
19	20	21	22	23	24	25
26	27	28	29	30	31	

7

JANUARY
S	M	T	W	T	F	S
						1
2	3	4	5	6	7	8
9	10	11	12	13	14	15
16	17	18	19	20	21	22
23	24	25	26	27	28	29
30	31					

FEBRUARY
S	M	T	W	T	F	S
		1	2	3	4	5
6	7	8	9	10	11	12
13	14	15	16	17	18	19
20	21	22	23	24	25	26
27	28					

MARCH
S	M	T	W	T	F	S
		1	2	3	4	5
6	7	8	9	10	11	12
13	14	15	16	17	18	19
20	21	22	23	24	25	26
27	28	29	30	31		

APRIL
S	M	T	W	T	F	S
					1	2
3	4	5	6	7	8	9
10	11	12	13	14	15	16
17	18	19	20	21	22	23
24	25	26	27	28	29	30

MAY
S	M	T	W	T	F	S
1	2	3	4	5	6	7
8	9	10	11	12	13	14
15	16	17	18	19	20	21
22	23	24	25	26	27	28
29	30	31				

JUNE
S	M	T	W	T	F	S
			1	2	3	4
5	6	7	8	9	10	11
12	13	14	15	16	17	18
19	20	21	22	23	24	25
26	27	28	29	30		

JULY
S	M	T	W	T	F	S
					1	2
3	4	5	6	7	8	9
10	11	12	13	14	15	16
17	18	19	20	21	22	23
24	25	26	27	28	29	30
31						

AUGUST
S	M	T	W	T	F	S
	1	2	3	4	5	6
7	8	9	10	11	12	13
14	15	16	17	18	19	20
21	22	23	24	25	26	27
28	29	30	31			

SEPTEMBER
S	M	T	W	T	F	S
				1	2	3
4	5	6	7	8	9	10
11	12	13	14	15	16	17
18	19	20	21	22	23	24
25	26	27	28	29	30	

OCTOBER
S	M	T	W	T	F	S
						1
2	3	4	5	6	7	8
9	10	11	12	13	14	15
16	17	18	19	20	21	22
23	24	25	26	27	28	29
30	31					

NOVEMBER
S	M	T	W	T	F	S
		1	2	3	4	5
6	7	8	9	10	11	12
13	14	15	16	17	18	19
20	21	22	23	24	25	26
27	28	29	30			

DECEMBER
S	M	T	W	T	F	S
				1	2	3
4	5	6	7	8	9	10
11	12	13	14	15	16	17
18	19	20	21	22	23	24
25	26	27	28	29	30	31

8

JANUARY
S	M	T	W	T	F	S
1	2	3	4	5	6	7
8	9	10	11	12	13	14
15	16	17	18	19	20	21
22	23	24	25	26	27	28
29	30	31				

FEBRUARY
S	M	T	W	T	F	S
			1	2	3	4
5	6	7	8	9	10	11
12	13	14	15	16	17	18
19	20	21	22	23	24	25
26	27	28	29			

MARCH
S	M	T	W	T	F	S
				1	2	3
4	5	6	7	8	9	10
11	12	13	14	15	16	17
18	19	20	21	22	23	24
25	26	27	28	29	30	31

APRIL
S	M	T	W	T	F	S
1	2	3	4	5	6	7
8	9	10	11	12	13	14
15	16	17	18	19	20	21
22	23	24	25	26	27	28
29	30					

MAY
S	M	T	W	T	F	S
		1	2	3	4	5
6	7	8	9	10	11	12
13	14	15	16	17	18	19
20	21	22	23	24	25	26
27	28	29	30	31		

JUNE
S	M	T	W	T	F	S
					1	2
3	4	5	6	7	8	9
10	11	12	13	14	15	16
17	18	19	20	21	22	23
24	25	26	27	28	29	30

JULY
S	M	T	W	T	F	S
1	2	3	4	5	6	7
8	9	10	11	12	13	14
15	16	17	18	19	20	21
22	23	24	25	26	27	28
29	30	31				

AUGUST
S	M	T	W	T	F	S
			1	2	3	4
5	6	7	8	9	10	11
12	13	14	15	16	17	18
19	20	21	22	23	24	25
26	27	28	29	30	31	

SEPTEMBER
S	M	T	W	T	F	S
						1
2	3	4	5	6	7	8
9	10	11	12	13	14	15
16	17	18	19	20	21	22
23	24	25	26	27	28	29
30						

OCTOBER
S	M	T	W	T	F	S
	1	2	3	4	5	6
7	8	9	10	11	12	13
14	15	16	17	18	19	20
21	22	23	24	25	26	27
28	29	30	31			

NOVEMBER
S	M	T	W	T	F	S
				1	2	3
4	5	6	7	8	9	10
11	12	13	14	15	16	17
18	19	20	21	22	23	24
25	26	27	28	29	30	

DECEMBER
S	M	T	W	T	F	S
						1
2	3	4	5	6	7	8
9	10	11	12	13	14	15
16	17	18	19	20	21	22
23	24	25	26	27	28	29
30	31					

9

JANUARY
```
S  M  T  W  T  F  S
      1  2  3  4  5  6
 7  8  9 10 11 12 13
14 15 16 17 18 19 20
21 22 23 24 25 26 27
28 29 30 31
```
FEBRUARY
```
S  M  T  W  T  F  S
            1  2  3
 4  5  6  7  8  9 10
11 12 13 14 15 16 17
18 19 20 21 22 23 24
25 26 27 28 29
```
MARCH
```
S  M  T  W  T  F  S
                1  2
 3  4  5  6  7  8  9
10 11 12 13 14 15 16
17 18 19 20 21 22 23
24 25 26 27 28 29 30
31
```
APRIL
```
S  M  T  W  T  F  S
    1  2  3  4  5  6
 7  8  9 10 11 12 13
14 15 16 17 18 19 20
21 22 23 24 25 26 27
28 29 30
```
MAY
```
S  M  T  W  T  F  S
          1  2  3  4
 5  6  7  8  9 10 11
12 13 14 15 16 17 18
19 20 21 22 23 24 25
26 27 28 29 30 31
```
JUNE
```
S  M  T  W  T  F  S
                   1
 2  3  4  5  6  7  8
 9 10 11 12 13 14 15
16 17 18 19 20 21 22
23 24 25 26 27 28 29
30
```
JULY
```
S  M  T  W  T  F  S
    1  2  3  4  5  6
 7  8  9 10 11 12 13
14 15 16 17 18 19 20
21 22 23 24 25 26 27
28 29 30 31
```
AUGUST
```
S  M  T  W  T  F  S
             1  2  3
 4  5  6  7  8  9 10
11 12 13 14 15 16 17
18 19 20 21 22 23 24
25 26 27 28 29 30 31
```
SEPTEMBER
```
S  M  T  W  T  F  S
 1  2  3  4  5  6  7
 8  9 10 11 12 13 14
15 16 17 18 19 20 21
22 23 24 25 26 27 28
29 30
```
OCTOBER
```
S  M  T  W  T  F  S
          1  2  3  4  5
 6  7  8  9 10 11 12
13 14 15 16 17 18 19
20 21 22 23 24 25 26
27 28 29 30 31
```
NOVEMBER
```
S  M  T  W  T  F  S
                1  2
 3  4  5  6  7  8  9
10 11 12 13 14 15 16
17 18 19 20 21 22 23
24 25 26 27 28 29 30
```
DECEMBER
```
S  M  T  W  T  F  S
 1  2  3  4  5  6  7
 8  9 10 11 12 13 14
15 16 17 18 19 20 21
22 23 24 25 26 27 28
29 30 31
```

10

JANUARY
```
S  M  T  W  T  F  S
          1  2  3  4  5
 6  7  8  9 10 11 12
13 14 15 16 17 18 19
20 21 22 23 24 25 26
27 28 29 30 31
```
FEBRUARY
```
S  M  T  W  T  F  S
                1  2
 3  4  5  6  7  8  9
10 11 12 13 14 15 16
17 18 19 20 21 22 23
24 25 26 27 28 29
```
MARCH
```
S  M  T  W  T  F  S
                   1
 2  3  4  5  6  7  8
 9 10 11 12 13 14 15
16 17 18 19 20 21 22
23 24 25 26 27 28 29
30 31
```
APRIL
```
S  M  T  W  T  F  S
       1  2  3  4  5
 6  7  8  9 10 11 12
13 14 15 16 17 18 19
20 21 22 23 24 25 26
27 28 29 30
```
MAY
```
S  M  T  W  T  F  S
             1  2  3
 4  5  6  7  8  9 10
11 12 13 14 15 16 17
18 19 20 21 22 23 24
25 26 27 28 29 30 31
```
JUNE
```
S  M  T  W  T  F  S
 1  2  3  4  5  6  7
 8  9 10 11 12 13 14
15 16 17 18 19 20 21
22 23 24 25 26 27 28
29 30
```
JULY
```
S  M  T  W  T  F  S
       1  2  3  4  5
 6  7  8  9 10 11 12
13 14 15 16 17 18 19
20 21 22 23 24 25 26
27 28 29 30 31
```
AUGUST
```
S  M  T  W  T  F  S
                1  2
 3  4  5  6  7  8  9
10 11 12 13 14 15 16
17 18 19 20 21 22 23
24 25 26 27 28 29 30
31
```
SEPTEMBER
```
S  M  T  W  T  F  S
    1  2  3  4  5  6
 7  8  9 10 11 12 13
14 15 16 17 18 19 20
21 22 23 24 25 26 27
28 29 30
```
OCTOBER
```
S  M  T  W  T  F  S
          1  2  3  4
 5  6  7  8  9 10 11
12 13 14 15 16 17 18
19 20 21 22 23 24 25
26 27 28 29 30 31
```
NOVEMBER
```
S  M  T  W  T  F  S
                   1
 2  3  4  5  6  7  8
 9 10 11 12 13 14 15
16 17 18 19 20 21 22
23 24 25 26 27 28 29
30
```
DECEMBER
```
S  M  T  W  T  F  S
    1  2  3  4  5  6
 7  8  9 10 11 12 13
14 15 16 17 18 19 20
21 22 23 24 25 26 27
28 29 30 31
```

11

JANUARY
```
S  M  T  W  T  F  S
             1  2  3  4
 5  6  7  8  9 10 11
12 13 14 15 16 17 18
19 20 21 22 23 24 25
26 27 28 29 30 31
```
FEBRUARY
```
S  M  T  W  T  F  S
                   1
 2  3  4  5  6  7  8
 9 10 11 12 13 14 15
16 17 18 19 20 21 22
23 24 25 26 27 28
```
MARCH
```
S  M  T  W  T  F  S
 1  2  3  4  5  6  7
 8  9 10 11 12 13 14
15 16 17 18 19 20 21
22 23 24 25 26 27 28
29 30 31
```
APRIL
```
S  M  T  W  T  F  S
          1  2  3  4
 5  6  7  8  9 10 11
12 13 14 15 16 17 18
19 20 21 22 23 24 25
26 27 28 29 30
```
MAY
```
S  M  T  W  T  F  S
                1  2
 3  4  5  6  7  8  9
10 11 12 13 14 15 16
17 18 19 20 21 22 23
24 25 26 27 28 29 30
31
```
JUNE
```
S  M  T  W  T  F  S
    1  2  3  4  5  6
 7  8  9 10 11 12 13
14 15 16 17 18 19 20
21 22 23 24 25 26 27
28 29 30
```
JULY
```
S  M  T  W  T  F  S
          1  2  3  4
 5  6  7  8  9 10 11
12 13 14 15 16 17 18
19 20 21 22 23 24 25
26 27 28 29 30 31
```
AUGUST
```
S  M  T  W  T  F  S
                   1
 2  3  4  5  6  7  8
 9 10 11 12 13 14 15
16 17 18 19 20 21 22
23 24 25 26 27 28 29
30 31
```
SEPTEMBER
```
S  M  T  W  T  F  S
       1  2  3  4  5
 6  7  8  9 10 11 12
13 14 15 16 17 18 19
20 21 22 23 24 25 26
27 28 29 30
```
OCTOBER
```
S  M  T  W  T  F  S
                1  2  3
 4  5  6  7  8  9 10
11 12 13 14 15 16 17
18 19 20 21 22 23 24
25 26 27 28 29 30 31
```
NOVEMBER
```
S  M  T  W  T  F  S
 1  2  3  4  5  6  7
 8  9 10 11 12 13 14
15 16 17 18 19 20 21
22 23 24 25 26 27 28
29 30
```
DECEMBER
```
S  M  T  W  T  F  S
       1  2  3  4  5
 6  7  8  9 10 11 12
13 14 15 16 17 18 19
20 21 22 23 24 25 26
27 28 29 30 31
```

12

JANUARY
```
S  M  T  W  T  F  S
                1  2  3
 4  5  6  7  8  9 10
11 12 13 14 15 16 17
18 19 20 21 22 23 24
25 26 27 28 29 30 31
```
FEBRUARY
```
S  M  T  W  T  F  S
 1  2  3  4  5  6  7
 8  9 10 11 12 13 14
15 16 17 18 19 20 21
22 23 24 25 26 27 28
29
```
MARCH
```
S  M  T  W  T  F  S
    1  2  3  4  5  6
 7  8  9 10 11 12 13
14 15 16 17 18 19 20
21 22 23 24 25 26 27
28 29 30 31
```
APRIL
```
S  M  T  W  T  F  S
             1  2  3
 4  5  6  7  8  9 10
11 12 13 14 15 16 17
18 19 20 21 22 23 24
25 26 27 28 29 30
```
MAY
```
S  M  T  W  T  F  S
                   1
 2  3  4  5  6  7  8
 9 10 11 12 13 14 15
16 17 18 19 20 21 22
23 24 25 26 27 28 29
30 31
```
JUNE
```
S  M  T  W  T  F  S
       1  2  3  4  5
 6  7  8  9 10 11 12
13 14 15 16 17 18 19
20 21 22 23 24 25 26
27 28 29 30
```
JULY
```
S  M  T  W  T  F  S
             1  2  3
 4  5  6  7  8  9 10
11 12 13 14 15 16 17
18 19 20 21 22 23 24
25 26 27 28 29 30 31
```
AUGUST
```
S  M  T  W  T  F  S
 1  2  3  4  5  6  7
 8  9 10 11 12 13 14
15 16 17 18 19 20 21
22 23 24 25 26 27 28
29 30 31
```
SEPTEMBER
```
S  M  T  W  T  F  S
          1  2  3  4
 5  6  7  8  9 10 11
12 13 14 15 16 17 18
19 20 21 22 23 24 25
26 27 28 29 30
```
OCTOBER
```
S  M  T  W  T  F  S
                1  2
 3  4  5  6  7  8  9
10 11 12 13 14 15 16
17 18 19 20 21 22 23
24 25 26 27 28 29 30
31
```
NOVEMBER
```
S  M  T  W  T  F  S
    1  2  3  4  5  6
 7  8  9 10 11 12 13
14 15 16 17 18 19 20
21 22 23 24 25 26 27
28 29 30
```
DECEMBER
```
S  M  T  W  T  F  S
          1  2  3  4
 5  6  7  8  9 10 11
12 13 14 15 16 17 18
19 20 21 22 23 24 25
26 27 28 29 30 31
```

13

JANUARY
```
S  M  T  W  T  F  S
                   1  2
 3  4  5  6  7  8  9
10 11 12 13 14 15 16
17 18 19 20 21 22 23
24 25 26 27 28 29 30
31
```
FEBRUARY
```
S  M  T  W  T  F  S
    1  2  3  4  5  6
 7  8  9 10 11 12 13
14 15 16 17 18 19 20
21 22 23 24 25 26 27
28 29
```
MARCH
```
S  M  T  W  T  F  S
    1  2  3  4  5
 6  7  8  9 10 11 12
13 14 15 16 17 18 19
20 21 22 23 24 25 26
27 28 29 30 31
```
APRIL
```
S  M  T  W  T  F  S
                1  2
 3  4  5  6  7  8  9
10 11 12 13 14 15 16
17 18 19 20 21 22 23
24 25 26 27 28 29 30
```
MAY
```
S  M  T  W  T  F  S
 1  2  3  4  5  6  7
 8  9 10 11 12 13 14
15 16 17 18 19 20 21
22 23 24 25 26 27 28
29 30 31
```
JUNE
```
S  M  T  W  T  F  S
          1  2  3  4
 5  6  7  8  9 10 11
12 13 14 15 16 17 18
19 20 21 22 23 24 25
26 27 28 29 30
```
JULY
```
S  M  T  W  T  F  S
                1  2
 3  4  5  6  7  8  9
10 11 12 13 14 15 16
17 18 19 20 21 22 23
24 25 26 27 28 29 30
31
```
AUGUST
```
S  M  T  W  T  F  S
    1  2  3  4  5  6
 7  8  9 10 11 12 13
14 15 16 17 18 19 20
21 22 23 24 25 26 27
28 29 30 31
```
SEPTEMBER
```
S  M  T  W  T  F  S
                1  2  3
 4  5  6  7  8  9 10
11 12 13 14 15 16 17
18 19 20 21 22 23 24
25 26 27 28 29 30
```
OCTOBER
```
S  M  T  W  T  F  S
                   1
 2  3  4  5  6  7  8
 9 10 11 12 13 14 15
16 17 18 19 20 21 22
23 24 25 26 27 28 29
30 31
```
NOVEMBER
```
S  M  T  W  T  F  S
       1  2  3  4  5
 6  7  8  9 10 11 12
13 14 15 16 17 18 19
20 21 22 23 24 25 26
27 28 29 30
```
DECEMBER
```
S  M  T  W  T  F  S
             1  2  3
 4  5  6  7  8  9 10
11 12 13 14 15 16 17
18 19 20 21 22 23 24
25 26 27 28 29 30 31
```

14

JANUARY
```
S  M  T  W  T  F  S
                   1
 2  3  4  5  6  7  8
 9 10 11 12 13 14 15
16 17 18 19 20 21 22
23 24 25 26 27 28 29
30 31
```
FEBRUARY
```
S  M  T  W  T  F  S
       1  2  3  4  5
 6  7  8  9 10 11 12
13 14 15 16 17 18 19
20 21 22 23 24 25 26
27 28 29
```
MARCH
```
S  M  T  W  T  F  S
          1  2  3  4
 5  6  7  8  9 10 11
12 13 14 15 16 17 18
19 20 21 22 23 24 25
26 27 28 29 30 31
```
APRIL
```
S  M  T  W  T  F  S
                   1
 2  3  4  5  6  7  8
 9 10 11 12 13 14 15
16 17 18 19 20 21 22
23 24 25 26 27 28 29
30
```
MAY
```
S  M  T  W  T  F  S
    1  2  3  4  5  6
 7  8  9 10 11 12 13
14 15 16 17 18 19 20
21 22 23 24 25 26 27
28 29 30 31
```
JUNE
```
S  M  T  W  T  F  S
                1  2  3
 4  5  6  7  8  9 10
11 12 13 14 15 16 17
18 19 20 21 22 23 24
25 26 27 28 29 30
```
JULY
```
S  M  T  W  T  F  S
                   1
 2  3  4  5  6  7  8
 9 10 11 12 13 14 15
16 17 18 19 20 21 22
23 24 25 26 27 28 29
30 31
```
AUGUST
```
S  M  T  W  T  F  S
       1  2  3  4  5
 6  7  8  9 10 11 12
13 14 15 16 17 18 19
20 21 22 23 24 25 26
27 28 29 30 31
```
SEPTEMBER
```
S  M  T  W  T  F  S
                1  2
 3  4  5  6  7  8  9
10 11 12 13 14 15 16
17 18 19 20 21 22 23
24 25 26 27 28 29 30
```
OCTOBER
```
S  M  T  W  T  F  S
 1  2  3  4  5  6  7
 8  9 10 11 12 13 14
15 16 17 18 19 20 21
22 23 24 25 26 27 28
29 30 31
```
NOVEMBER
```
S  M  T  W  T  F  S
          1  2  3  4
 5  6  7  8  9 10 11
12 13 14 15 16 17 18
19 20 21 22 23 24 25
26 27 28 29 30
```
DECEMBER
```
S  M  T  W  T  F  S
                1  2
 3  4  5  6  7  8  9
10 11 12 13 14 15 16
17 18 19 20 21 22 23
24 25 26 27 28 29 30
31
```

Important Dates in the United States and Canada, 2004–2007

Event	2004	2005	2006	2007
New Year's Day[1]	Jan. 1	Jan. 1	Jan. 1	Jan. 1
Martin Luther King Day[1]	Jan. 19	Jan. 17	Jan. 16	Jan. 15
Groundhog Day	Feb. 2	Feb. 2	Feb. 2	Feb. 2
St. Valentine's Day	Feb. 14	Feb. 14	Feb. 14	Feb. 14
Susan B. Anthony Day	Feb. 15	Feb. 15	Feb. 15	Feb. 15
Presidents' Day[1]	Feb. 16	Feb. 21	Feb. 20	Feb. 19
Mardi Gras	Feb. 24	Mar. 8	Feb. 28	Feb. 5
St. Patrick's Day	Mar. 17	Mar. 17	Mar. 17	Mar. 17
April Fool's Day	Apr. 1	Apr. 1	Apr. 1	Apr. 1
Daylight saving time begins	Apr. 4	Apr. 3	Apr. 2	Apr. 1
Arbor Day	Apr. 30	Apr. 29	Apr. 28	Apr. 27
National Teacher Day	May 4	May 3	May 9	May 1
Mother's Day	May 9	May 8	May 14	May 13
Armed Forces Day	May 15	May 14	May 20	May 19
Victoria Day[2]	May 17	May 23	May 22	May 21
National Maritime Day	May 22	May 22	May 22	May 22
Memorial Day[1]	May 31	May 30	May 29	May 28
Flag Day	June 14	June 14	June 14	June 14
Father's Day	June 20	June 19	June 11	June 17
Canada Day[2]	July 1	July 1	July 1	July 1
Independence Day[1]	July 4	July 4	July 4	July 4
Labor Day[1,2]	Sept. 6	Sept. 5	Sept. 4	Sept. 3
Citizenship Day	Sept. 17	Sept. 17	Sept. 17	Sept. 17
Columbus Day[1]	Oct. 11	Oct. 10	Oct. 9	Oct. 8
Thanksgiving Day (Canada)[2]	Oct. 11	Oct. 10	Oct. 9	Oct. 8
United Nations Day	Oct. 24	Oct. 24	Oct. 24	Oct. 24
Daylight saving time ends	Oct. 31	Oct. 30	Oct. 29	Oct. 28
Halloween	Oct. 31	Oct. 31	Oct. 31	Oct. 31
Election Day (U.S.)	Nov. 2	Nov. 8	Nov. 7	Nov. 6
Veterans Day[1,3]	Nov. 11	Nov. 11	Nov. 11	Nov. 11
Remembrance Day[2]	Nov. 11	Nov. 11	Nov. 11	Nov. 11
Thanksgiving Day (U.S.)[1]	Nov. 25	Nov. 24	Nov. 23	Nov. 22
Christmas Day[1,2]	Dec. 25	Dec. 25	Dec. 25	Dec. 25
Boxing Day[2]	Dec. 26	Dec. 26	Dec. 26	Dec. 26
New Year's Eve	Dec. 31	Dec. 31	Dec. 31	Dec. 31

1. Federal holiday in United States. 2. Federal holiday in Canada.
3. Also known as Armistice Day.

Major World Holidays

January 1 New Year's Day throughout the Western world and in India, Indonesia, Japan, Korea, the Philippines, Singapore, Taiwan, and Thailand; founding of Republic of China (Taiwan)

January 2 Berchtoldstag in Switzerland

January 3 Genshi-Sai (First Beginning) in Japan

January 5 Twelfth Night (Wassail Eve or Eve of Epiphany) in England

January 6 Epiphany, observed by Catholics throughout Europe and Latin America

mid-January Martin Luther King Jr.'s birthday on the third Monday in the Virgin Islands

January 15 Adults' Day in Japan

January 20 St. Agnes Eve in Great Britain

January 24 Australia Day in Australia

January 26 Republic Day in India

January–February Chinese New Year and Vietnamese New Year (Tet)

February Hamstrom on the first Sunday in Switzerland

February 3 Setsubun (Bean-throwing Festival) in Japan

February 5 Promulgation of the Constitution Day in Mexico

February 11 National Foundation Day in Japan

February 27 Independence Day in the Dominican Republic

March 1 Independence Movement Day in Korea; Constitution Day in Panama

March 8 Women's Day in many socialist countries

March 17 St. Patrick's Day in Ireland and Northern Ireland

March 19 St. Joseph's Day in Colombia, Costa Rica, Italy, and Spain

March 21 Benito Juárez's Birthday in Mexico

March 22 Arab League Day in Arab League countries

March 23 Pakistan Day in Pakistan

March 25 Independence Day in Greece; Lady Day (Quarter Day) in Great Britain

March 26 Fiesta del Árbol (Arbor Day) in Spain

March 29 Youth and Martyr's Day in Taiwan

March 30 Muslim New Year in Indonesia

March–April Carnival/Lent/Easter; The pre-Lenten celebration of Carnival (Mardi Gras) and the post-Lenten celebration of Easter are moveable feasts widely observed in Christian countries

April 1 Victory Day in Spain; April Fools' Day (All Fools' Day) in Great Britain

April 5 Arbor Day in Korea

April 6 Van Riebeeck Day in South Africa

April 7 World Health Day in UN member nations

April 8 Buddha's Birthday in Korea and Japan; Hana Matsuri (Flower Festival) in Japan

April 14 Pan American Day in the Americas

April 19 Declaration of Independence Day in Venezuela

April 22 Queen Isabella Day in Spain

April 23 St. George's Day in England

April 25 Liberation Day in Italy; ANZAC Day in Australia and New Zealand

April 29 Emperor's Day in Japan

April 30 Queen's Birthday in the Netherlands; Walpurgis Night in Germany and Scandinavia

May Constitution Day on first Monday in Japan

May 1 May Day–Labor Day in Russia and most of Europe and Latin America

May 5 Children's Day in Japan and Korea; Victory of General Zaragoza Day in Mexico; Liberation Day in the Netherlands

May 8 V-E Day in Europe

May 9 Victory over Fascism Day in Russia

May 19 Victory Day in Canada

May 31 Republic Day in South Africa

June 2 Founding of the Republic Day in Italy

June 5 Constitution Day in Denmark

June 6 Memorial Day in Korea; Flag Day in Sweden

June 8 Muhammad's Birthday in Indonesia

June 10 Portugal Day in Portugal

June 12 Independence Day in the Philippines

mid-June Queen's Official Birthday on second Saturday in Great Britain

June 16 Soweto Day in UN member nations

June 17 German Unity Day in Germany

June 20 Flag Day in Argentina

June 22 Midsummer's Day in Finland

June 24 Midsummer's Day in Great Britain

June 29 Feasts of Saints Peter and Paul in Chile, Colombia, Italy, Peru, Spain, and Venezuela

July 1 Canada Day in Canada; Half-year Holiday in Hong Kong; Bank Holiday in Taiwan

July 5 Independence Day in Venezuela

July 9 Independence Day in Argentina

July 10 Bon (Feast of Fortune) in Japan

July 12 Orangemen's Day in Northern Ireland

July 14 Bastille Day in France

mid-July Féria de San Fermín during second week in Spain

July 17 Constitution Day in Korea

July 18 National Day in Spain

July 20 Independence Day in Colombia

July 21–22 National Holiday in Belgium

July 22 National Liberation Day in Poland

July 24 Simón Bolívar's Birthday in Ecuador and Venezuela

July 25 St. James Day in Spain

July 28–29 Independence Day in Peru

August Holiday on first Monday in Fiji, Grenada, Guyana, Hong Kong, Ireland, and Malawi; Independence Day on first Tuesday in Jamaica

August 1 Lammas Day in England; National Day in Switzerland

August 5 Discovery Day in Trinidad and Tobago

August 9 National Day in Singapore

August 10 Independence Day in Ecuador

August 12 Queen's Birthday in Thailand

August 14 Independence Day in Pakistan

August 15 Independence Day in India and Korea; Assumption Day in Catholic countries

August 16 National Restoration Day in the Dominican Republic

August 17 Independence Day in Indonesia

August 31 Independence Day in Trinidad and Tobago

September Rose of Tralee Festival in Ireland

September 7 Independence Day in Brazil

September 9 Choxo-no-Sekku (Chrysanthemum Day) in Japan

September 14 Battle of San Jacinto Day in Nicaragua

mid-September Sherry Wine Harvest in Spain

September 15 Independence Day in Costa Rica, Guatemala, and Nicaragua; Respect for the Aged Day in Japan

September 16 Independence Day in Mexico and Papua New Guinea

September 18–19 Independence Day in Chile; St. Gennaro Day in Italy

September 28 Confucius's Birthday in Taiwan

October 1 National Day in People's Republic of China; Armed Forces Day in Korea; National Holiday in Nigeria

October 2 National Day in People's Republic of China; Mahatma Gandhi's Birthday in India

October 3 National Foundation Day in Korea

October 5 Proclamation of the Portuguese Republic Day in Portugal

October 7 Foundation in the German Democratic Republic

October 9 Korean Alphabet Day in Korea

October 10 Kruger Day in South Africa; Founding of the Republic of China in Taiwan

October 12 Columbus Day in Spain and widely throughout Mexico, and Central and South America

October 19 Ascension of Muhammad Day in Indonesia

October 20 Revolution Day in Guatemala; Kenyatta Day in Kenya

October 24 United Nations Day in UN member nations

October 26 National Holiday in Austria

October 28 Greek National Day in Greece

November 1 All Saints' Day, observed by Catholics in most countries

November 2 All Souls' Day in Ecuador, El Salvador, Luxembourg, Macao, Mexico (Day of the Dead), San Marino, Uruguay, and Vatican City

November 4 National Unity Day in Italy

November 5 Guy Fawkes Day in Great Britain

November 7–8 October Revolution Day in Russia

November 11 Armistice Day in Belgium, France, French Guiana, and Tahiti; Remembrance Day in Canada

November 12 Sun Yat-sen's Birthday in Taiwan

November 15 Proclamation of the Republic Day in Brazil

November 17 Day of Penance in Federal Republic of Germany

November 19 National Holiday in Monaco

November 20 Anniversary of the Revolution in Mexico

November 23 Kinro-Kansha-no-Hi (Labor Thanksgiving Day) in Japan

November 30 National Heroes' Day in the Philippines

December 5 Discovery by Columbus Day in Haiti; Constitution Day in Russia

December 6 Independence Day in Finland

December 8 Feast of the Immaculate Conception, widely observed in Catholic countries

December 10 Constitution Day in Thailand; Human Rights Day in UN member nations

December 12 Janhuri Day in Kenya; Guadalupe Day in Mexico

mid-December Nine Days of Posada during third week in Mexico

December 25 Christmas Day, widely observed in all Christian countries

December 26 St. Stephen's Day in Austria, Ireland, Italy, Liechtenstein, San Marino, Switzerland, and Barcelona (Spain); Boxing Day in Canada, Australia, and the U.K.

December 26–January 1 Kwanzaa in the United States

December 28 National Day in Nepal

December 31 New Year's Eve throughout the world; Omisoka (Grand Last Day) in Japan; Hogmanay Day in Scotland

Major Holidays on the American Calendar

JANUARY

New Year's Day (January 1): This holiday has its origins in Roman times, when sacrifices were offered to the god Janus in the wintertime. Janus was a two-faced god who looked back on the past and forward to the future at the same time.

Epiphany (January 6): Celebrated on the twelfth day after Christmas. This holiday is in observance of the manifestation of Jesus as the Son of God. Epiphany originally marked the beginning of the carnival season that preceded Lent.

Martin Luther King Day (observed on the third Monday in January): Honors the birthday of the slain civil rights leader who preached nonviolence and led the March on Washington in 1963. Dr. King's most famous speech is entitled "I Have a Dream."

FEBRUARY

Groundhog Day (February 2): According to legend, if a groundhog in Punxsutawney, Pennsylvania, peeks his head out of his burrow and sees his shadow, he'll return to his hole and there will be six more weeks of winter.

Abraham Lincoln's Birthday (February 12): Honors the 16th president of the United States, who led the nation through the Civil War (1861–1865) and was then assassinated. This holiday was first formally observed in Washington, D.C., in 1866, when both houses of Congress gathered to pay tribute to the slain president.

Valentine's Day (February 14): This holiday of love originated as a festival for two martyrs from the third century, both named St. Valentine. The holiday's association with romance may have come from an ancient belief that birds mate on this day.

Presidents' Day (second Monday in February): This official government holiday was created in observance of both Washington's and Lincoln's birthdays.

Washington's Birthday (February 22): Honors the first president of the United States, known as the Father of Our Country. This holiday was first observed in America in 1796, a year before Washington left office.

Shrove Tuesday (February or March): Observed on the day before Ash Wednesday. This holiday marks the end of carnival season.

Ash Wednesday (February or March): This is the first day of the Lenten season, which lasts a total of 40 days. This day of penance has been observed by Roman Catholics since before A.D. 1000.

MARCH AND APRIL

St. Patrick's Day (March 17): Honors the patron saint of Ireland. Most often celebrated in the United States with parties and special dinners, the most famous event is the annual St. Patrick's Day parade on Fifth Avenue in New York City.

Palm Sunday (Sunday before Easter): Commemorates the entry of Jesus into Jerusalem.

Good Friday (Friday before Easter): Commemorates the crucifixion of Jesus Christ, which is retold during the services.

Passover (March or April): Also called the Feast of Unleavened Bread, this holiday is observed by Jews all over the world. The focus of the holiday is a special feast called a seder, which incorporates foods that commemorate the escape of the Jews from Ancient Egypt.

Easter Sunday (March or April): Commemorates the resurrection of Jesus Christ; celebrated on the first Sunday after the full moon that occurs on or after March 21. (Easter is usually between March 22 and April 25.)

MAY

Mother's Day (second Sunday in May): First proposed by Anna Jarvis of Philadelphia in 1907, this holiday has become a national time for family gatherings and showing appreciation to mothers.

Memorial Day (last Monday in May): Also known as Decoration Day, this legal holiday was created in 1868 by order of General John A. Logan as a day on which the graves of Civil War soldiers would be decorated. Since that time, the day has been set aside to honor all American soldiers who have given their lives for their country.

JUNE

Flag Day (June 14): Set aside to commemorate the adoption of the Stars and Stripes by the Continental Congress on June 14,1777. It is a legal holiday only in Pennsylvania but is generally acknowleged and observed in many states each year.

Father's Day (third Sunday in June): Honors the role of the father in the American family, as Mother's Day honors the role of the mother.

JULY

Independence Day (July 4): Anniversary of the signing of the Declaration of Independence, July 4, 1776. The holiday has been celebrated nationwide since 1777, the first anniversary of the signing.

SEPTEMBER

Labor Day (first Monday in September): First proposed by Peter J. McGuire in New York in 1882, this holiday was created to honor the labor unions and workers who built the nation.

Rosh Hashanah (September): On the Hebrew calendar, this marks the Jewish New Year. It also begins a 10-day period of penitence that leads to Yom Kippur.

Yom Kippur (September–October): Also known as the Day of Atonement, this is the most holy of all Jewish holidays.

OCTOBER

Columbus Day (October 12): Commemorates the "discovery" of the "New World" by Italian explorer Christopher Columbus in 1492. Even though the land was already populated by Native Americans when Columbus arrived, this "discovery" marks the beginning of European influence in America.

United Nations Day (October 24): Marks the founding of the United Nations, which began in its present capacity in 1945 but had already been in operation as the League of Nations.

Halloween (October 31): Also known as All Hallows' Eve, this holiday has its origins in ancient Celtic rituals that marked the beginning of winter with bonfires, masquerades, and the telling of ghost stories.

NOVEMBER

Election Day (first Tuesday after the first Monday in November): Since it was declared an official holiday by Congress in 1845, presidential elections have been taking place on this day every four years. Most statewide elections are also held on this day, but election years vary according to state.

Veterans Day (November 11): Originally called Armistice Day, this holiday was created to celebrate the end of World War I in 1918. In June 1954, Congress changed the name of the holiday to Veterans Day and declared that the day would honor all men and women who have served in America's armed forces.

Thanksgiving (fourth Thursday in November): President Lincoln was the first president to proclaim Thanksgiving a national holiday in1863. Most people believe the tradition of reserving a day of thanks began with an order given by Governor Bradford of Plymouth Colony in New England in 1621.

DECEMBER

Hanukkah (usually December): Also known as the Festival of Lights, this Jewish holiday commemorates the repurification of the Temple of Jerusalem in 162 A.D. Purification

involved the burning of holy oil, and a one-day supply miraculously burned for eight days. Today, on each of the eight nights, an additional candle is added to the menorah, or candelabra.

Christmas (December 25): This day, which celebrates the birth of Jesus, is the most widely celebrated holiday of the Christian year. Customs associated with Christmas are centuries old. The use of mistletoe, for example, comes from the Druids.

Kwanzaa (December 26): This is a spiritual festival for African Americans that celebrates the goodness of life.

CHEMISTRY

One Tired Turkey?

Some people fall asleep before the big game on Thanksgiving. L-tryptophan, an amino acid in turkey, is often blamed for making people sleepy. It helps the body produce niacin, an important B vitamin. The niacin then allows the body to produce serotonin, a neurotransmitter that makes people feel sleepy. However, L-tryptophan has to be taken on an empty stomach to make people feel sleepy, so it's probably the large meal rather than the turkey that makes people drowsy.

Seeing Sparks

A spark occurs when energy is input into atoms from heat, friction, or electricity. The electrons in the atom absorb this energy. When the electrons return to their usual state, the energy is released in the form of light. One way to observe this is with a wintergreen LifeSavers candy. Crush the candy with pliers in a dark room. Rubbing two sugar cubes together in the dark will also work.

Color Change

The color of a leaf results from an interaction of different pigments produced by the plant. The main pigments responsible for leaf color are porphyrins, carotenoids, and flavonoids. The color that we see depends on the amounts and types of pigments that are present. Chemical interactions within the plant, mainly in response to acidity or pH, also affect the leaf color.

The Formulas of Food

Chemistry plays a major part in most food products. Soda may contain many different acids. The acid that produces bubbles is carbonic acid. BHA and BHT are two chemicals commonly used as preservatives in food. They keep fats from turning rancid. Chocolate and cocoa naturally contain relatively high levels of cadmium and lead.

Timeline of Notable Discoveries in Chemistry

1627–1691 Robert Boyle (1627–1691), an English chemist, helps found the modern science of chemistry. He studies calcination of metals and develops the standard definition of *element*.

1669 Phosphorus discovered by Hennig Brand (died c. 1692).

1735 Cobalt discovered by Georg Brandt (1694–1768).

1735 Platinum discovered by Antonio de Ulloa (1716–1795).

1751 Nickel discovered by Baron Axel F. Cronstedt (1722–1765).

1766 English chemist and physicist Henry Cavendish (1731–1810) discovers hydrogen.

1772 Nitrogen discovered by Daniel Rutherford (1749–1819).

1774 Oxygen is discovered by Joseph Priestley (1733–1804). He calls it "dephlogisticated air." Previous discovery by Karl W. Schleele (1742–1786) is not published until 1777.

1774 Chlorine and manganese discovered by Karl W. Schleele (1742–1786).

1789 Uranium and zirconium discovered by Martin H. Klaproth (1743–1817).

1791 Titanium discovered by William Gregor (1761–1817).

1800 Italian physicist Alessandro Volta (1745–1827) invents the first battery, proving that electricity can be generated by chemical action. His "voltaic pile" uses disks of silver and zinc.

1807 Sodium and potassium discovered by Sir Humphry Davy (1778–1829).

1808 Barium, calcium, strontium, and magnesium discovered by Sir Humphry Davy.

1808–1810 English chemist John Dalton (1766–1844) publishes his revolutionary atomic theory of matter in his *New System of Chemical Philosophy*. He holds that all elements are made of tiny atoms, each of same weight. His work further confirms Joseph Louis Proust's theory of constant proportions.

1811 Iodine discovered by Bernard Courtois (1777–1838).

1817 Cadmium discovered by Friedrich Stromeyer (1776–1835).

1817 Lithium discovered by Johan A. Arfwedson (1792–1841).

1818 Selenium discovered by Jöns Jakob Berzelius (1779–1848).

c. 1824 Silicon discovered by Jöns Jakob Berzelius.

1825 Aluminum discovered by Hans C. Oersted (1777–1851).

1826 Bromine discovered by Antoine J. Balard (1802–1876).

1833 British chemist and physicist Michael Faraday (1791–1867) formulates his law of electrolysis.

1868 Helium discovered by Pierre Janssen (1824–1907) and Joseph N. Lockyer (1836–1920).

1869 Dmitry Mendeleyev (1834–1907) first publishes his periodic table of elements.

1886 Fluorine discovered by Henri Moissan (1852–1907).

1894 Argon discovered by John Strutt, Baron Rayleigh (1842–1919), and Sir William Ramsay (1852–1916).

1898 Krypton, neon, and xenon discovered by Sir William Ramsay (1852–1916) and Morris W. Travers (1872–1961).

1898 Radium and polonium (first element discovered by radiochemical analysis) discovered by Pierre Curie (1859–1906) and Marie Curie (1867–1934).

1900 Radon discovered by Friedrich E. Dorn (1848–1916).

1931 U.S. chemist Linus Pauling (1901–1994) introduces chemical theory of resonance to explain bonding of atoms in certain molecules, notably benzene.

1940 Plutonium discovered by Glenn T. Seaborg (b. 1912).

1957 Polypropylene, lightweight plastic, is created.

c. 1964 Simplified technique for synthesizing proteins is introduced by American researcher Bruce Merrifield (b. 1921). It soon is adapted to automatic machines and becomes important in gene synthesis in 1980s.

1970 Human growth hormone is synthesized.

1983 American Chemical Society reports the number of chemicals it has recorded to date has reached six million. Millions of others are believed known but not formally recorded.

The Periodic Table of Elements

alkali metals I A	alkaline earth metals II A					transition metals									III B	IV A	V A	VI A	VII A	noble gases 0
Period 1 1 **H** 1.01 Hydrogen																				2 **He** 4.00 Helium
Period 2 3 **Li** 6.94 Lithium	4 **Be** 9.01 Beryllium														5 **B** 10.81 Boron	6 **C** 12.01 Carbon	7 **N** 14.01 Nitrogen	8 **O** 16.00 Oxygen	9 **F** 19.00 Flourine	10 **Ne** 20.18 Neon
Period 3 11 **Na** 22.99 Sodium	12 **Mg** 24.31 Magnesium	III B	IV B	V B	VI B	VII B	VIII			I B	II B				13 **Al** 26.98 Aluminum	14 **Si** 28.09 Silicon	15 **P** 30.97 Phosphorus	16 **S** 32.07 Sulphur	17 **Cl** 35.45 Chlorine	18 **Ar** 39.95 Argon
Period 4 19 **K** 39.10 Potassium	20 **Ca** 40.08 Calcium	21 **Sc** 44.96 Scandium	22 **Ti** 47.88 Titanium	23 **V** 50.94 Vanadium	24 **Cr** 52.00 Chromium	25 **Mn** 54.95 Manganese	26 **Fe** 55.84 Iron	27 **Co** 58.93 Cobalt	28 **Ni** 58.70 Nickel	29 **Cu** 63.55 Copper	30 **Zn** 65.39 Zinc				31 **Ga** 69.72 Gallium	32 **Ge** 72.61 Germanium	33 **As** 74.92 Arsenic	34 **Se** 78.96 Selenium	35 **Br** 79.90 Bromine	36 **Kr** 83.80 Krypton
Period 5 37 **Rb** 85.47 Rubidium	38 **Sr** 87.62 Strontium	39 **Y** 88.91 Yttrium	40 **Zr** 95.94 Zirconium	41 **Nb** 92.91 Niobium	42 **Mo** 95.94 Molybdenum	43 **Tc** (98) Technetium	44 **Ru** 101.07 Ruthenium	45 **Rh** 102.91 Rhodium	46 **Pd** 106.4 Palladium	47 **Ag** 107.87 Silver	48 **Cd** 112.41 Cadmium				49 **In** 114.82 Indium	50 **Sn** 118.71 Tin	51 **Sb** 121.74 Antimony	52 **Te** 127.60 Tellurium	53 **I** 126.90 Iodine	54 **Xe** 131.29 Xenon
Period 6 55 **Cs** 132.91 Cesium	56 **Ba** 137.33 Barium	Lanthanide series (see below)	72 **Hf** 178.49 Hafnium	73 **Ta** 180.94 Tantalum	74 **W** 183.85 Tungsten	75 **Re** 186.21 Rhenium	76 **Os** 190.23 Osmium	77 **Ir** 192.22 Iridium	78 **Pt** 195.08 Platinum	79 **Au** 196.97 Gold	80 **Hg** 200.59 Mercury				81 **Tl** 204.38 Thallium	82 **Pb** 207.2 Lead	83 **Bi** 208.98 Bismuth	84 **Po** (209) Polonium	85 **At** (210) Astatine	86 **Rn** (222) Radon
Period 7 87 **Fr** (223) Francium	88 **Ra** 226.03 Radium	Actinide series (see below)	104 **Rf** 261 Rutherfordium	105 **Ha/Db** 262 Hahnium/Dubnium	106 **Sg** 266 Seaborgium	107 **Bh** 267 Bohrium	108 **Hs** 269 Hassium	109 **Mt** 268 Meitnerium	110 (273)	111 (272)	112 (277)				113	114	115	116	117	118

other metals

rare earth elements— Lanthanide series	57 **La** 138.91 Lanthanum	58 **Ce** 140.12 Cerium	59 **Pr** 140.91 Praseodymium	60 **Nd** 144.24 Neodymium	61 **Pm** (145) Promethium	62 **Sm** 150.4 Samarium	63 **Eu** 151.96 Europium	64 **Gd** 157.25 Gadolinium	65 **Tb** 158.93 Terbium	66 **Dy** 162.50 Dysprosium	67 **Ho** 164.93 Holmium	68 **Er** 167.26 Erbium	69 **Tm** 168.93 Thulium	70 **Yb** 173.04 Ytterbium	71 **Lu** 174.97 Luetium
Actinide series	89 **Ac** 227.03 Actinium	90 **Th** 232.04 Thorium	91 **Pa** 231.04 Protactinium	92 **U** 238.03 Uranium	93 **Np** 237.03 Neptunium	94 **Pu** (244) Plutonium	95 **Am** (243) Americium	96 **Cm** (247) Curium	97 **Bk** (247) Berkelium	98 **Cf** (251) Californium	99 **Es** (252) Einsteinium	100 **Fm** (257) Fermium	101 **Md** (258) Mendelevium	102 **No** (259) Nobelium	103 **Lr** (260) Lawrencium

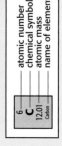

Key:
- 6 — atomic number
- **C** — chemical symbol
- 12.01 — atomic mass
- Carbon — name of element

Source: *New York Times Almanac,* 2003

COMMUNICATION

Beeper Bonanza

About 2.2 million of the 53 million pager users in the United States are under the age of 18. Most of those pagers were purchased by parents so they could communicate more easily with their children. While the average pager user in the United States receives 25 pages per week, those under 18 receive more than 30 per week.

Mail Mania

The U.S Postal Service handles more than 200 billion pieces of mail per year. That's equivalent to five pieces of mail every day to every address in the United States! The postal service serves more than 7 million customers daily at 38,000 postal retail outlets. In addition, mail carriers collect mail from more than 326,000 street mail collection boxes across the country.

It's for You

The number of calls made from the United States to other countries totaled 6.6 billion in 2000 for a total international phone bill of about $14.9 billion!

A Quick Connection

High-speed Internet connection lines are growing quickly in popularity. High-speed access to the Internet increased by 36% in just one year to total 9.6 million connection lines in December 2001. By 2004, high-speed Internet will be in place in 25 million homes and provider revenue will total $13.3 billion.

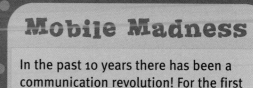

Mobile Madness

In the past 10 years there has been a communication revolution! For the first time, Americans now use their mobile phones more than traditional landline phones. The average person's monthly mobile-phone use exceeds 490 minutes, while monthly landline use is approximately 480 minutes.

Postal Abbreviations for States and Territories

Northern Mariana Islands	CM
Puerto Rico	PR
Trust Territory of the Pacific	TT
Virgin Islands	VI

Internet Definitions and Terms

Browser
Short for Web browser, it is a program that allows you to search the Internet for information.

Download

The transfer of information from the Internet to your computer.

E-mail
Electronic mail that allows you to send and receive messages though the Internet.

Http

Hypertext Transfer Protocol. A set of rules that tells computers how to communicate with one another.

URL
Uniform Resource Locator. The address of an Internet site.

WWW

World Wide Web. The multimedia database of information on the Internet.

Top 5 Most Linked-To Sites on the World Wide Web

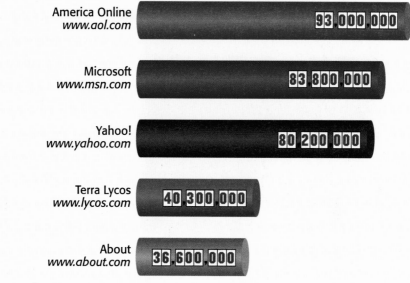

America Online
www.aol.com
93,000,000

Microsoft
www.msn.com
83,800,000

Yahoo!
www.yahoo.com
80 200 000

Terra Lycos
www.lycos.com
40,300,000

About
www.about.com
36,600,000

Source: Media Metrix, 2001

Radio Formats of the United States
(as percentage of total listeners)

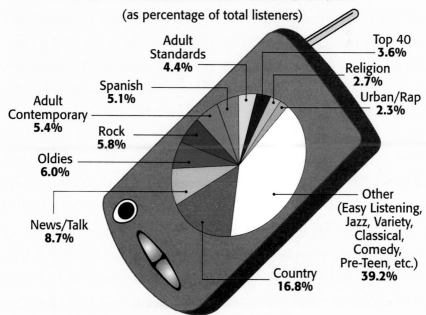

Adult Standards
4.4%

Top 40
3.6%

Spanish
5.1%

Religion
2.7%

Adult Contemporary
5.4%

Urban/Rap
2.3%

Rock
5.8%

Oldies
6.0%

Other
(Easy Listening,
Jazz, Variety,
Classical,
Comedy,
Pre-Teen, etc.)
39.2%

News/Talk
8.7%

Country
16.8%

Source: International Telecommunications Union, 2002

Top 5 Countries With the Most Post Offices

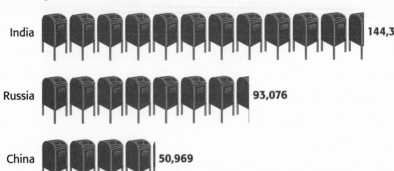

India	144,396
Russia	93,076
China	50,969
United States	39,270
Turkey	28,086

Source: *CIA World Factbook*, 2001

Top 5 Countries With the Most Cellular Phone Users
(in millions)

United States	127.0M
Japan	74.8M
Germany	56.2M
Italy	48.7M
United Kingdom	47.0M

Source: International Telecommunications Union, 2001

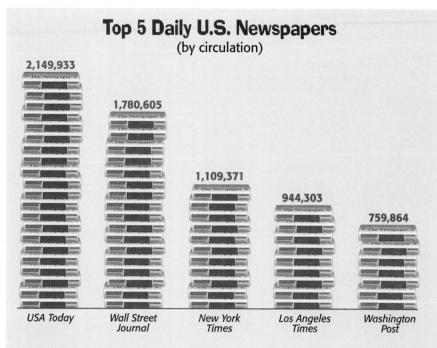

Top 5 Daily U.S. Newspapers
(by circulation)

2,149,933 — USA Today

1,780,605 — Wall Street Journal

1,109,371 — New York Times

944,303 — Los Angeles Times

759,864 — Washington Post

Source: *Editor & Publisher International Handbook*, 2001

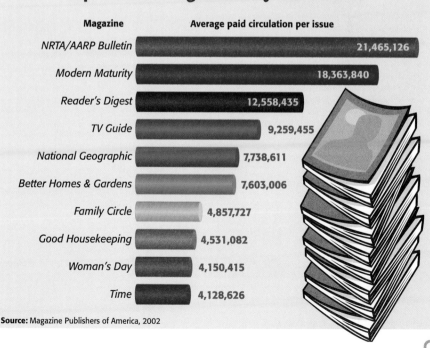

Top 10 U.S. Magazines by Circulation

Magazine	Average paid circulation per issue
NRTA/AARP Bulletin	21,465,126
Modern Maturity	18,363,840
Reader's Digest	12,558,435
TV Guide	9,259,455
National Geographic	7,738,611
Better Homes & Gardens	7,603,006
Family Circle	4,857,727
Good Housekeeping	4,531,082
Woman's Day	4,150,415
Time	4,128,626

Source: Magazine Publishers of America, 2002

Top-Selling U.S. Kids' Magazines
(based on total paid circulation)

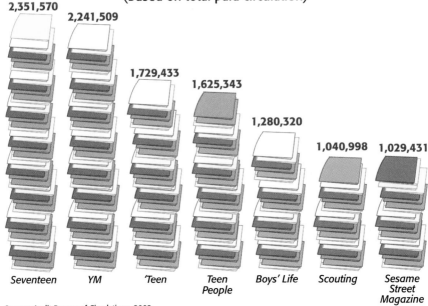

Seventeen	YM	'Teen	Teen People	Boys' Life	Scouting	Sesame Street Magazine
2,351,570	2,241,509	1,729,433	1,625,343	1,280,320	1,040,998	1,029,431

Source: Audit Bureau of Circulations, 2002

Top 10 Magazine Genres in the U.S.

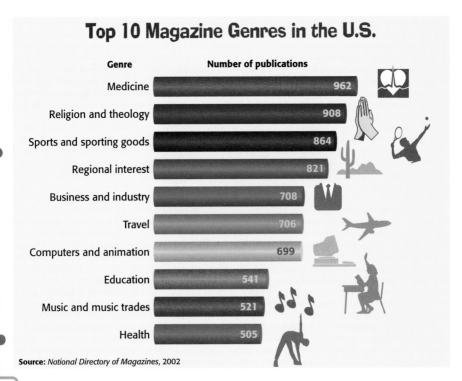

Genre	Number of publications
Medicine	962
Religion and theology	908
Sports and sporting goods	864
Regional interest	821
Business and industry	708
Travel	706
Computers and animation	699
Education	541
Music and music trades	521
Health	505

Source: *National Directory of Magazines*, 2002

Selected Hot Lines and Information Services

AIDS hot line	(800) 342-AIDS
Auto safety hot line	(800) 424-9393
	(202) 426-0123 in Washington, DC
Child abuse hot line	(800) 4-A-CHILD
College money hot line	(800) 638-6700
	(800) 492-6602 in Maryland
Drug hot line	(800) 662-HELP
National Center for Missing and Exploited Children	(800) 843-5678
Parents Anonymous/Abuse prevention hot line	(800) 421-0353
Parents who have kidnapped their children hot line	(800) A-WAY-OUT
Poison hot line	(800) 343-2722
Consumer Product Safety Commission product safety hot line	(800) 638-2772
Runaway hot line	(800) 621-4000
	(800) 972-6004 in Illinois
Shriner's Hospital free children's hospital care referral line	(800) 237-5055

How to Get in Touch With Selected Government Agencies

SENATE

Senator's name
United States Senate
Washington, DC 20510

HOUSE OF REPRESENTATIVES

Representative's name
United States House
of Representatives
Washington, DC 20510

DEPARTMENT OF AGRICULTURE

1400 Independence Avenue SW
Washington, DC 20250
Main number: (202) 720-2791
Web site: http://www.usda.gov/

For information on: **animal and plant health; consumer affairs; family nutrition; food safety and inspection; human nutrition; veterinary medicine.**

DEPARTMENT OF COMMERCE

1401 Constitution Avenue NW
Washington, DC 20230
Main number: (202) 482-2000
Reference: (202) 377-2161
Web site: http://www.commerce.gov/

For information on: **business outlook analyses; economic and demographic statistics; engineering; imports and exports; minority-owned businesses; patents and trademarks; technology; travel; weather and atmosphere.**

DEPARTMENT OF DEFENSE

The Pentagon
1400 Defense Pentagon,
  Rm 3A750
Washington, DC 20301-1400
Main number: (703) 545-6700
Web site: http://www.dod.gov/

For information on: **atomic energy; foreign country security; mapping; military history; nuclear operations and technology; tactical warfare.**

DEPARTMENT OF EDUCATION

400 Maryland Avenue SW
Washington, DC 20202
Main office: (800) USA-LEARN
Web site: http://www.ed.gov/

For information on: **adult education; bilingual education; civil rights; educational statistics; elementary and secondary education; access and services for the disabled; higher education; libraries; special education.**

DEPARTMENT OF ENERGY

Forrestal Building
1000 Independence Avenue SW
Washington, DC 20585
Main number: (202) DIAL-DOE
Public affairs: (202) 586-6827
Web site: http://www.doe.gov/

For information on: **coal liquids, gas, shale, oil; conservation; energy emergencies; fusion energy; inventions; nuclear energy; nuclear physics.**

DEPARTMENT OF HEALTH AND HUMAN SERVICES

200 Independence Avenue SW
Washington, DC 20201
Main number: (202) 619-0257
Web site: http://www.os.dhhs.gov/

For information on: **AIDS; alcohol abuse; diseases; drug abuse; drug research; family planning; food safety; minority health; occupational safety; smoking; statistical data; toxic substances; veterinary medicine.**

DEPARTMENT OF THE INTERIOR

1849 C Street NW
Washington, DC 20240
Main number: (202) 208-3100
Web site: http://www.doi.gov/

For information on: **archaeology; fish and wildlife; geology; mapping; minerals; Native Americans; natural resources; water.**

DEPARTMENT OF JUSTICE

950 Pennsylvania Avenue NW
Washington, DC 20530
Office of the Attorney
  General: (202) 514-2001
Public affairs: (202) 616-2777
Web site: http://www.usdoj.gov/

For information on: **civil rights; drug enforcement; immigration; justice statistics; juvenile justice; prisons.**

DEPARTMENT OF TRANSPORTATION

400 7th Street SW
Washington, DC 20590
Main number: (202) 366-4000
Public affairs: (202) 366-4570
Web site: http://www.dot.gov/

For information on: **automobile safety; aviation safety; aviation standards; boating; hazardous materials transportation; highway safety; mass transit; railroad safety; shipbuilding; vehicle accident statistics; vehicle crashworthiness.**

DEPARTMENT OF THE TREASURY

1500 Pennsylvania Avenue NW
Washington, DC 20220
Main number: (202) 622-2000
Web site: http://www.ustreas.gov/

For information on: **coin and medal production; currency production; currency research and development; customs; savings bonds; Secret Service protection; taxpayer assistance; tax return investigation.**

ENVIRONMENTAL PROTECTION AGENCY

1200 Pennsylvania Avenue NW
Washington, DC 20460
Main number: (202) 272-0167
Web site: http://www.epa.gov/

For information on: **air and radiation; pesticides and toxic substances; acid deposition; environmental monitoring and quality assurance; solid waste and emergency response; water; noise control.**

FEDERAL COMMUNICATIONS COMMISSION

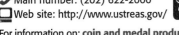

445 12th Street SW
Washington, DC 20554
Main number: (888) CALL-FCC
Web site: http://www.fcc.gov/

For information on: **cable television; broadcast stations; radio regulation.**

NATIONAL AERONAUTICS AND SPACE ADMINISTRATION

300 E Street SW
Washington, DC 20546
Main number: (202) 358-0000
Web site: http://www.nasa.gov/

For information on: **aeronautics and space technology; life sciences; astrophysics; earth sciences; solar system exploration; space shuttle payload; Mars observer program; microgravity science; upper atmosphere research; solar flares.**

NATIONAL ENDOWMENT FOR THE ARTS

1100 Pennsylvania Avenue NW
Washington, DC 20506
Main number: (202) 682-5400
Web site: http://www.arts.endow.gov/

For information on: **literature; museums; folk arts; visual arts; dance arts; theater; opera; history; language.**

NATIONAL ENDOWMENT FOR THE HUMANITIES

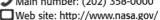

1100 Pennsylvania Avenue NW, Room 406
Washington, DC 20506
Main number: (202) 606-8400
Web site: http://www.neh.fed.us/

For information on: **literature; museums; folk arts; visual arts; dance arts; music arts; theater arts and musical theater; opera; media arts (film, radio, TV); history; language.**

NATIONAL SCIENCE FOUNDATION

4201 Wilson Boulevard
Arlington, VA 22230
Main number: (703) 292-5111
Web site: http://www.nsf.gov/

For information on: **atmospheric/astronomical and earth-ocean sciences; mathematical and physical sciences; Arctic and Antarctic research; anthropology; engineering; biology; genetic biology; chemistry; computer science; earthquakes; economics; ethics and science; meteorology; galactic and extragalactic astronomy; geography; geology; history and philosophy of science; nutrition; linguistics; marine chemistry; minority research; science and technology to aid the disabled.**

COMPUTERS

Speediest Stats per Second

The Earth Simulator in Yokohama, Japan, is the world's fastest computer. It can perform 35.86 trillion calculations per second—4.5 times more than the next fastest machine. The Earth Simulator is used to study the planet's climate.

Index Insanity

In December 2001, the Google Web site achieved a new record for search engines, with 1.5 billion documents indexed. Every time you do a search on Google, your key terms are filtered through each of the indexed pages to find potential matches.

What's in a Name?

The United States has more than 11 million domain names—or Web site address—of the 15.8 million that exist worldwide. Some names are considered more valuable than others. The most expensive Internet domain name—business.com—sold for $7.5 million in December 1999.

Kids Choose Computers

Kids like their computers . . . a lot! In a 2002 survey, some 33% of children and teens polled said they would keep their computer if they could have only one communication device. Another 26% chose television, some 21% picked telephone, and just 15% chose radio.

Call a Doctor!

Approximately 50,000 computer viruses are currently in existence—with as many as 10 new viruses being created each day. To date, the "I Love You" virus has been one of the most destructive. More than half a year after it hit, some 50 versions of the virus were still attacking computers worldwide.

Computers in Use: U.S. vs. the World

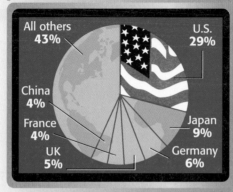

All others **43%**

U.S. **29%**

China **4%**

France **4%**

Japan **9%**

UK **5%**

Germany **6%**

Source: Based on data from *Computer Industry Almanac*, 2002

Computers per Capita: U.S. vs. the World

 United States 585 per 1,000 people

 Worldwide Average  104 per 1,000 people

Source: U.S. Census Bureau, 2001

Internet Timeline

1969 ARPA (Advanced Research Projects Agency) goes online in December. It connects four major U.S. universities. Designed for research, education, and government organizations, it provides a communications network linking the country in the event that a military attack destroys conventional communications systems.

1972 Electronic mail is introduced. Queen Elizabeth sends her first e-mail in 1976.

1973 Transmission Control Protocol/Internet Protocol (TCP/IP) is designed. In 1983 it becomes the standard for communicating between computers over the Internet. One of these protocols, FTP (File Transfer Protocol), allows users to log on to a remote computer, list the files on that computer, and download files from that computer.

1989 Peter Deutsch at McGill University in Montreal, Canada, is the first to index the Internet. He devises Archie, an archive of FTP sites. Tim Berners-Lee of CERN (European Laboratory for Particle Physics) develops a new technique for distributing information on the Internet, which is eventually called the World Wide Web. The Web is based on hypertext, which permits the user to connect from one document to another at different sites on the Internet via hyperlinks (specially programmed words, phrases, buttons, or graphics). Unlike other Internet protocols, such as FTP and e-mail, the Web is accessible through a graphical user interface.

1991 Gopher, the first user-friendly interface, is created at the University of Minnesota and named after the school mascot. Gopher becomes the most popular interface for several years.

1993 Mosaic is developed by Marc Andreessen at the National Center for Supercomputing Applications (NCSA). It becomes the dominant navigating system for the World Wide Web, which, at this time, accounts for only 1% of all Internet traffic.

1994 The White House launches its own Web page. Also, initial commerce sites are established and mass marketing campaigns are launched via e-mail, introducing the term "spamming" to the Internet vocabulary.

1996 The number of Internet users grows to approximately 45 million, with roughly 30 million of those in North America (United States and Canada), 9 million in Europe, and 6 million in Asia/Pacific (Australia, Japan, etc.). 43.2 million (44%) of U.S. households own a personal computer, and 14 million of them are online.

1997 Approximately 66% of North American computer owners, 15% of those in Europe, and 14% of those in Asia/Pacific are online.

2002 More than 164 million Americans are online. Some 544 million people worldwide use the Internet. About 9.8 billion electronic messages are sent daily.

Sources: International Data Corporation, the W3C Consortium, and the Internet Society

Who's on the World Wide Web?

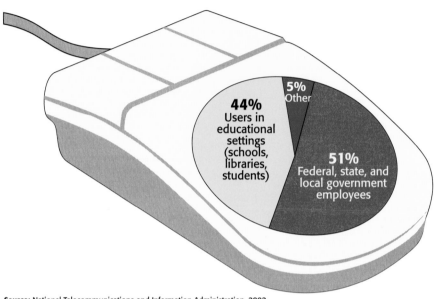

5%
Other

44%
Users in educational settings (schools, libraries, students)

51%
Federal, state, and local government employees

Source: National Telecommunications and Information Administration, 2002

Internet Use Grows at the Library

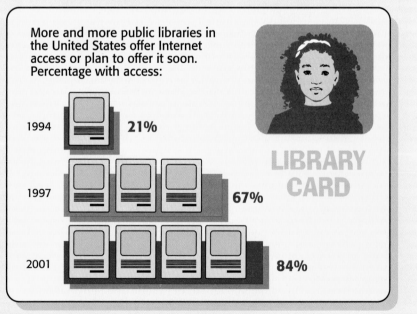

More and more public libraries in the United States offer Internet access or plan to offer it soon. Percentage with access:

1994   **21%**

1997   **67%**

2001   **84%**

LIBRARY CARD

Source: American Library Association

U.S. Online Users Profile

(as a percentage of each sex and individual age group*)

AGE

Under 25	67.0%
25–49	63.9%
50 and over	37.1%

SEX*

Women	53.8%
Men	53.9%

*Estimates vary widely.

How many households use dial-up Internet access?
Estimate: **43.1 million**

How many use high-speed alternatives?
Estimate: **15.4 million**

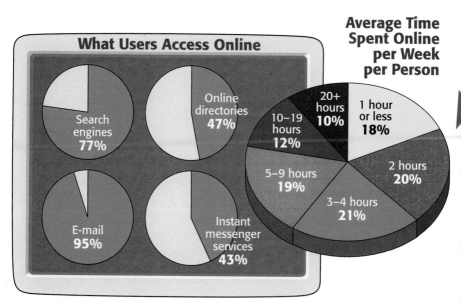

What Users Access Online

Search engines **77%**

Online directories **47%**

E-mail **95%**

Instant messenger services **43%**

Average Time Spent Online per Week per Person

20+ hours **10%**

1 hour or less **18%**

10–19 hours **12%**

5–9 hours **19%**

2 hours **20%**

3–4 hours **21%**

Source: Based on information from the U.S. Census Bureau, 2001

93

U.S. Internet Users Under 18, 1995 vs. 2002

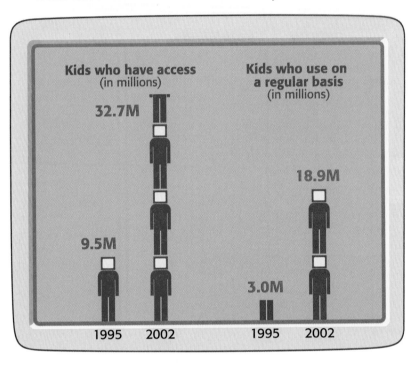

Kids who have access
(in millions)

32.7M

9.5M

1995   2002

**Kids who use on
a regular basis**
(in millions)

18.9M

3.0M

1995   2002

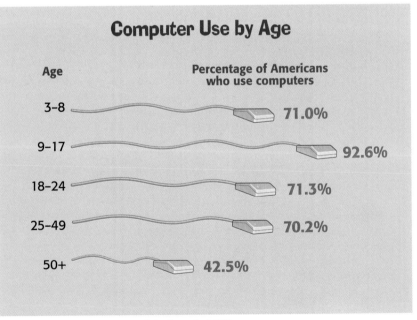

Computer Use by Age

Age	Percentage of Americans who use computers
3–8	71.0%
9–17	92.6%
18–24	71.3%
25–49	70.2%
50+	42.5%

Source: U.S. Census Bureau; *Current Population Survey*, Sept. 2001

Activities of Individuals Online
(percentage of Internet users)

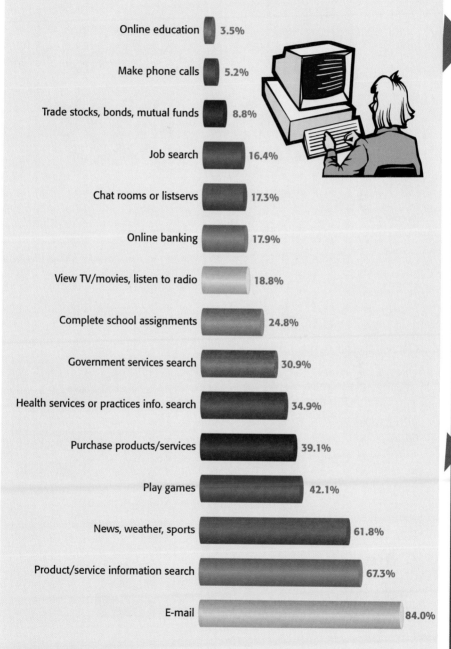

Activity	Percentage
Online education	3.5%
Make phone calls	5.2%
Trade stocks, bonds, mutual funds	8.8%
Job search	16.4%
Chat rooms or listservs	17.3%
Online banking	17.9%
View TV/movies, listen to radio	18.8%
Complete school assignments	24.8%
Government services search	30.9%
Health services or practices info. search	34.9%
Purchase products/services	39.1%
Play games	42.1%
News, weather, sports	61.8%
Product/service information search	67.3%
E-mail	84.0%

Source: NTIA and ESA, U.S. Department of Commerce, 2002

TVs, Phones, and Computers in the U.S.
(percentage of households)

TVs  98%

Telephones 98%

Computers  60%

Source: Nielsen Media Research, 2002

U.S. Computer Users, by Race
(in millions)

Asian-American & Pacific Islander — 71.2M

White — 70.0M

Black — 55.7M

Hispanic — 48.8M

Source: U.S. Census Bureau, 2001

Percentage of Kids in the U.S. . . .

(ages 3 to 17)

. . . With Access to Computers

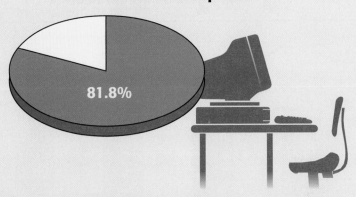

81.8%

. . . Who Use Computers at Home

92.3%

. . . Who Use Computers at School

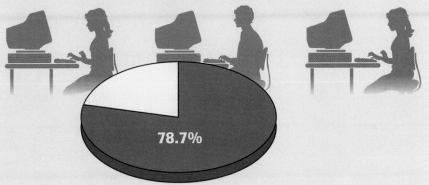

78.7%

Source: U.S. Census Bureau, 2001

Young U.S. Computer Users, by Activity
(percentage of U.S. population under 25 years old)

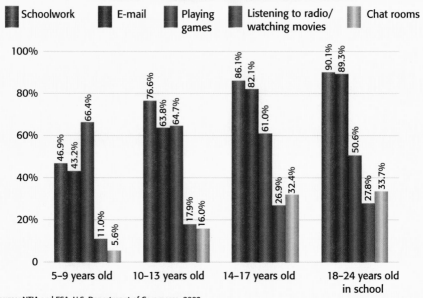

Legend: Schoolwork · E-mail · Playing games · Listening to radio/watching movies · Chat rooms

5–9 years old: 46.9%, 43.2%, 66.4%, 11.0%, 5.6%
10–13 years old: 76.6%, 63.8%, 64.7%, 17.9%, 16.0%
14–17 years old: 86.1%, 82.1%, 61.0%, 26.9%, 32.4%
18–24 years old in school: 90.1%, 89.3%, 50.6%, 27.8%, 33.7%

Source: NTIA and ESA, U.S. Department of Commerce, 2002

Internet Use by Location
(percent of U.S. population who access the Internet)

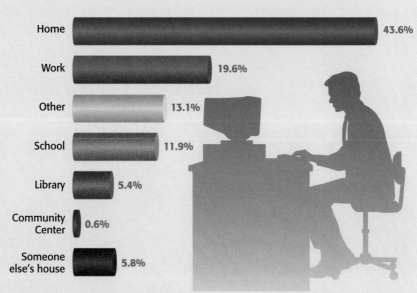

- Home: 43.6%
- Work: 19.6%
- Other: 13.1%
- School: 11.9%
- Library: 5.4%
- Community Center: 0.6%
- Someone else's house: 5.8%

Source: NTIA and ESA, U.S. Department of Commerce, 2002

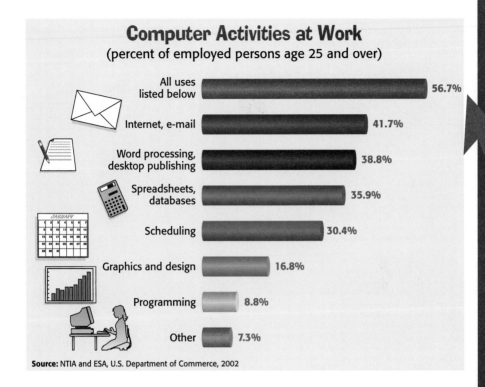

Computer Activities at Work
(percent of employed persons age 25 and over)

- All uses listed below — 56.7%
- Internet, e-mail — 41.7%
- Word processing, desktop publishing — 38.8%
- Spreadsheets, databases — 35.9%
- Scheduling — 30.4%
- Graphics and design — 16.8%
- Programming — 8.8%
- Other — 7.3%

Source: NTIA and ESA, U.S. Department of Commerce, 2002

Computers in U.S. Homes
(percentage of total U.S. households)

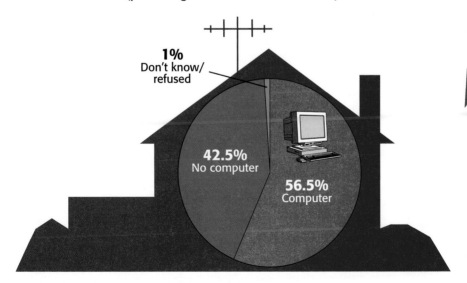

1%
Don't know/ refused

42.5%
No computer

56.5%
Computer

Source: NTIA, 2001

EARTH SCIENCE

Is It Over Yet?

The longest hurricane on record occurred in 1994 when Hurricane/ Typhoon John lasted 31 days. It was formed and named in the Northeast Pacific and reached hurricane force there. It then moved across the international date line and was renamed Typhoon John. Finally, it moved back across the dateline and was renamed Hurricane John.

Tree Power

Just 1 acre (0.4 ha) of trees can remove about 13 tons (11.8 t) of dust and gases from the surrounding environment each year, making the air we breathe cleaner.

Volcano Vitals

The largest volcano in the world is Mauna Loa, in Hawaii, with a volume of about 9,596 cubic miles (40,000 cu km) and an above–sea level area of 1,999 square miles (5,125 sq km). The tallest volcano is Mauna Kea—also in Hawaii—with a base-to-summit height of more than 30,000 feet (9,100 m).

Earth-Shaking Statistics

Alaska and California have the highest number of earthquakes in the United States each year because they sit on major fault lines. In fact, 10 of the 13 largest earthquakes in the United States occurred in Alaska. North Dakota and Florida have the fewest.

Twisted Tornadoes

Each year about 1,000 tornadoes are reported across the United States. The most violent tornadoes, with wind speeds of 250 mph (402 kph) or more, are capable of tremendous destruction. Damage paths can be in excess of 1 mile (1.6 km) wide and 50 miles (80 km) long.

Earth's Layers

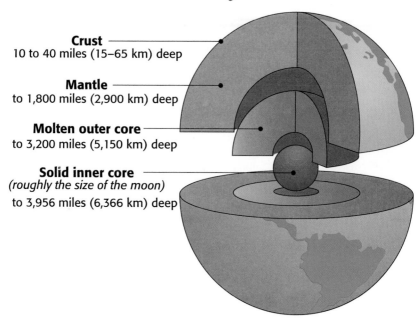

Crust
10 to 40 miles (15–65 km) deep

Mantle
to 1,800 miles (2,900 km) deep

Molten outer core
to 3,200 miles (5,150 km) deep

Solid inner core
(roughly the size of the moon)
to 3,956 miles (6,366 km) deep

What's in Earth's Crust?

Earth's crust is the outermost solid layer of the planet. Under the continents, the crust varies from 19 to 37 miles (30 to 60 km) in thickness. Under the oceans it is generally much thinner, only 3 to 5 miles (5 to 8 km) thick. Continental crust is made up of granite and other relatively light rocks, while oceanic crust is chiefly made up of basalt. The crust that is accessible to accurate scientific measurements contains the following principal elements:

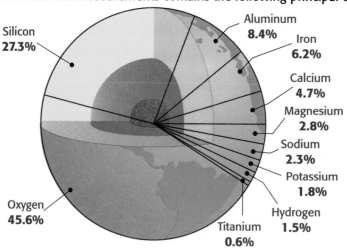

Silicon
27.3%

Aluminum
8.4%

Iron
6.2%

Calcium
4.7%

Magnesium
2.8%

Sodium
2.3%

Potassium
1.8%

Oxygen
45.6%

Titanium
0.6%

Hydrogen **1.5%**

The Geologic Timeline

BYA = Billion years ago **MYA = Million years ago**

PRECAMBRIAN ERA 4.6 BYA–545 MYA		Few life-forms, limited to oceans; bacteria and algae; possibly sponges, corals, and jellyfish
PALEOZOIC ERA 545–251 MYA	**Cambrian Period** 545–505 MYA	First shell-bearing marine invertebrates; plant life is algae; no known land life
	Ordovician Period 505–440 MYA	Many sea invertebrates; microscopic animals, mollusks, and urchinlike creatures; first known vertebrates (armored jawless fish)
	Silurian Period 440–410 MYA	Most animal forms still invertebrates; large, scorpion-like arthropods, and coral reefs; primitive fish in streams; first true land plants; first true land animals resembling scorpions and millipedes
	Devonian Period 410–360 MYA	Many fish, including sharks, lungfish, and bony fish; appearance of first true land vertebrates (amphibians); rise of trees similar to present-day ferns, horsetails, and club mosses; first seed plants
	Mississippian Period 360–320 MYA	Amphibians and possibly first reptiles; large sharks; swamps with forests on land, spore-producing trees
	Pennsylvanian Period 320–290 MYA	First true reptiles; many amphibians; appearance of first true insects (huge cockroaches and dragonflies); land covered by swamps and dense forests of mosses, ferns, rushes, horsetails, and early cone-bearing trees
	Permian Period 290–251 MYA	Many land animals, freshwater fish; mammal-like reptiles; insects; spread of cone-bearing trees
MESOZOIC ERA 251–65 MYA	**Triassic Period** 251–205 MYA	Age of reptiles begins; early dinosaurs; large amphibians
	Jurassic Period 205–145 MYA	Many kinds of dinosaurs; flying "dragons," "sea serpents," and giant lizards; first true mammals; first birds; appearance of frogs and toads; first flowering plants
	Cretaceous Period 145–65 MYA	Dominance of dinosaurs and reptiles on land; first snakes; large marine invertebrates; by end, total extinction of most typical mesozoic life-forms, including dinosaurs
CENOZOIC ERA 65 MYA–Present	**Tertiary Period** 65–1.6 MYA	Rise and dominance of advanced mammals; rise of primates and human ancestors; giant toothless birds resembling ostriches and emus
	Quaternary Period 1.6 MYA–Present	Appearance of modern life-forms; extinction of many earlier life-forms (mammoths, woolly rhinoceroses, and mastodons); rise of humans

The Structure of Earth's Atmosphere

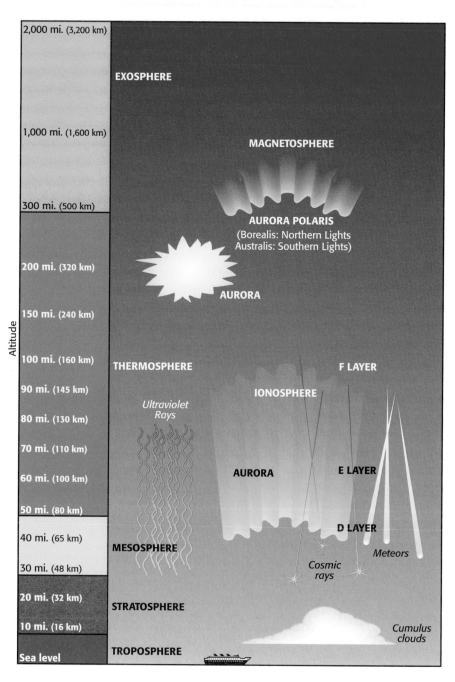

Altitude

2,000 mi. (3,200 km)

EXOSPHERE

1,000 mi. (1,600 km)

MAGNETOSPHERE

300 mi. (500 km)

AURORA POLARIS
(Borealis: Northern Lights
Australis: Southern Lights)

200 mi. (320 km)

AURORA

150 mi. (240 km)

100 mi. (160 km)

THERMOSPHERE   **F LAYER**

90 mi. (145 km)   **IONOSPHERE**

80 mi. (130 km)   *Ultraviolet Rays*

70 mi. (110 km)

60 mi. (100 km)   **AURORA**   **E LAYER**

50 mi. (80 km)

40 mi. (65 km)   **D LAYER**

MESOSPHERE   *Meteors*

30 mi. (48 km)   *Cosmic rays*

20 mi. (32 km)   STRATOSPHERE

10 mi. (16 km)   *Cumulus clouds*

Sea level   TROPOSPHERE

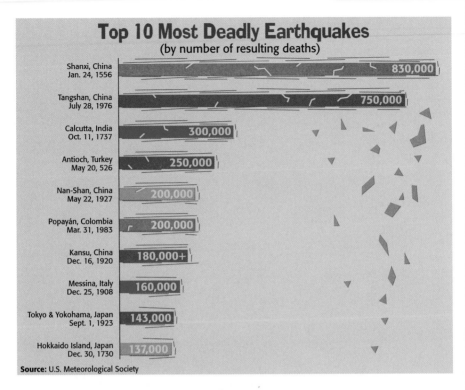

Top 10 Most Deadly Earthquakes
(by number of resulting deaths)

Shanxi, China Jan. 24, 1556	830,000
Tangshan, China July 28, 1976	750,000
Calcutta, India Oct. 11, 1737	300,000
Antioch, Turkey May 20, 526	250,000
Nan-Shan, China May 22, 1927	200,000
Popayán, Colombia Mar. 31, 1983	200,000
Kansu, China Dec. 16, 1920	180,000+
Messina, Italy Dec. 25, 1908	160,000
Tokyo & Yokohama, Japan Sept. 1, 1923	143,000
Hokkaido Island, Japan Dec. 30, 1730	137,000

Source: U.S. Meteorological Society

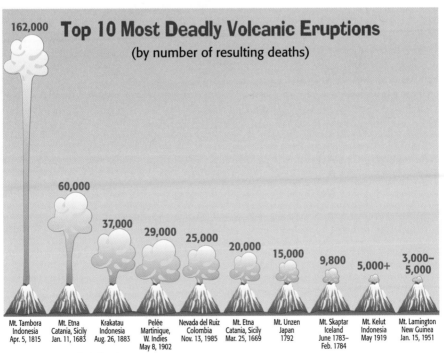

Top 10 Most Deadly Volcanic Eruptions
(by number of resulting deaths)

Deaths	Volcano	Location	Date
162,000	Mt. Tambora	Indonesia	Apr. 5, 1815
60,000	Mt. Etna	Catania, Sicily	Jan. 11, 1683
37,000	Krakatau	Indonesia	Aug. 26, 1883
29,000	Pelée	Martinique, W. Indies	May 8, 1902
25,000	Nevada del Ruiz	Colombia	Nov. 13, 1985
20,000	Mt. Etna	Catania, Sicily	Mar. 25, 1669
15,000	Mt. Unzen	Japan	1792
9,800	Mt. Skaptar	Iceland	June 1783– Feb. 1784
5,000+	Mt. Kelut	Indonesia	May 1919
3,000– 5,000	Mt. Lamington	New Guinea	Jan. 15, 1951

Source: U.S. Meteorological Society

EDUCATION

Homeschool Happenings

Approximately 850,000 students nationwide are homeschooled. This amounts to 1.7% of all U.S. students aged 5 to 17. About 82% were homeschooled only, and about 18% were enrolled in public or private schools part-time.

Super-sized with Students

Higher learning is on the rise in the United States. The three U.S. colleges and universities with the highest enrollments are the University of Texas at Austin, with 49,009 students, Ohio State University Main Campus, with 48,003, and Miami Dade Community College, with 47,152 students.

A City of Students

The City Montessori School in Lucknow, India, is the world's largest private school in a single city, with 26,312 pupils. It is also the only school to receive the UNESCO Prize for Peace Education (2002).

School Size Stats

Mexico and China have more schools for their young people than any other countries in the world. Mexico has the largest number of universities and colleges, with 10,341. China has the largest number of elementary schools, with 849,123.

Artful Education

In addition to reading, writing, and arithmetic, many public schools try to incorporate the arts into their curriculum. On average in the United States, 94% of public schools offer music classes, about 87% offer visual arts classes, some 20% offer dance classes, and approximately 19% offer drama and theater classes.

U.S. School Enrollment by Grade

(public and private)

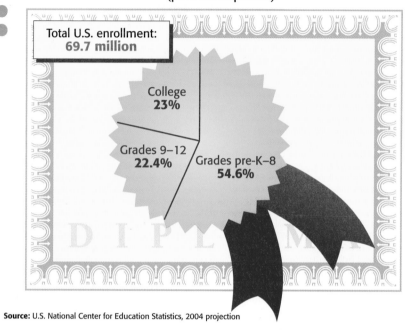

Total U.S. enrollment:
69.7 million

College
23%

Grades 9–12
22.4%

Grades pre-K–8
54.6%

Source: U.S. National Center for Education Statistics, 2004 projection

Highest Education Level Achieved Nationwide

(of people with some education)

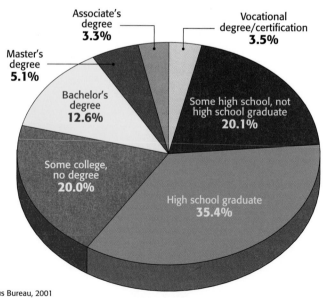

Associate's
degree
3.3%

Vocational
degree/certification
3.5%

Master's
degree
5.1%

Bachelor's
degree
12.6%

Some high school, not
high school graduate
20.1%

Some college,
no degree
20.0%

High school graduate
35.4%

Source: U.S. Census Bureau, 2001

U.S. Population:
Level of Education, Ages 25 and Over

All persons

4+ years of high school **84.1%**

College **25.6%**

By sex—male

4+ years of high school **84.2%**

College **27.8%**

By sex—female

4+ years of high school **84.0%**

College **23.6%**

By race—white

4+ years of high school **84.9%**

College **26.1%**

By race—black

4+ years of high school **78.5%**

College **16.5%**

By race—Hispanic

4+ years of high school **57.0%**

College **10.6%**

By age: 25–34 years

4+ years of high school **88.1%**

College **29.3%**

By age: 35–54 years

4+ years of high school **88.6%**

College **28.1%**

By age: 55 years+

4+ years of high school **74.8%**

College **25.0%**

By residence: metropolitan

4+ years of high school **84.9%**

College **27.8%**

By residence: nonmetropolitan

4+ years of high school **80.8%**

College **16.3%**

Source: U.S. Bureau of the Census, *Current Population Survey*, 2001

U.S. School Enrollment, 1966–2006*
(in millions)

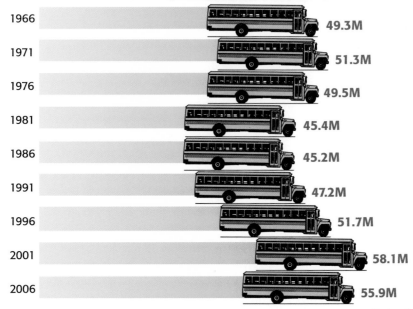

Year	Enrollment
1966	49.3M
1971	51.3M
1976	49.5M
1981	45.4M
1986	45.2M
1991	47.2M
1996	51.7M
2001	58.1M
2006	55.9M

Source: National Education Association survey; American Association of Colleges for Teacher Education   *Projected

U.S. Teachers, by Race

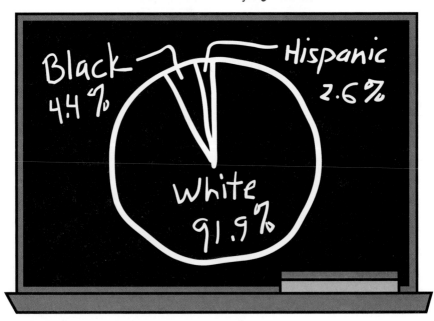

Black 4.4%   Hispanic 2.6%   White 91.9%

Source: U.S. Department of Education, 2001

Top 10 States With the Fewest Students

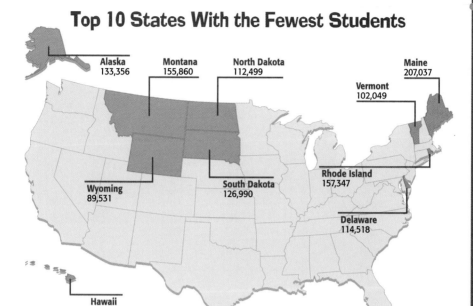

Alaska
133,356

Montana
155,860

North Dakota
112,499

Maine
207,037

Vermont
102,049

Wyoming
89,531

South Dakota
126,990

Rhode Island
157,347

Delaware
114,518

Hawaii
182,328

Source: National Education Association, *Rankings of States,* 2001

Top 10 States With the Most Students

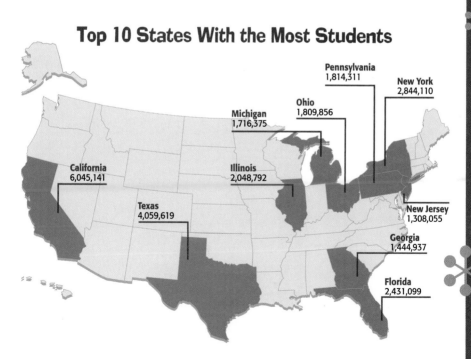

Pennsylvania
1,814,311

New York
2,844,110

Ohio
1,809,856

Michigan
1,716,375

California
6,045,141

Illinois
2,048,792

New Jersey
1,308,055

Texas
4,059,619

Georgia
1,444,937

Florida
2,431,099

Source: National Education Association, *Rankings of States,* 2001

Mean SAT Scores, Math and Verbal Combined, 1980–2001

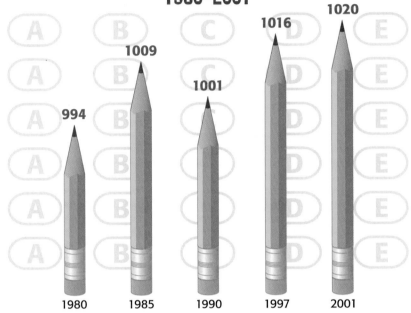

994 — 1980
1009 — 1985
1001 — 1990
1016 — 1997
1020 — 2001

Source: The College Board

Top 10 Most Popular Majors Among Incoming College Freshmen

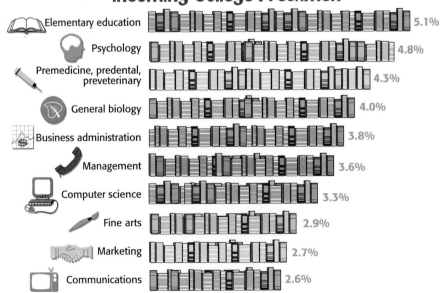

Elementary education — 5.1%
Psychology — 4.8%
Premedicine, predental, preveterinary — 4.3%
General biology — 4.0%
Business administration — 3.8%
Management — 3.6%
Computer science — 3.3%
Fine arts — 2.9%
Marketing — 2.7%
Communications — 2.6%

Source: Higher Education Research Institute, University of California, Los Angeles,
The American Freshman: National Norms for the Fall, 2001

Selected Degrees and Their Abbreviations

Abbreviation		Degree
A.B. or B.A.		Bachelor of Arts
B.F.A.		Bachelor of Fine Arts
B.S. or S.B.		Bachelor of Science
D.D.S.		Doctor of Dental Surgery or Doctor of Dental Science
D.V.M.		Doctor of Veterinary Medicine
Ed.D.		Doctor of Education
LL.B.		Bachelor of Laws
M.A.		Master of Arts
M.B.A.		Master of Business Administration
M.D.		Doctor of Medicine
M.Div.		Master of Divinity
M.E.		Master of Engineering
M.Ed.		Master of Education
M.F.A.		Master of Fine Arts
M.L.S.		Master of Library Science
M.S.		Master of Science
M.S.W.		Master of Social Work
Ph.D.		Doctor of Philosophy

Average Cost of 4-Year Colleges, 1978–2003

(tuition and fees, per year)

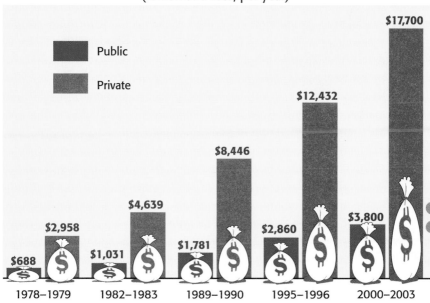

Public
Private

$17,700
$12,432
$8,446
$4,639
$2,958
$2,860
$3,800
$1,781
$1,031
$688

1978–1979 1982–1983 1989–1990 1995–1996 2000–2003

Source: The College Board

ENERGY

Paper Planet

Americans use about 67 million tons (68 million t) of paper each year. This averages out to about 580 pounds (263 kg) per person. Not surprisingly, paper products make up about 40% of the nation's trash. In fact, American businesses generate enough paper each year to circle Earth 20 times!

From Soup to Nuts

There's more to crude oil than meets the eye. There are about 3,000 products that are made from crude oil. Besides gasoline, diesel fuel, and heating oil, crude oil is used to make products such as ink, crayons, bubble gum, dishwashing liquids, deodorant, eyeglasses, records, tires, ammonia, and artificial heart valves.

What a Traffic Jam

If all the family vehicles in the United States were lined up, they would reach from Earth to the moon and back again.

Gas Guzzling by the Gallon

Most Americans drive their cars at least once a day. Each year, personal vehicles in the United States consume enough gas to cover a football field to a depth of about 40 miles (64 km).

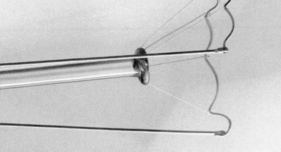

A Bright Idea

If 10,000 schools turned off all their lights for just one minute, they would save more than $81,000. If those same schools turned off their lights every time they went to recess, they would save more than $4.9 million!

Leading Energy
Producers of the World

(by percentage of total produced)

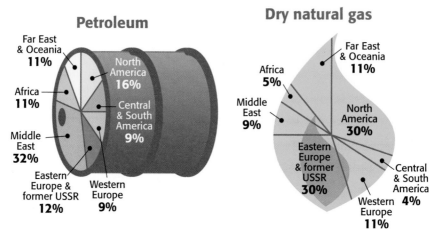

Petroleum

Far East
& Oceania
11%

North
America
16%

Africa
11%

Central
& South
America
9%

Middle
East
32%

Eastern
Europe &
former USSR
12%

Western
Europe
9%

Dry natural gas

Far East
& Oceania
11%

Africa
5%

Middle
East
9%

North
America
30%

Eastern
Europe
& former
USSR
30%

Central
& South
America **4%**

Western
Europe
11%

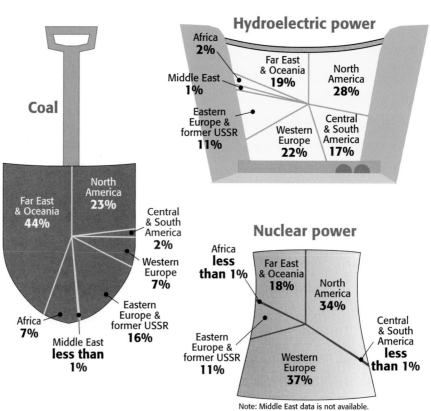

Hydroelectric power

Africa
2%

Far East
& Oceania
19%

North
America
28%

Middle East
1%

Eastern
Europe &
former USSR
11%

Western
Europe
22%

Central
& South
America
17%

Coal

North
America
23%

Far East
& Oceania
44%

Central
& South
America
2%

Western
Europe
7%

Eastern
Europe &
former USSR
16%

Africa
7%

Middle East
**less than
1%**

Nuclear power

Africa
**less
than 1%**

Far East
& Oceania
18%

North
America
34%

Eastern
Europe &
former USSR
11%

Western
Europe
37%

Central
& South
America
**less
than 1%**

Note: Middle East data is not available.

Source: Energy Information Administration, 2001

Leading Energy Consumers of the World

(by percentage of total consumed)

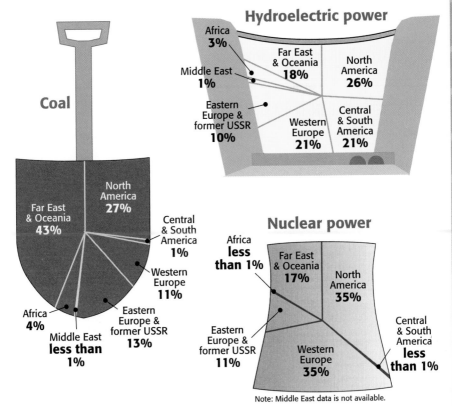

Petroleum

Far East & Oceania **28%**

North America **30%**

Africa **3%**

Middle East **6%**

Central & South America **7%**

Eastern Europe & former USSR **6%**

Western Europe **20%**

Dry natural gas

Africa **2%**

Far East & Oceania **12%**

Middle East **8%**

North America **31%**

Eastern Europe & former USSR **26%**

Western Europe **17%**

Central & South America **4%**

Hydroelectric power

Africa **3%**

Far East & Oceania **18%**

North America **26%**

Middle East **1%**

Eastern Europe & former USSR **10%**

Western Europe **21%**

Central & South America **21%**

Coal

North America **27%**

Far East & Oceania **43%**

Central & South America **1%**

Western Europe **11%**

Africa **4%**

Middle East **less than 1%**

Eastern Europe & former USSR **13%**

Nuclear power

Africa **less than 1%**

Far East & Oceania **17%**

North America **35%**

Central & South America **less than 1%**

Eastern Europe & former USSR **11%**

Western Europe **35%**

Note: Middle East data is not available.

Source: Energy Information Administration, 2001

117

World Primary Energy Production by Source

(as percentage of all energy produced)

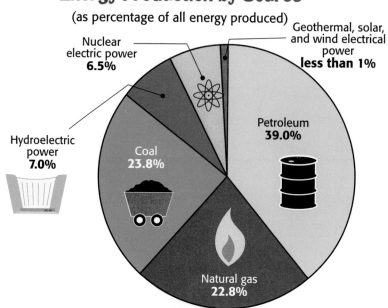

Nuclear electric power
6.5%

Geothermal, solar, and wind electrical power
less than 1%

Petroleum
39.0%

Hydroelectric power
7.0%

Coal
23.8%

Natural gas
22.8%

Source: Energy Information Adminstration, U.S. Department of Energy, 2001

U.S. Energy Production

(as percentage of all energy produced)

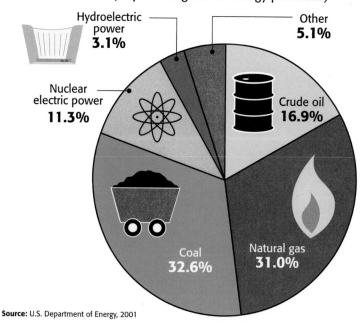

Hydroelectric power
3.1%

Other
5.1%

Nuclear electric power
11.3%

Crude oil
16.9%

Coal
32.6%

Natural gas
31.0%

Source: U.S. Department of Energy, 2001

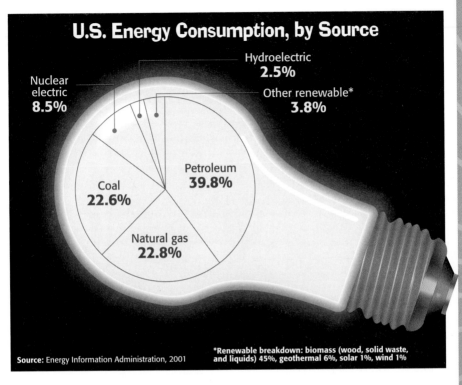

U.S. Energy Consumption, by Source

Hydroelectric
2.5%

Nuclear electric
8.5%

Other renewable*
3.8%

Petroleum
39.8%

Coal
22.6%

Natural gas
22.8%

Source: Energy Information Administration, 2001

*Renewable breakdown: biomass (wood, solid waste, and liquids) 45%, geothermal 6%, solar 1%, wind 1%

U.S. Consumption of Foreign Oil, 1986–2001
(as percentage of all U.S. oil consumption)

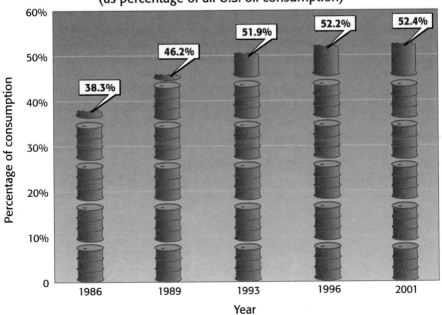

38.3%
46.2%
51.9%
52.2%
52.4%

Percentage of consumption

Year

1986   1989   1993   1996   2001

Source: American Petroleum Institute

Who Supplies U.S. Oil?

The United States imports about half of all the oil it consumes. That means that each day, nearly 9 million barrels are imported. Half of that amount comes from the OPEC (Organization of Petroleum Exporting Countries) nations. The rest comes from Canada, Mexico, and other countries.

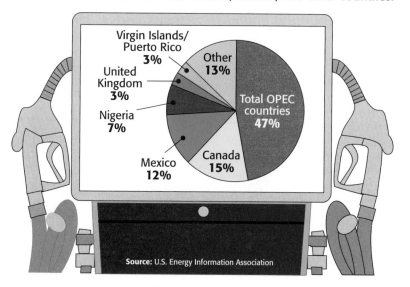

Virgin Islands/
Puerto Rico
3%

United
Kingdom
3%

Nigeria
7%

Other
13%

Total OPEC
countries
47%

Canada
15%

Mexico
12%

Source: U.S. Energy Information Association

How U.S. Homes Are Heated

(by heat source, in percentage of homes)

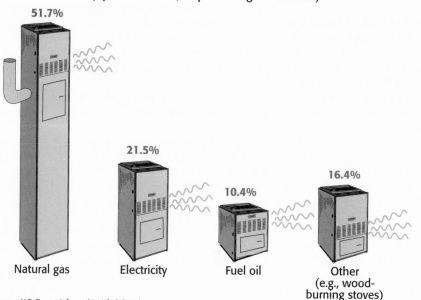

51.7%

21.5%

10.4%

16.4%

Natural gas   Electricity   Fuel oil   Other
(e.g., wood-
burning stoves)

Source: U.S. Energy Information Administration

U.S. Energy Use, by Household

(how energy is used in U.S. households, by percentage)

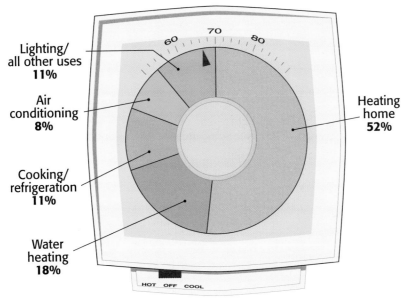

Lighting/
all other uses
11%

Air
conditioning
8%

Cooking/
refrigeration
11%

Water
heating
18%

Heating
home
52%

Source: U.S. Energy Information Agency, 2001

Commercial Nuclear Plants in Operation, by State

As of September 2003, there were
103 operable nuclear reactors in 31 states.

Source: U.S. Energy Information Agency, 2003

Appliance Ownership
(as percentage of all U.S. households)

Electrical appliances

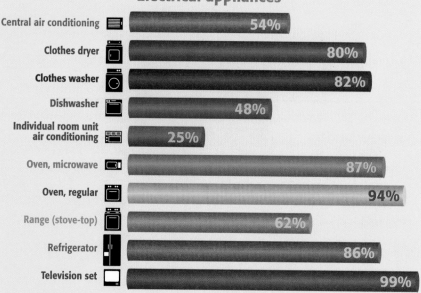

Central air conditioning — 54%
Clothes dryer — 80%
Clothes washer — 82%
Dishwasher — 48%
Individual room unit air conditioning — 25%
Oven, microwave — 87%
Oven, regular — 94%
Range (stove-top) — 62%
Refrigerator — 86%
Television set — 99%

Gas appliances

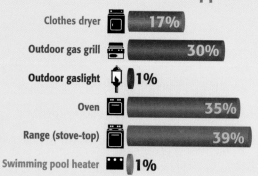

Clothes dryer — 17%
Outdoor gas grill — 30%
Outdoor gaslight — 1%
Oven — 35%
Range (stove-top) — 39%
Swimming pool heater — 1%

Source: Energy Information Administration, U.S. Department of Energy, *Annual Energy Review,* 2001

Fuel Efficiency of Motor Vehicles in the United States, 1980–2001

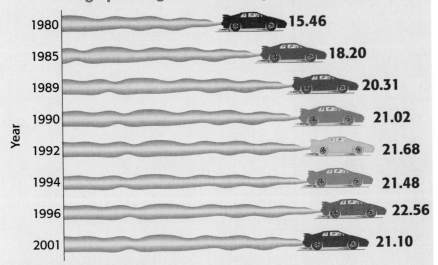

Average passenger cars, miles per gallon of gas

Year

1980	15.46
1985	18.20
1989	20.31
1990	21.02
1992	21.68
1994	21.48
1996	22.56
2001	21.10

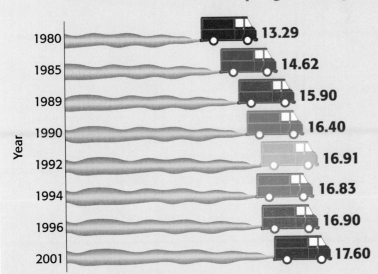

All motor vehicles, miles per gallon of gas

Year

1980	13.29
1985	14.62
1989	15.90
1990	16.40
1992	16.91
1994	16.83
1996	16.90
2001	17.60

Source: U.S. Department of Transportation, Federal Highway Administration

ENVIRONMENT

Water Wonders

There is the same amount of water on Earth today as there was when the planet was formed. So, the water that you drink today could possibly contain the same molecules that a dinosaur drank.

Recycling Reminder

It's important to recycle paper because it decreases garbage and provides inexpensive material for new products. Each ton of recycled paper can save 17 trees, 380 gallons (1,440 l) of oil, 3 cubic yards (2.3 cu m) of landfill space, 4,000 kilowatts of energy, and 7,000 gallons (26,500 l) of water!

Water Warning

Here's another reason to conserve Earth's water. Approximately 97% of the world's water is salty and undrinkable. Another 2% is frozen in glaciers and polar ice caps. This means humans have access to just 1% of the planet's water for all our needs.

Trash Talking

The average U.S. citizen produces about 4 pounds (1.8 kg) of waste per day. This is equivalent to more than 1,600 pounds (726 kg) of trash per year per person. That's more than 64 tons (58 t) of waste being produced in a lifetime!

Don't Be a Drip

Each person in the United States uses about 50 gallons (189 l) of water every day. One of the biggest water wastes is a dripping faucet. One drop per second wastes 2,700 gallons (10,220 l) of water per year!

Which Materials Get Recycled Most?

(percent of total waste recovered; averages)

80%

60%

56%

37%

31%

23%

| Asphalt | Aluminum cans | Newsprint | Plastic soft drink bottles | Glass beverage bottles | Magazines |

Source: Federal Highway Administration, 2002

Top 10 Paper-Recycling Countries

Paper products recycled per 1,000 people, in tons

Austria	Sweden	Switzerland	Netherlands	United States	Germany	Finland	Japan	France	South Korea
163.49	159.69	158.58	155.95	148.35	134.02	132.44	116.77	97.54	82.78

Country

Source: Food and Agriculture Organization of the United Nations, 2001

Rising Carbon Dioxide Levels, Rising Temperatures, 1865–2001

The concentration of carbon dioxide (CO_2) in the atmosphere, shown in the chart below, has been rising for the past century and a half, largely as a result of people burning fuel. But has Earth's temperature risen as a result? After studying global temperature charts, such as the one at the bottom of the page, most experts have concluded that it has.

Rise in CO_2 Concentration in the Atmosphere

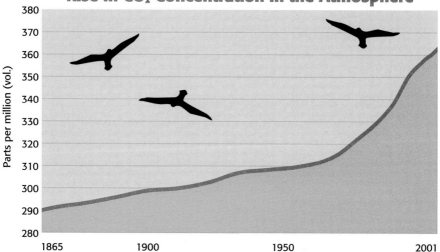

Parts per million (vol.)

380
370
360
350
340
330
320
310
300
290
280

1865   1900   1950   2001

Rise in Global Annual Temperature

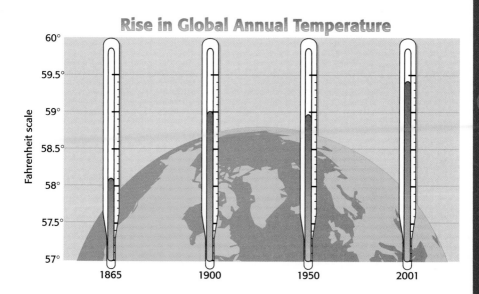

Fahrenheit scale

60°
59.5°
59°
58.5°
58°
57.5°
57°

1865   1900   1950   2001

Source: IPCC, NASA

The World's Top 10 Worst Carbon Dioxide Producing Countries
(millions of pounds per year)

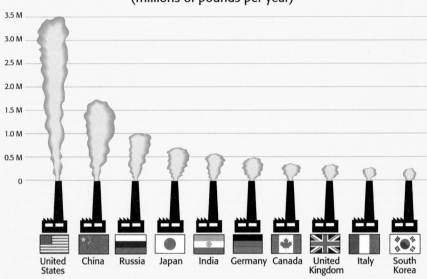

Source: U.S. Department of Energy, 2001

Top 5 Worst U.S. Metropolitan Areas for Carbon Monoxide
(percentage of days when air quality was unhealthful)

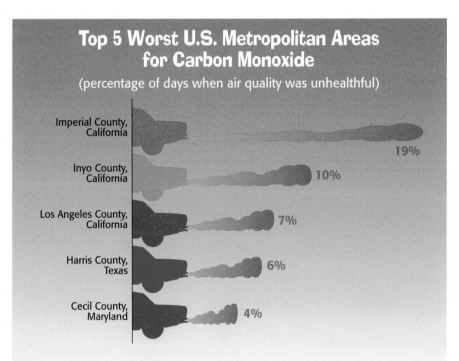

Source: U.S. Environmental Protection Agency, 2001

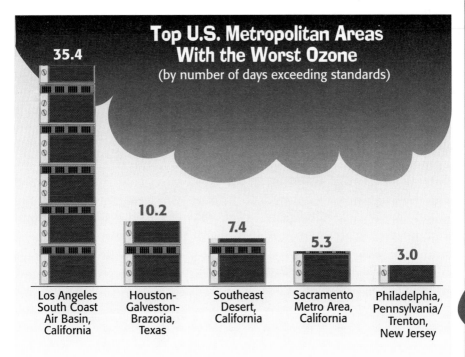

Top U.S. Metropolitan Areas With the Worst Ozone
(by number of days exceeding standards)

35.4 — Los Angeles South Coast Air Basin, California

10.2 — Houston-Galveston-Brazoria, Texas

7.4 — Southeast Desert, California

5.3 — Sacramento Metro Area, California

3.0 — Philadelphia, Pennsylvania/Trenton, New Jersey

Source: U.S. Environmental Protection Agency, 2001

U.S. Waters Receiving the Greatest Amounts of Toxic Discharges, 1995–2000
(by amount of discharge, in pounds/kilograms)

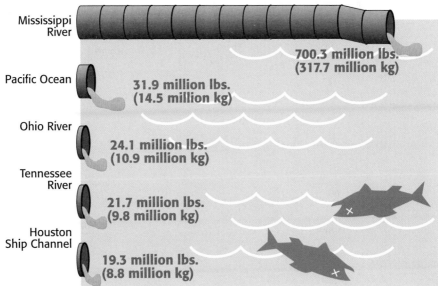

Mississippi River — 700.3 million lbs. (317.7 million kg)

Pacific Ocean — 31.9 million lbs. (14.5 million kg)

Ohio River — 24.1 million lbs. (10.9 million kg)

Tennessee River — 21.7 million lbs. (9.8 million kg)

Houston Ship Channel — 19.3 million lbs. (8.8 million kg)

Source: Environmental Working Group, U.S. PIRG

What Americans Throw Away

(percentage of the total garbage Americans throw away each year)

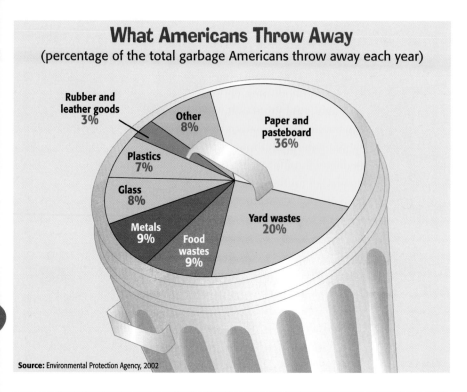

Rubber and leather goods
3%

Other
8%

Paper and pasteboard
36%

Plastics
7%

Glass
8%

Metals
9%

Food wastes
9%

Yard wastes
20%

Source: Environmental Protection Agency, 2002

Rate of Deforestation of Tropical Forests, 1981–2000

(in millions of hectares lost)

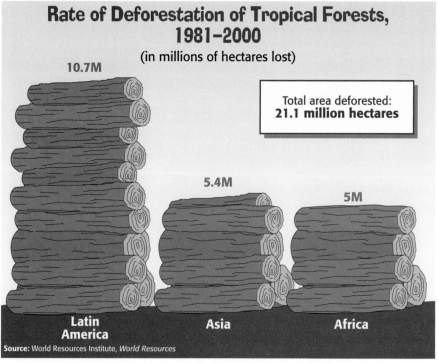

10.7M

Total area deforested:
21.1 million hectares

5.4M

5M

Latin America

Asia

Africa

Source: World Resources Institute, *World Resources*

Top 5 Worst Oil Spills
(100,000 tons or more)

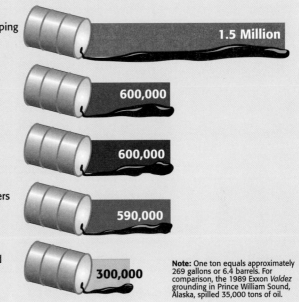

Sea Island, Kuwait
Iraq begins deliberately dumping
oil into Persian Gulf
January 25, 1991

1.5 Million

Southern Gulf of Mexico
Itox I oil well blows up
June 3, 1979

600,000

Persian Gulf
Blowout of Norwuz oil field
February 1983

600,000

U.S., East Coast
German U-boats attack tankers
after U.S. enters World War II
January–June 1942

590,000

Off Trinidad and Tobago
Tankers *Atlantic Empress* and
Aegean Captain collide
July 1, 1979

300,000

Source: United Nations Data

Note: One ton equals approximately
269 gallons or 6.4 barrels. For
comparison, the 1989 Exxon *Valdez*
grounding in Prince William Sound,
Alaska, spilled 35,000 tons of oil.

The Top 5 Costliest Natural Disasters in U.S. History
(in billions of dollars)

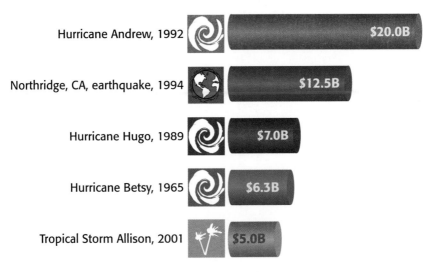

Hurricane Andrew, 1992 — **$20.0B**

Northridge, CA, earthquake, 1994 — **$12.5B**

Hurricane Hugo, 1989 — **$7.0B**

Hurricane Betsy, 1965 — **$6.3B**

Tropical Storm Allison, 2001 — **$5.0B**

Source: Insurance Information Institute; University of Colorado Natural Hazards Center, Federal Emergency Management

GEOGRAPHY (U.S.)

Exploring Underground

Mammoth Cave in central Kentucky is the longest cave system in the world, with 345 miles (555 km) of underground passageways, which contain entire lakes and rivers!

Stuck in the Middle

The geographic center of the 50 states, which includes the continental states as well as Alaska and Hawaii, is Butte County, South Dakota. The geographic center of the 48 contiguous states is Smith County, Kansas.

Directional Distances

The "four corners" of the United States can be compared somewhat to a compass. The northernmost spot in the United States is Point Barrow, Alaska. The southernmost point is Ka Lae, Hawaii. The easternmost part of the country is West Quoddy Head, Maine, while the westernmost point is Cape Wrangell, Alaska.

Across the Miles

The longest distance it is possible to travel within the 50 states is from Log Point on Elliot Key in Florida to Kure Island in Hawaii. This trip would be 5,859 miles (9,429 km).

Going to Extremes

The topography of the United States varies greatly. The highest point in the country is Mount McKinley, at 20,320 feet (6,198 m) above sea level in Alaska. The lowest point is Death Valley in California, at 282 feet (86 m) below sea level. The average elevation in the country is about 2,500 feet (763 m).

U.S. States and Their Capital Cities

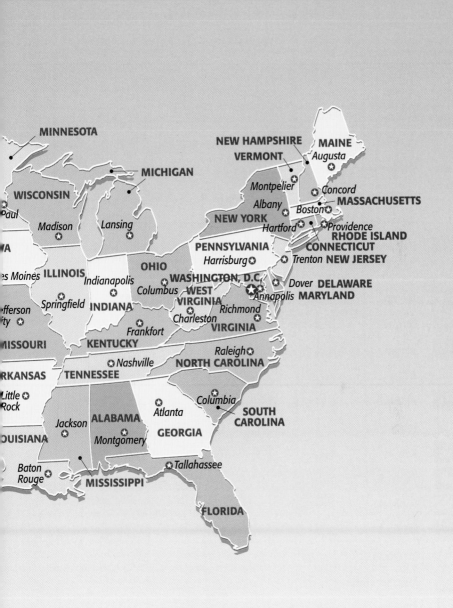

MINNESOTA

MICHIGAN

WISCONSIN

Paul

Madison ✪   Lansing ✪

WA

es Moines   ILLINOIS   Indianapolis ✪

Springfield ✪   INDIANA

fferson
ty ✪

MISSOURI   KENTUCKY

Frankfort ✪

RKANSAS   TENNESSEE

✪ Nashville

Little ✪
Rock

Jackson   ALABAMA   Atlanta ✪

OUISIANA   ✪
Montgomery

Baton
Rouge ✪

MISSISSIPPI

NEW HAMPSHIRE   MAINE
VERMONT   Augusta ✪

Montpelier   ✪ Concord
Albany ✪   ✪ Boston   MASSACHUSETTS
NEW YORK   Hartford ✪   Providence
                          RHODE ISLAND
PENNSYLVANIA   CONNECTICUT
Harrisburg ✪   ✪ Trenton   NEW JERSEY
OHIO   WASHINGTON, D.C.
Columbus ✪   ✪ Dover   DELAWARE
        WEST   ✪ Annapolis   MARYLAND
        VIRGINIA
Charleston ✪   Richmond ✪
                VIRGINIA

Raleigh ✪
NORTH CAROLINA

Columbia ✪
SOUTH
CAROLINA

GEORGIA

✪ Tallahassee

FLORIDA

The States at a Glance

Flag	State	Capital	Nickname	Area	Rank in area
	Alabama	Montgomery	The Heart of Dixie	51,718 sq. mi. 133,950 sq. km	29
	Alaska	Juneau	Last Frontier	587,878 sq. mi. 1,522,596 sq. km	1
	Arizona	Phoenix	Grand Canyon State	114,007 sq. mi. 295,276 sq. km	6
	Arkansas	Little Rock	Land of Opportunity	53,183 sq. mi. 137,742 sq. km	27
	California	Sacramento	Golden State	158,648 sq. mi. 410,896 sq. km	3
	Colorado	Denver	Centennial State	104,100 sq. mi. 269,618 sq. km	8
	Connecticut	Hartford	Constitution State	5,006 sq. mi. 12,966 sq. km	48
	Delaware	Dover	First State	2,026 sq. mi. 5,246 sq. km	49
	Florida	Tallahassee	Sunshine State	58,681 sq. mi. 151,982 sq. km	22
	Georgia	Atlanta	Empire State of the South	58,930 sq. mi. 152,627 sq. km	21
	Hawaii	Honolulu	Aloha State	6,459 sq. mi. 16,729 sq. km	47
	Idaho	Boise	Gem State	83,574 sq. mi. 216,456 sq. km	13
	Illinois	Springfield	Land of Lincoln	56,343 sq. mi. 145,928 sq. km	24
	Indiana	Indianapolis	Hoosier State	36,185 sq. mi. 93,720 sq. km	38
	Iowa	Des Moines	Hawkeye State	56,276 sq. mi. 145,754 sq. km	25
	Kansas	Topeka	Sunflower State	82,282 sq. mi. 213,110 sq. km	14
	Kentucky	Frankfort	Bluegrass State	40,411 sq. mi. 104,655 sq. km	37
	Louisiana	Baton Rouge	Pelican State	47,720 sq. mi. 123,593 sq. km	31
	Maine	Augusta	Pine Tree State	33,128 sq. mi. 85,801 sq. km	39
	Maryland	Annapolis	Old Line State	10,455 sq. mi. 27,077 sq. km	42
	Massachusetts	Boston	Bay State	8,262 sq. mi. 21,398 sq. km	45
	Michigan	Lansing	Wolverine State	58,513 sq. mi. 151,548 sq. km	23
	Minnesota	St. Paul	Gopher State	84,397 sq. mi. 218,587 sq. km	12
	Mississippi	Jackson	Magnolia State	47,695 sq. mi. 123,530 sq. km	32
	Missouri	Jefferson City	Show Me State	69,709 sq. mi. 180,546 sq. km	19

Flag	State	Capital	Nickname	Area	Rank in area
	Montana	Helena	Treasure State	147,047 sq. mi. 380,849 sq. km	4
	Nebraska	Lincoln	Cornhusker State	77,359 sq. mi. 200,358 sq. km	15
	Nevada	Carson City	Silver State	110,567 sq. mi. 286,367 sq. km	7
	New Hampshire	Concord	Granite State	9,283 sq. mi. 24,044 sq. km	44
	New Jersey	Trenton	Garden State	7,790 sq. mi. 20,175 sq. km	46
	New Mexico	Santa Fe	Land of Enchantment	121,599 sq. mi. 314,939 sq. km	5
	New York	Albany	Empire State	49,112 sq. mi. 127,200 sq. km	30
	North Carolina	Raleigh	Tar Heel State	52,672 sq. mi. 136,421 sq. km	28
	North Dakota	Bismarck	Flickertail State	70,704 sq. mi. 183,123 sq. km	17
	Ohio	Columbus	Buckeye State	41,328 sq. mi. 107,040 sq. km	35
	Oklahoma	Oklahoma City	Sooner State	69,903 sq. mi. 181,048 sq. km	18
	Oregon	Salem	Beaver State	97,052 sq. mi. 251,365 sq. km	10
	Pennsylvania	Harrisburg	Keystone State	45,310 sq. mi. 117,351 sq. km	33
	Rhode Island	Providence	Ocean State	1,213 sq. mi. 3,142 sq. km	50
	South Carolina	Columbia	Palmetto State	31,117 sq. mi. 80,593 sq. km	40
	South Dakota	Pierre	Mount Rushmore State	77,122 sq. mi. 199,744 sq. km	16
	Tennessee	Nashville	Volunteer State	42,146 sq. mi. 109,158 sq. km	34
	Texas	Austin	Lone Star State	266,874 sq. mi. 691,201 sq. km	2
	Utah	Salt Lake City	Beehive State	84,905 sq. mi. 219,902 sq. km	11
	Vermont	Montpelier	Green Mountain State	9,615 sq. mi. 24,903 sq. km	43
	Virginia	Richmond	Old Dominion	40,598 sq. mi. 105,149 sq. km	36
	Washington	Olympia	Evergreen State	68,126 sq. mi. 176,446 sq. km	20
	West Virginia	Charleston	Mountain State	24,231 sq. mi. 62,759 sq. km	41
	Wisconsin	Madison	Badger State	56,145 sq. mi. 145,414 sq. km	26
	Wyoming	Cheyenne	Equality State	97,818 sq. mi. 253,349 sq. km	9

Source: *World Book*

Top 10 States in Land Area
(ranked by size in square miles and square kilometers)

Alaska — 587,878 sq. mi. (1,522,596 sq. km)

Texas — 266,874 sq. mi. (691,201 sq. km)

California — 158,648 sq. mi. (410,896 sq. km)

Montana — 147,047 sq. mi. (380,849 sq. km)

New Mexico — 121,599 sq. mi. (314,939 sq. km)

Arizona — 114,007 sq. mi. (295,276 sq. km)

Nevada — 110,567 sq. mi. (286,367 sq. km)

Colorado — 104,100 sq. mi. (269,618 sq. km)

Wyoming — 97,818 sq. mi. (253,349 sq. km)

Oregon — 97,052 sq. mi. (251,365 sq. km)

Source: U.S. Census Bureau

Top 10 Smallest States in Land Area
(ranked by size in square miles and square kilometers)

Rhode Island — 1,213 sq. mi. (3,142 sq. km)

Delaware — 2,026 sq. mi. (5,246 sq. km)

Connecticut — 5,006 sq. mi. (12,966 sq. km)

Hawaii — 6,459 sq. mi. (16,729 sq. km)

New Jersey — 7,790 sq. mi. (20,175 sq. km)

Massachusetts — 8,262 sq. mi. (21,398 sq. km)

New Hampshire — 9,283 sq. mi. (24,044 sq. km)

Vermont — 9,615 sq. mi. (24,903 sq. km)

Maryland — 10,455 sq. mi. (27,077 sq. km)

West Virginia — 24,231 sq. mi. (62,759 sq. km)

Source: U.S. Census Bureau

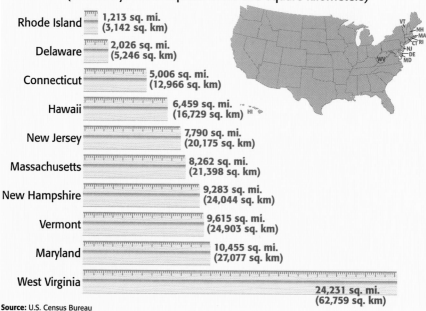

Topographical Map of the Continental United States

CANADA

Atlantic
Ocean

Pacific
Ocean

Key
Highest
elevation

Lowest
elevation

MEXICO

Gulf of
Mexico

Top 5 Highest U.S. Mountains
(by elevation)

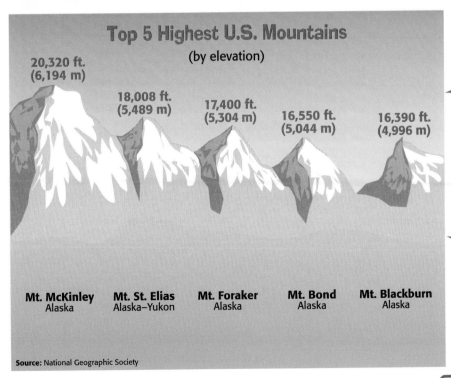

20,320 ft.
(6,194 m)

18,008 ft.
(5,489 m)

17,400 ft.
(5,304 m)

16,550 ft.
(5,044 m)

16,390 ft.
(4,996 m)

Mt. McKinley
Alaska

Mt. St. Elias
Alaska–Yukon

Mt. Foraker
Alaska

Mt. Bond
Alaska

Mt. Blackburn
Alaska

Source: National Geographic Society

The Great Lakes—Facts and Figures

NAME	AREA		BORDERS	MAJOR PORTS
	Square miles	Square kilometers		
Lake Superior	31,820	82,414	Minnesota, Wisconsin, Michigan (United States); Ontario (Canada)	Duluth, Superior, Sault Ste. Marie (United States); Sault Ste. Marie, Thunder Bay (Canada)
Lake Huron	23,010	59,596	Michigan (United States); Ontario (Canada)	Port Huron (United States); Sarnia (Canada)
Lake Michigan	22,400	58,016	Illinois, Indiana, Michigan, Wisconsin (United States)	Milwaukee, Racine, Kenosha, Chicago, Gary, Muskegon (United States)
Lake Erie	9,940	25,745	Michigan, New York, Ohio, Pennsylvania (United States); Ontario (Canada)	Toledo, Sandusky, Lorain, Cleveland, Erie, Buffalo (United States)
Lake Ontario	7,540	19,529	New York (United States); Ontario (Canada)	Rochester, Oswego (United States); Toronto, Hamilton (Canada)
Total Area	97,710	245,300		

Source: *Principal Rivers and Lakes of the World*, 2000

Top 10 Longest U.S. Rivers
(in miles and kilometers)

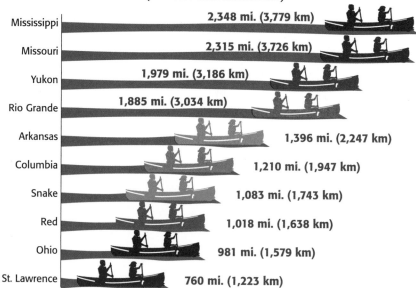

Mississippi	2,348 mi. (3,779 km)
Missouri	2,315 mi. (3,726 km)
Yukon	1,979 mi. (3,186 km)
Rio Grande	1,885 mi. (3,034 km)
Arkansas	1,396 mi. (2,247 km)
Columbia	1,210 mi. (1,947 km)
Snake	1,083 mi. (1,743 km)
Red	1,018 mi. (1,638 km)
Ohio	981 mi. (1,579 km)
St. Lawrence	760 mi. (1,223 km)

Source: *Principal Rivers and Lakes of the World*, 2000

Top 10 Most Populous States
(ranked by estimated census data)

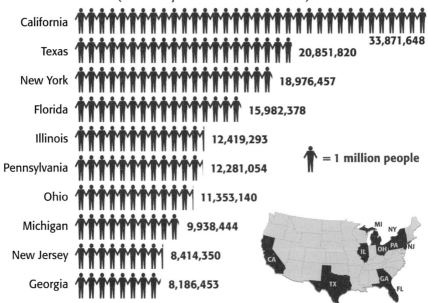

California	33,871,648
Texas	20,851,820
New York	18,976,457
Florida	15,982,378
Illinois	12,419,293
Pennsylvania	12,281,054
Ohio	11,353,140
Michigan	9,938,444
New Jersey	8,414,350
Georgia	8,186,453

= 1 million people

Top 10 Least Populous States
(ranked by estimated census data)

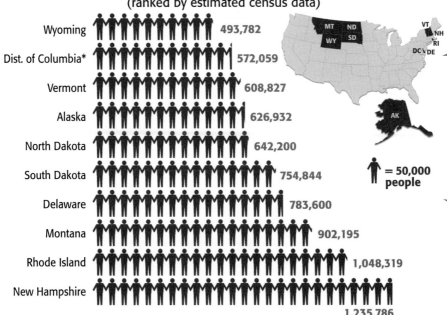

Wyoming	493,782
Dist. of Columbia*	572,059
Vermont	608,827
Alaska	626,932
North Dakota	642,200
South Dakota	754,844
Delaware	783,600
Montana	902,195
Rhode Island	1,048,319
New Hampshire	1,235,786

= 50,000 people

Source: U.S. Census Bureau, 2000   *Washington, D.C., is our nation's capital and is independent from all the states.

States With the Most Land for Recreation and Conservation

(by total acreage [hectares] of state parks and recreation areas)

3.2 million acres (1.3M h)

Alaska

California — 1.3 million acres (526,000 h)

Texas — 501,000 acres (203,000 h)

Florida — 444,000 acres (180,000 h)

Illinois — 403,000 acres (163,000 h)

Iowa — 391,000 acres (158,000 h)

Colorado — 340,000 acres (138,000 h)

Kansas — 324,000 acres (131,000 h)

New Jersey — 305,000 acres (123,000 h)

Pennsylvania — 277,000 acres (112,000 h)

Source: National Association of State Park Directors

Top 10 Largest National Historical Parks

(by total acreage [hectares])

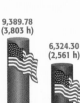

- 32,840.14 (13,300 h) — Chaco Culture (NM)
- 20,433.19 (8,275 h) — Cumberland Gap (KY/TN/VA)
- 19,236.60 (7,784 h) — Chesapeake and Ohio Canal (MD/WV/DC)
- 11,665.32 (4,724 h) — Jean Lafitte (LA)
- 9,389.78 (3,803 h) — Colonial (VA)
- 6,324.30 (2,561 h) — Pecos (NM)
- 3,006.07 (1,217 h) — Valley Forge (PA)
- 2,884.88 (1,168 h) — Saratoga (NY)
- 2,418.93 (980 h) — Klondike Goldrush (AK/WA)
- 2,023.67 (820 h) — Nez Perce (ID)

Source: Department of the Interior, National Park Service

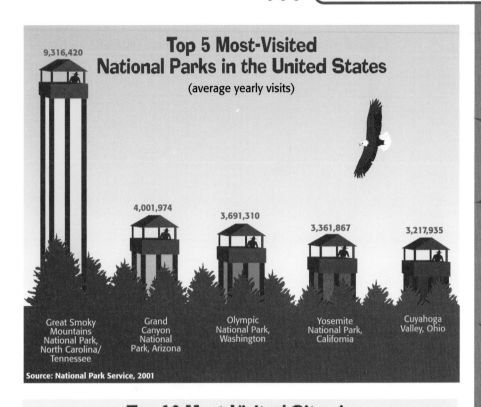

Top 5 Most-Visited National Parks in the United States
(average yearly visits)

9,316,420 — Great Smoky Mountains National Park, North Carolina/Tennessee

4,001,974 — Grand Canyon National Park, Arizona

3,691,310 — Olympic National Park, Washington

3,361,867 — Yosemite National Park, California

3,217,935 — Cuyahoga Valley, Ohio

Source: National Park Service, 2001

Top 10 Most-Visited Sites in the National Park System
(by number of visits)

Blue Ridge Parkway (NC, VA) — 21,538,760

Golden Gate National Recreation Area (CA) — 13,961,267

Great Smoky Mountains National Park (TN, NC) — 9,316,420

Gateway National Recreation Area (NY, NJ) — 9,014,438

Lake Mead National Recreation Area (AZ, NV) — 7,550,284

George Washington Memorial National Parkway (VA, MD, DC) — 7,419,375

Natchez Trace Parkway (AL, MS, TN) — 5,643,170

Delaware Water Gap National Recreation Area (PA, NJ) — 5,165,415

Gulf Islands National Seashore (FL, MS) — 4,561,862

Cape Cod National Seashore (MA) — 4,455,931

Source: National Park Service, Department of the Interior, 2002

Locations of U.S. National Memorials
(as designated by the National Park Service)

1. **Arkansas Post** Arkansas—First permanent French settlement in the lower Mississippi River valley.

2. **Arlington House, the Robert E. Lee Memorial** Virginia—Lee's home overlooking the Potomac.

3. **Chamizal** El Paso, Texas—Commemorates 1963 settlement of 99-year border dispute with Mexico.

4. **Coronado** Arizona—Commemorates first European exploration of the Southwest.

5. **DeSoto** Florida—Commemorates 16th-century Spanish explorations.

6. **Father Marquette** Michigan—Commemorates Father Jacques Marquette, a French Jesuit missionary who helped establish Michigan's first European settlement at Sault Ste. Marie in 1668.

7. **Federal Hall** New York—First seat of U.S. government under the Constitution.

8. **Flight 93** Pennsylvania—Commemorates the passengers and crew of Flight 93 who lost their lives to bring down a plane headed to attack the nation's capital.

9. **Fort Caroline** Florida—On St. Johns River, overlooks site of a French Huguenot colony.

10. **Fort Clatsop** Oregon—Lewis and Clark encampment, 1805–1806.

11. **Franklin Delano Roosevelt** New York—Statues of Pres. Roosevelt and Eleanor Roosevelt, as well as waterfalls and gardens. Dedicated May 2, 1997.

12. **General Grant** New York—Grant's tomb.

13. **Hamilton Grange** New York—Home of Alexander Hamilton.

14. **Jefferson National Expansion Memorial** St. Louis, Missouri—Commemorates westward expansion.

15. **Johnstown Flood** Pennsylvania—Commemorates tragic flood of 1889.

16. **Korean War Veterans** Washington, D.C.—Dedicated in 1995, honors those who served in the Korean War.

17. **Lincoln Boyhood** Indiana—Abraham Lincoln grew up here.

18. **Lincoln Memorial** Washington, D.C.—Marble statue of the 16th U.S. president.

19. **Lyndon B. Johnson Grove on the Potomac** Washington, D.C.—Overlooks the Potomac River vista of the capital.

20. **Mount Rushmore** South Dakota—World-famous sculpture of four presidents.

21. **Oklahoma City** Oklahoma—Established to commemorate the April 19, 1995 bombing of the Alfred P. Murrah Federal Building.

22. **Perry's Victory and International Peace Memorial** Put-in-Bay, Ohio—The world's most massive Doric column, constructed 1912–1915, promotes pursuit of international peace through arbitration and disarmament.

23. **Roger Williams** Providence, Rhode Island—Memorial to founder of Rhode Island.

24. **Thaddeus Kosciuszko** Pennsylvania—Memorial to Polish hero of American Revolution.

25. **Theodore Roosevelt Island** Washington, D.C.—Statue of Roosevelt in wooded island sanctuary.

26. **Thomas Jefferson Memorial** Washington, D.C.—Statue of Jefferson in an inscribed circular, colonnaded structure.

27. **USS *Arizona*** Hawaii—Memorializes American losses at Pearl Harbor.

28. **Vietnam Veterans** Washington, D.C.—Black granite wall inscribed with names of those missing or killed in action in the Vietnam War.

29. **Washington Monument** Washington, D.C.—Obelisk honoring the first U.S. president.

30. **Wright Brothers** North Carolina—Site of first powered flight.

Source: National Park Service

Locations of U.S. National Battlefields

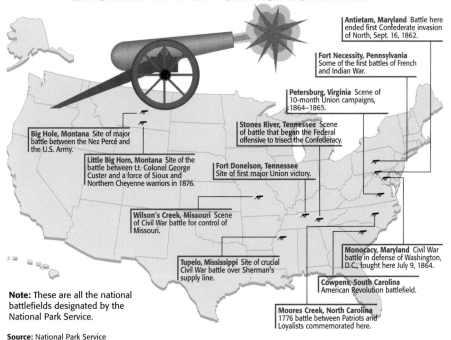

Antietam, Maryland Battle here ended first Confederate invasion of North, Sept. 16, 1862.

Fort Necessity, Pennsylvania Some of the first battles of French and Indian War.

Petersburg, Virginia Scene of 10-month Union campaigns, 1864–1865.

Stones River, Tennessee Scene of battle that began the Federal offensive to trisect the Confederacy.

Big Hole, Montana Site of major battle between the Nez Percé and the U.S. Army.

Little Big Horn, Montana Site of the battle between Lt. Colonel George Custer and a force of Sioux and Northern Cheyenne warriors in 1876.

Fort Donelson, Tennessee Site of first major Union victory.

Wilson's Creek, Missouri Scene of Civil War battle for control of Missouri.

Monocacy, Maryland Civil War battle in defense of Washington, D.C., fought here July 9, 1864.

Tupelo, Mississippi Site of crucial Civil War battle over Sherman's supply line.

Cowpens, South Carolina American Revolution battlefield.

Moores Creek, North Carolina 1776 battle between Patriots and Loyalists commemorated here.

Note: These are all the national battlefields designated by the National Park Service.

Source: National Park Service

Stats on the Statue of Liberty

Dimensions	Ft.	In.
Height from heel to torch (45.3 m)	151	1
Height from base of pedestal to torch (91.5 m)	305	1
Height from heel to top of head (33.8 m)	111	1
Length of hand (5 m)	16	5
Index finger (2.4 m)	8	0
Circumference at second joint (1 m)	3	6
Size of fingernail (33 cm x 25 cm)		13x10
Head from chin to cranium (5 m)	17	3
Head thickness from ear to ear (3 m)	10	0
Distance across the eye (.76 m)	2	6
Length of nose (1.4 m)	4	6
Right arm, length (12.8 m)	42	0
Right arm, greatest thickness (3.7 m)	12	0
Thickness of waist (10.7 m)	35	0
Width of mouth (1 m)	3	0
Tablet, length (7.2 m)	23	7
Tablet, width (4.1 m)	13	7
Tablet, thickness (.60 m)	2	0

Source: National Park Service

Selected National Sites of Washington, D.C.

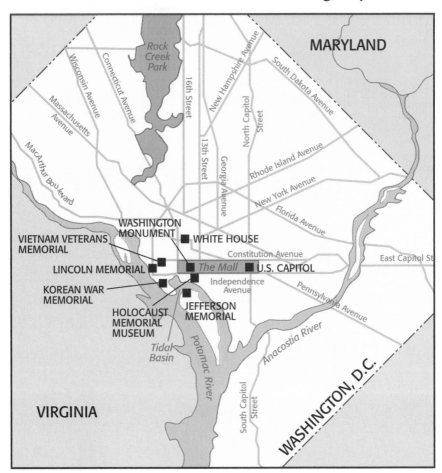

U.S. Capitol

The Capitol is open to the public for guided tours only from 9:00 A.M.– 4:30 P.M. Monday through Saturday. Free tickets are available on a first come, first served basis at the Capitol Guide Service kiosk located on the sidewalk southwest of the Capitol.
Phone: (202) 225-6827

Holocaust Memorial Museum

The museum is open daily, 10:00 A.M.– 5:30 P.M., except Yom Kippur and Dec. 25. 100 Raoul Wallenburg Pl., SW (formerly 15th St., SW), near Independence Ave.
Phone: (202) 488-0400

Jefferson Memorial

The memorial, which is located on the south edge of the Tidal Basin, is open daily, 8:00 A.M.–midnight. An elevator and curb ramps for the disabled are in service.
Phone: (202) 426-6841

Korean War Memorial

The $18 million military memorial, which was funded by private donations, is open 8:00 A.M.– midnight daily.
Phone: (202) 426-6841

Lincoln Memorial

The memorial, which is located in West Potomac Park, is open daily, 8:00 A.M.–midnight. An elevator and curb ramps for the disabled are in service.
Phone: (202) 426-6841

Vietnam Veterans Memorial

The memorial is open daily except Dec. 25, 8:00 A.M.–midnight.
Phone: (202) 426-6841

Washington Monument

Open daily except Dec. 25, 9:00 A.M.– 4:30 P.M.. Tickets are required for entry and can either be reserved ahead of time or picked up same day.
Phone: (202) 426-6841

White House

Free reserved tickets for guided tours can be obtained 8–10 weeks in advance from your local congressperson or senator. 1600 Pennsylvania Ave.
Phone: (202) 456-7041

Source: Washington Convention and Visitor's Bureau

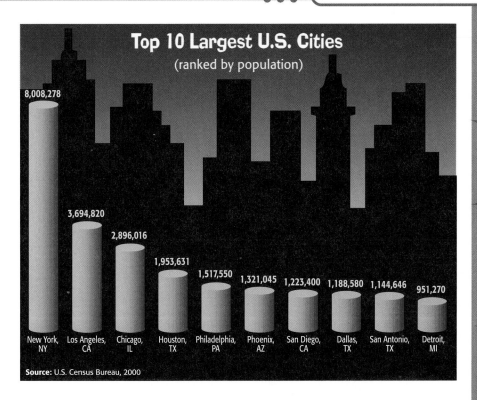

Top 10 Largest U.S. Cities
(ranked by population)

City	Population
New York, NY	8,008,278
Los Angeles, CA	3,694,820
Chicago, IL	2,896,016
Houston, TX	1,953,631
Philadelphia, PA	1,517,550
Phoenix, AZ	1,321,045
San Diego, CA	1,223,400
Dallas, TX	1,188,580
San Antonio, TX	1,144,646
Detroit, MI	951,270

Source: U.S. Census Bureau, 2000

Top 10 Major U.S. Cities With the Fastest-Declining Populations, 1990–2000

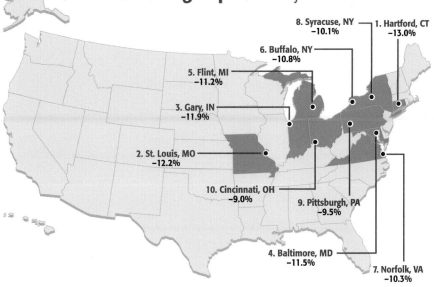

8. Syracuse, NY −10.1%
1. Hartford, CT −13.0%
6. Buffalo, NY −10.8%
5. Flint, MI −11.2%
3. Gary, IN −11.9%
2. St. Louis, MO −12.2%
10. Cincinnati, OH −9.0%
9. Pittsburgh, PA −9.5%
4. Baltimore, MD −11.5%
7. Norfolk, VA −10.3%

Source: U.S. Census Bureau, 2000

GEOGRAPHY (U.S.)

Top 10 Most Densely Populated U.S. Cities, 2001
(population per square mile)

New York, NY	San Francisco, CA	Jersey City, NJ	Chicago, IL	Santa Ana, CA
26,404	**16,632**	**16,111**	**12,752**	**12,471**

Boston, MA	Hialeah, FL	Newark, NJ	Philadelphia, PA	Yonkers, NY
12,172	**11,793**	**11,494**	**11,233**	**10,833**

Source: U.S. Census Bureau, 2001   ♦ = 1,000 people

Top 10 Fastest-Growing Major U.S. Cities, 1990–2000
(ranked by percent change)

Las Vegas, NV +85.2%
Plano, TX +72.5%
Scottsdale, AZ +55.8%
Glendale, AZ +47.7%
Bakersfield, CA +41.3%
Austin, TX +41.0%
Mesa, AZ +37.6%
Charlotte, NC +36.6%
Phoenix, AZ +34.3%
Raleigh, NC +32.8%

Source: U.S. Census Bureau, 2000

148

Profile: Top 10 Largest U.S. Cities, by Race

(percentage of population)

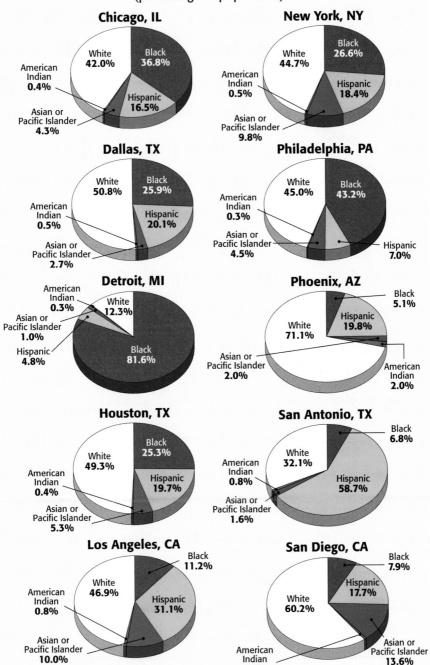

Chicago, IL
- White 42.0%
- Black 36.8%
- Hispanic 16.5%
- American Indian 0.4%
- Asian or Pacific Islander 4.3%

New York, NY
- White 44.7%
- Black 26.6%
- Hispanic 18.4%
- American Indian 0.5%
- Asian or Pacific Islander 9.8%

Dallas, TX
- White 50.8%
- Black 25.9%
- Hispanic 20.1%
- American Indian 0.5%
- Asian or Pacific Islander 2.7%

Philadelphia, PA
- White 45.0%
- Black 43.2%
- American Indian 0.3%
- Asian or Pacific Islander 4.5%
- Hispanic 7.0%

Detroit, MI
- American Indian 0.3%
- White 12.3%
- Asian or Pacific Islander 1.0%
- Hispanic 4.8%
- Black 81.6%

Phoenix, AZ
- Black 5.1%
- Hispanic 19.8%
- White 71.1%
- Asian or Pacific Islander 2.0%
- American Indian 2.0%

Houston, TX
- Black 25.3%
- White 49.3%
- Hispanic 19.7%
- American Indian 0.4%
- Asian or Pacific Islander 5.3%

San Antonio, TX
- Black 6.8%
- White 32.1%
- Hispanic 58.7%
- American Indian 0.8%
- Asian or Pacific Islander 1.6%

Los Angeles, CA
- Black 11.2%
- White 46.9%
- Hispanic 31.1%
- American Indian 0.8%
- Asian or Pacific Islander 10.0%

San Diego, CA
- Black 7.9%
- Hispanic 17.7%
- White 60.2%
- Asian or Pacific Islander 13.6%
- American Indian 0.6%

Source: U.S. Census Bureau, based on 2000 data

GEOGRAPHY (WORLD)

A Mountainous Growth Spurt?

Thanks to new satellite technology, the official height of Mount Everest was announced as 29,035 feet (8,850 m) in November 1999. This is 6 feet (2 m) higher than the previously accepted height, which had been listed for more than 100 years.

From Here to Timbuktu?

Timbuktu is an actual city in Mali, Africa, located near the Niger River and the Sahara Desert. It was a trading post many years ago, and people believed it contained a great deal of gold. Many adventurers died trying to reach Timbuktu, which is why people mention its name today when they are talking about a faraway location.

Home Away from Home

You can easily find the place on the exact opposite side of the world from your town. First, find the latitude of your location. Then reverse the direction. (If it's east, change it to west, for example.) Next, find the longitude of your location and subtract it from 180. Finally, reverse this direction, too. (If it's north, call it south.) The new latitude and longitude represent the opposite point on the globe. So, if you live in Kansas City, Missouri, which has a latitude of 39°N and a longitude of 94°W, your opposite coordinates would be 39°S and 86°E. This point can be found in the Taklinakan Desert in China.

Continental Contents

The African continent has some pretty impressive features: it contains the world's longest river—the Nile; the world's largest desert—the Sahara; and more countries than any other continent.

Cool Cave Creation

Lubang Nasib Bagus in Sarawak, Malaysia, is the world's largest cave chamber, or single room. It measures 2,300 feet (702 m) long and 1,480 feet (451 m) wide. The entire chamber is also at least 230 feet (70 m) high. That's more than twice the size of Radio City Music Hall in New York.

Countries of the World

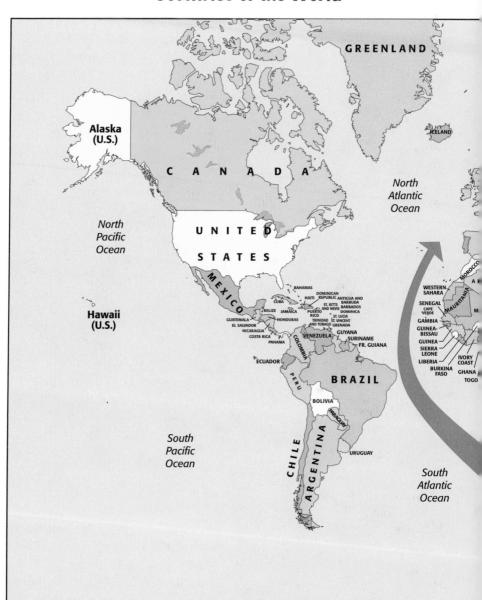

GREENLAND

Alaska
(U.S.)

ICELAND

C A N A D A

North
Atlantic
Ocean

North
Pacific
Ocean

U N I T E D
S T A T E S

M E X I C O

Hawaii
(U.S.)

BAHAMAS
DOMINICAN
HAITI REPUBLIC ANTIGUA AND
CUBA ST. KITTS BARBUDA
BELIZE JAMAICA AND NEVIS BARBADOS
PUERTO DOMINICA
RICO ST. LUCIA
GUATEMALA HONDURAS TRINIDAD ST. VINCENT
EL SALVADOR AND TOBAGO GRENADA
NICARAGUA VENEZUELA GUYANA
COSTA RICA SURINAME
PANAMA FR. GUIANA
COLOMBIA

ECUADOR

WESTERN
SAHARA
SENEGAL
CAPE
VERDE
GAMBIA
GUINEA-
BISSAU
GUINEA
SIERRA
LEONE
LIBERIA
IVORY
COAST
BURKINA GHANA
FASO TOGO

MOROCCO

MAURITANIA

M

P E R U

B R A Z I L

BOLIVIA

PARAGUAY

South
Pacific
Ocean

C H I L E

A R G E N T I N A

URUGUAY

South
Atlantic
Ocean

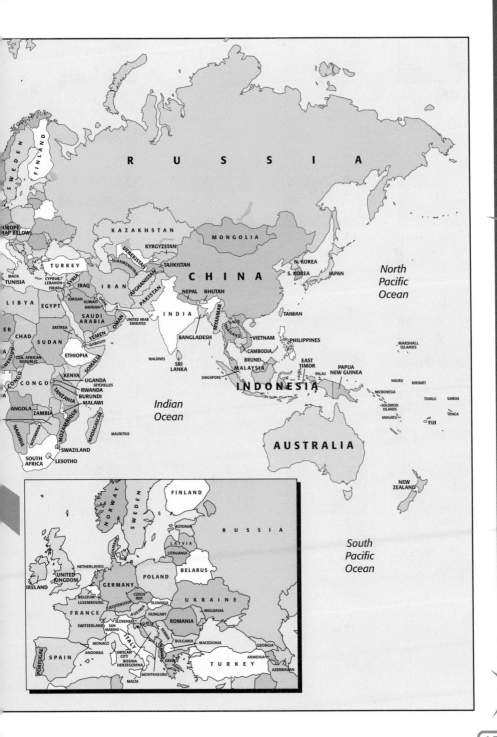

S W E D E N

F I N L A N D

R U S S I A

[UROPE MAP BELOW]

KAZAKHSTAN

MONGOLIA

KYRGYZSTAN

UZBEKISTAN

TURKMENISTAN

TAJIKISTAN

TURKEY

MALTA
TUNISIA

CYPRUS
LEBANON
ISRAEL

SYRIA

IRAQ

IRAN

AFGHANISTAN

PAKISTAN

NEPAL BHUTAN

C H I N A

N. KOREA

S. KOREA

JAPAN

North
Pacific
Ocean

LIBYA

EGYPT

JORDAN
KUWAIT
BAHRAIN

QATAR

SAUDI
ARABIA

OMAN

UNITED ARAB
EMIRATES

I N D I A

MYANMAR

TAIWAN

CHAD

SUDAN

ERITREA

YEMEN

DJIBOUTI

ETHIOPIA

SOMALIA

BANGLADESH

SRI
LANKA

THAILAND

LAOS

VIETNAM

CAMBODIA

PHILIPPINES

MARSHALL
ISLANDS

CEN. AFRICAN
REPUBLIC

MALDIVES

BRUNEI

EAST
TIMOR

PALAU

PAPUA
NEW GUINEA

NAURU

KIRIBATI

CONGO

KENYA

UGANDA

SEYCHELLES

RWANDA
BURUNDI

TANZANIA

MALAWI

SINGAPORE

MALAYSIA

I N D O N E S I A

MICRONESIA

SOLOMON
ISLANDS

TUVALU

SAMOA

ANGOLA

ZAMBIA

MOZAMBIQUE

MADAGASCAR

Indian
Ocean

VANUATU

TONGA

FIJI

NAMIBIA

BOTSWANA

MAURITIUS

A U S T R A L I A

SWAZILAND

SOUTH
AFRICA

LESOTHO

NEW
ZEALAND

South
Pacific
Ocean

N O R W A Y

S W E D E N

FINLAND

ESTONIA

R U S S I A

DENMARK

LATVIA

LITHUANIA

NETHERLANDS

UNITED
KINGDOM

POLAND

BELARUS

IRELAND

GERMANY

BELGIUM
LUXEMBOURG

CZECH
REP.

LIECHTENSTEIN

SLOVAKIA

U K R A I N E

FRANCE

AUSTRIA

HUNGARY

MOLDAVIA

SWITZERLAND

SLOVENIA

SAN
MARINO

ROMANIA

MONACO

I T A L Y

CROATIA

SERBIA

BULGARIA

MACEDONIA

GEORGIA

PORTUGAL

SPAIN

ANDORRA

VATICAN
CITY

BOSNIA
HERZEGOVINA

GREECE

ARMENIA

AZERBAIJAN

MONTENEGRO

T U R K E Y

MALTA

ALBANIA

Countries of the World

AFGHANISTAN

cap: Kabul
pop: 26,800,000
area (sq. mi.): 251,773
lang: Dari Persian, Pashtu,
  Uzbek
money: afghani
gov: In transition

ALBANIA

cap: Tiranë
pop: 3,500,000
area (sq. mi.): 11,100
lang: Albanian, Greek
money: lek
gov: Emerging democracy

ALGERIA

cap: Algiers
pop: 31,736,000
area (sq. mi.): 918,497
lang: Arabic, Berber, French
money: dinar
gov: Republic

ANDORRA

cap: Andorra la Vella
pop: 67,600
area (sq. mi.): 185
lang: Catalan, French, Spanish
money: euro
gov: Parliamentary democracy

ANGOLA

cap: Luanda
pop: 10,360,000
area (sq. mi.): 481,353
lang: Portuguese, Bantu
money: kwanza
gov: Multiparty democracy

ANTIGUA AND BARBUDA

cap: St. John's
pop: 66,970
area (sq. mi.): 171
lang: English
money: dollar
gov: Constitutional monarchy
  with British-style parliament

ARGENTINA

cap: Buenos Aires
pop: 37,384,000
area (sq. mi.): 1,065,189
lang: Spanish, Italian
money: peso
gov: Republic

ARMENIA

cap: Yerevan
pop: 3,336,000
area (sq. mi.): 11,306
lang: Armenian
money: dram
gov: Republic

AUSTRALIA

cap: Canberra
pop: 19,357,000
area (sq. mi.): 2,966,420
lang: English, aboriginal
  languages
money: dollar
gov: Democratic, federal state
  system

AUSTRIA

cap: Vienna
pop: 8,150,000
area (sq. mi.): 32,377
lang: German
money: euro
gov: Federal Republic

AZERBAIJAN

cap: Baku
pop: 7,771,000
area (sq. mi.): 33,400
lang: Azeri, Russian,
  Armenian
money: manat
gov: Republic

BAHAMAS

cap: Nassau
pop: 300,000
area (sq. mi.): 5,380
lang: English, Creole
money: dollar
gov: Independent
  commonwealth

BAHRAIN

cap: Manama
pop: 656,397
area (sq. mi.): 268
lang: Arabic, English, Farsi,
  Urdu
money: dinar
gov: Traditional monarchy

BANGLADESH

cap: Dhaka
pop: 133,376,000
area (sq. mi.): 55,813
lang: Bengali, Chakma, Bagh
money: taka
gov: Parliamentary
  democracy

BARBADOS

cap: Bridgetown
pop: 277,000
area (sq. mi.): 166
lang: English
money: dollar
gov: Parliamentary democracy

BELARUS

cap: Minsk
pop: 10,373,000
area (sq. mi.): 80,134
lang: Byelorussian, Russian
money: ruble
gov: Republic

BELGIUM

cap: Brussels
pop: 10,274,000
area (sq. mi.): 11,799
lang: Flemish, French, German
money: euro
gov: Parliamentary democracy

Countries of the World (cont.)

BELIZE

cap: Belmopan
pop: 263,000
area (sq. mi.): 8,867
lang: English, Spanish, Creole
money: dollar
gov: Parliamentary
democracy

BENIN

cap: Porto-Novo
pop: 6,787,000
area (sq. mi.): 43,483
lang: French, Fon, Yoruba
money: CFA franc
gov: Republic

BHUTAN

cap: Thimphu
pop: 2,094,000
area (sq. mi.): 18,147
lang: Dzongkha, Nepali,
Tibetan
money: ngultrum
gov: Monarchy

BOLIVIA

cap: Sucre
pop: 8,445,000
area (sq. mi.): 421,165
lang: Spanish, Quecha,
Aymara
money: boliviano
gov: Republic

BOSNIA AND HERZEGOVINA

cap: Sarajevo
pop: 3,964,000
area (sq. mi.): 19,741
lang: Serbo-Croatian
money: conv. mark
gov: Republic

BOTSWANA

cap: Gabarone
pop: 1,591,000
area (sq. mi.): 231,804
lang: English, Setswana
money: pula
gov: Parliamentary republic

BRAZIL

cap: Brasília
pop: 176,092,000
area (sq. mi.): 3,286,470
lang: Portuguese
money: real
gov: Federal republic

BRUNEI DARUSSALAM

cap: Bandar Seri Begawan
pop: 351,000
area (sq. mi.): 2,226
lang: Malay, English, Chinese
money: dollar
gov: Independent sultanate

BULGARIA

cap: Sofia
pop: 7,621,000
area (sq. mi.): 44,365
lang: Bulgarian, Turkish
money: lev
gov: Republic

BURKINA FASO

cap: Ouagadougou
pop: 12,603,000
area (sq. mi.): 105,869
lang: French, Sudanic
languages
money: CFA franc
gov: Republic

BURUNDI

cap: Bujumbura
pop: 6,373,000
area (sq. mi.): 10,759
lang: French, Kirundi, Swahili
money: franc
gov: In transition

CAMBODIA

cap: Phnom Penh
pop: 12,775,000
area (sq. mi.): 70,238
lang: Khmer, French
money: riel
gov: Constitutional monarchy

CAMEROON

cap: Yaoundé
pop: 16,184,000
area (sq. mi.): 179,714
lang: English, French, others
money: CFA franc
gov: Republic

CANADA

cap: Ottawa
pop: 31,902,000
area (sq. mi.): 3,849,672
lang: English, French
money: dollar
gov: Confederation with
parliamentary democracy

CAPE VERDE

cap: Praia
pop: 408,760
area (sq. mi.): 1,557
lang: Portuguese, Crioulo
money: escudo
gov: Republic

**CENTRAL AFRICAN
REPUBLIC**

cap: Bangui
pop: 3,642,000
area (sq. mi.): 240,534
lang: French, Sangho, others
money: CFA franc
gov: Republic

Countries of the World (cont.)

CHAD

cap: N'Djamena
pop: 8,997,000
area (sq. mi.): 495,755
lang: French, Arabic, others
money: CFA franc
gov: Republic

CHILE

cap: Santiago
pop: 15,499,000
area (sq. mi.): 302,779
lang: Spanish
money: peso
gov: Republic

CHINA, People's Rep. of

cap: Beijing
pop: 1,284,303,00
area (sq. mi.): 3,696,100
lang: Mandarin, Yue, others
money: yuan
gov: Communist Party–led
state

CHINA, Rep. of (Taiwan)

cap: Taipei
pop: 22,548,000
area (sq. mi.): 13,885
lang: Mandarin, Malay, others
money: dollar (yuan)
gov: Democracy

COLOMBIA

cap: Bogotá
pop: 41,008,000
area (sq. mi.): 439,735
lang: Spanish
money: peso
gov: Republic

COMOROS

cap: Moroni
pop: 614,382
area (sq. mi.): 838
lang: Arabic, French, Comoran
money: franc
gov: In transition

CONGO, Democratic Republic of the

cap: Kinshasa
pop: 55,225,000
area (sq. mi.): 905,563
lang: French, Kongo, others
money: Congolese franc
gov: In transition

CONGO, Republic of the

cap: Brazzaville
pop: 2,958,000
area (sq. mi.): 132,046
lang: French, Kongo, Teke
money: CFA franc
gov: Republic

COSTA RICA

cap: San José
pop: 3,384,000
area (sq. mi.): 19,652
lang: Spanish, English
money: colón
gov: Republic

CÔTE D'IVOIRE (Ivory Coast)

cap: Yamoussoukro
pop: 16,804,000
area (sq. mi.): 124,503
lang: French, Dioula, others
money: CFA franc
gov: Republic

CROATIA

cap: Zagreb
pop: 4,391,000
area (sq. mi.): 21,829
lang: Serbo-Croatian
money: kuna
gov: Parliamentary democracy

CUBA

cap: Havana
pop: 11,200,000
area (sq. mi.): 44,218
lang: Spanish
money: peso
gov: Communist state

CYPRUS

cap: Nicosia
pop: 767,314
area (sq. mi.): 44,218
lang: Greek, Turkish, English
money: pound
gov: Republic

CZECH REPUBLIC

cap: Prague
pop: 10,256,000
area (sq. mi.): 30,449
lang: Czech, Slovak
money: koruna
gov: Republic

DENMARK

cap: Copenhagen
pop: 5,368,000
area (sq. mi.): 16,633
lang: Danish
money: krone
gov: Constitutional monarchy

DJIBOUTI

cap: Djibouti
pop: 472,810
area (sq. mi.): 8,950
lang: French, Arabic, Afar, Somali
money: franc
gov: Republic

Countries of the World (cont.)

DOMINICA

cap: Roseau
pop: 70,158
area (sq. mi.): 290
lang: English, Creole
money: dollar
gov: Parliamentary
    democracy

DOMINICAN REPUBLIC

cap: Santo Domingo
pop: 8,721,000
area (sq. mi.): 18,704
lang: Spanish
money: peso
gov: Republic

EAST TIMOR

cap: Dili
pop: 825,000
area (sq. mi.): 5,641
lang: Portuguese, Tetum
money: U.S. dollar
gov: In transition

ECUADOR

cap: Quito
pop: 13,447,000
area (sq. mi.): 109,483
lang: Spanish, Quechua,
    Jivaroan
money: dollar
gov: Republic

EGYPT

cap: Cairo
pop: 70,712,000
area (sq. mi.): 386,650
lang: Arabic, English, French
money: pound
gov: Republic

EL SALVADOR

cap: San Salvador
pop: 6,353,000
area (sq. mi.): 8,124
lang: Spanish, Nahuatl
money: colón
gov: Republic

EQUATORIAL GUINEA

cap: Malabo
pop: 498,000
area (sq. mi.): 10,832
lang: Spanish, Fang, Bubi
money: CFA franc
gov: Republic

ERITREA

cap: Asmara
pop: 4,465,000
area (sq. mi.): 36,170
lang: Tigre, Kunama, others
money: nafka
gov: In transition

ESTONIA

cap: Tallinn
pop: 1,415,000
area (sq. mi.): 17,413
lang: Estonian, Russian,
    Latvian
money: kroon
gov: Republic

ETHIOPIA

cap: Addis Ababa
pop: 67,673,000
area (sq. mi.): 435,606
lang: Amharic, Tigre, Galla
money: birr
gov: Federal republic

FIJI

cap: Suva
pop: 856,000
area (sq. mi.): 7,056
lang: English, Fijian, Hindi
money: dollar
gov: In transition

FINLAND

cap: Helsinki
pop: 5,183,000
area (sq. mi.): 130,119
lang: Finnish, Swedish
money: euro
gov: Constitutional republic

FRANCE

cap: Paris
pop: 59,765,000
area (sq. mi.): 220,668
lang: French
money: euro
gov: Republic

GABON

cap: Libreville
pop: 1,223,000
area (sq. mi.): 103,346
lang: French, Fang, others
money: CFA franc
gov: Republic

GAMBIA

cap: Banjul
pop: 1,455,000
area (sq. mi.): 4,127
lang: English, Mandinka,
    Wolof
money: dalasi
gov: Republic

GEORGIA

cap: Tbilisi
pop: 4,960,000
area (sq. mi.): 26,911
lang: Georgian, Russian,
    Armenian
money: lari
gov: Republic

Countries of the World (cont.)

GERMANY

cap: Berlin
pop: 83,251,000
area (sq. mi.): 137,838
lang: German
money: euro
gov: Federal republic

GHANA

cap: Accra
pop: 20,244,000
area (sq. mi.): 92,098
lang: English, various African
   languages
money: cedi
gov: Republic

GREECE

cap: Athens
pop: 10,645,000
area (sq. mi.): 51,146
lang: Greek, English
money: euro
gov: Parliamentary republic

GRENADA

cap: St. George's
pop: 89,210
area (sq. mi.): 133
lang: English, French patois
money: dollar
gov: Parliamentary democracy

GUATEMALA

cap: Guatemala City
pop: 13,314,000
area (sq. mi.): 42,042
lang: Spanish, Mayan
money: quetzal
gov: Republic

GUINEA

cap: Conakry
pop: 7,775,000
area (sq. mi.): 94,964
lang: French, Peul, Mande
money: franc
gov: Republic

GUINEA-BISSAU

cap: Bissau
pop: 1,345,000
area (sq. mi.): 13,948
lang: Portuguese, Crioulo,
   others
money: CFA franc
gov: Republic

GUYANA

cap: Georgetown
pop: 698,000
area (sq. mi.): 83,000
lang: English, Indian languages
money: dollar
gov: Republic

HAITI

cap: Port-au-Prince
pop: 7,063,000
area (sq. mi.): 10,579
lang: French, Creole
money: gourde
gov: Republic

HONDURAS

cap: Tegucigalpa
pop: 6,560,000
area (sq. mi.): 43,277
lang: Spanish, Indian
   languages
money: lempira
gov: Republic

HUNGARY

cap: Budapest
pop: 10,075,000
area (sq. mi.): 35,919
lang: Hungarian
money: forint
gov: Parliamentary democracy

ICELAND

cap: Reykjavik
pop: 279,384
area (sq. mi.): 39,769
lang: Icelandic
money: krona
gov: Constitutional republic

INDIA

cap: New Dehli
pop: 1,045,845,000
area (sq. mi.): 1,266,595
lang: Hindi, English, others
money: rupee
gov: Federal republic

INDONESIA

cap: Jakarta
pop: 232,073,000
area (sq. mi.): 735,268
lang: Bahasa Indonesia,
   Javanese, others
money: rupiah
gov: Republic

IRAN

cap: Tehran
pop: 66,620,000
area (sq. mi.): 636,293
lang: Farsi, Turkic, Kurdish
money: rial
gov: Islamic republic

IRAQ

cap: Baghdad
pop: 24,001,000
area (sq. mi.): 167,924
lang: Arabic, Kurdish
money: dinar
gov: In transition

Countries of the World (cont.)

IRELAND

cap: Dublin
pop: 3,883,000
area (sq. mi.): 27,137
lang: English, Gaelic
money: euro
gov: Parliamentary republic

ISRAEL

cap: Jerusalem
pop: 6,029,000
area (sq. mi.): 7,847
lang: Hebrew, Arabic, English
money: shekel
gov: Republic

ITALY

cap: Rome
pop: 57,715,000
area (sq. mi.): 116,303
lang: Italian
money: euro
gov: Republic

JAMAICA

cap: Kingston
pop: 2,680,000
area (sq. mi.): 4,232
lang: English, Jamaican
Creole
money: dollar
gov: Parliamentary
democracy

JAPAN

cap: Tokyo
pop: 126,974,000
area (sq. mi.): 145,856
lang: Japanese
money: yen
gov: Parliamentary democracy

JORDAN

cap: Amman
pop: 5,307,000
area (sq. mi.): 37,737
lang: Arabic, English
money: dinar
gov: Constitutional monarchy

KAZAKHSTAN

cap: Almaty
pop: 16,741,000
area (sq. mi.): 1,049,200
lang: Kazakh, Russian, German
money: tenge
gov: Republic

KENYA

cap: Nairobi
pop: 31,138,000
area (sq. mi.): 224,960
lang: Swahili, English, others
money: shilling
gov: Republic

KIRIBATI

cap: Tarawa
pop: 96,335
area (sq. mi.): 266
lang: English, Gilbertese
money: dollar
gov: Republic

KOREA, Dem. People's Rep. of (North Korea)

cap: Pyongyang
pop: 22,224,000
area (sq. mi.): 46,540
lang: Korean
money: won
gov: Communist state

KOREA, Rep. of (South Korea)

cap: Seoul
pop: 48,324,000
area (sq. mi.): 38,025
lang: Korean
money: won
gov: Republic, with power
centralized in a strong
executive

KUWAIT

cap: Kuwait
pop: 2,111,000
area (sq. mi.): 6,880
lang: Arabic, English
money: dinar
gov: Constitutional
monarchy

KYRGYZSTAN

cap: Bishkek
pop: 4,882,000
area (sq. mi.): 76,642
lang: Russian
money: som
gov: Republic

LAOS

cap: Vientiane
pop: 5,777,000
area (sq. mi.): 91,428
lang: Lao, French, Sino-
Tibetan languages
money: kip
gov: Communist state

LATVIA

cap: Riga
pop: 2,366,000
area (sq. mi.): 24,900
lang: Latvian, Lithuanian,
Russian
money: lat
gov: Republic

LEBANON

cap: Beirut
pop: 3,667,000
area (sq. mi.): 4,015
lang: Arabic, French, others
money: pound
gov: Republic

Countries of the World (cont.)

LESOTHO

cap: Maseru
pop: 2,207,000
area (sq. mi.): 11,716
lang: English, Sesotho, others
money: maluti
gov: Modified constitutional monarchy

LIBERIA

cap: Monrovia
pop: 3,228,000
area (sq. mi.): 38,250
lang: English, Niger-Congo languages
money: dollar
gov: Republic

LIBYA

cap: Tripoli
pop: 5,368,000
area (sq. mi.): 679,359
lang: Arabic, Italian, English
money: dinar
gov: Islamic Arabic Socialist "mass-state"

LIECHTENSTEIN

cap: Vaduz
pop: 32,842
area (sq. mi.): 62
lang: German, Alemannic dialect
money: Swiss franc
gov: Hereditary constitutional monarchy

LITHUANIA

cap: Vilnius
pop: 3,601,000
area (sq. mi.): 25,170
lang: Lithuanian, Polish, Russian
money: litas
gov: Republic

LUXEMBOURG

cap: Luxembourg
pop: 448,569
area (sq. mi.): 998
lang: French, German, Luxembourgisch
money: euro
gov: Constitutional monarchy

MACEDONIA

cap: Skopje
pop: 2,054,000
area (sq. mi.): 9,928
lang: Macedonian, Albanian, others
money: denar
gov: Republic

MADAGASCAR

cap: Antananarivo
pop: 16,473,000
area (sq. mi.): 226,657
lang: French, Malagasy
money: franc
gov: Republic

MALAWI

cap: Lilongwe
pop: 10,701,000
area (sq. mi.): 45,747
lang: English, Chichewa, Bantu languages
money: kwacha
gov: Multiparty democracy

MALAYSIA

cap: Kuala Lumpur
pop: 22,662,000
area (sq. mi.): 127,316
lang: Malay, English, others
money: ringgit
gov: Federal parliamentary democracy with a constitutional monarchy

MALDIVES

cap: Male
pop: 320,165
area (sq. mi.): 115
lang: Divehi, English
money: rufiyaa
gov: Republic

MALI

cap: Bamako
pop: 11,340,000
area (sq. mi.): 478,764
lang: French, Bambara, Senufo
money: CFA franc
gov: Republic

MALTA

cap: Valletta
pop: 400,000
area (sq. mi.): 122
lang: Maltese, English
money: lira
gov: Parliamentary democracy

MARSHALL ISLANDS

cap: Majuro
pop: 73,630
area (sq. mi.): 70
lang: English, Marshallese, Japanese
money: U.S. dollar
gov: Republic

MAURITANIA

cap: Nouakchott
pop: 2,828,000
area (sq. mi.): 419,212
lang: Hassanya Arabic, Wolof, others
money: ouguiya
gov: Islamic republic

MAURITIUS

cap: Port Louis
pop: 1,200,000
area (sq. mi.): 720
lang: English, Creole, others
money: rupee
gov: Republic

Countries of the World (cont.)

MEXICO

cap: Mexico City
pop: 103,400,000
area (sq. mi.): 761,604
lang: Spanish, Mayan, other
   indigenous languages
money: peso
gov: Federal republic

MICRONESIA

cap: Palikir
pop: 135,869
area (sq. mi.): 270
lang: English, Trukese, others
money: dollar
gov: Republic

MOLDOVA

cap: Chisinau
pop: 4,434,597
area (sq. mi.): 13,012
lang: Moldovan, Russian
money: leu
gov: Republic

MONACO

cap: Monaco
pop: 31,987
area (sq. mi.): 0.6
lang: French, English,
   Monegasque
money: euro
gov: Constitutional
   monarchy

MONGOLIA

cap: Ulan Bator
pop: 2,694,000
area (sq. mi.): 604,247
lang: Mongolian, Turkic,
   Russian
money: tugrik
gov: Republic

MOROCCO

cap: Rabat
pop: 31,167,000
area (sq. mi.): 172,413
lang: Arabic, Berber
   languages, French
money: dirham
gov: Constitutional
   monarchy

MOZAMBIQUE

cap: Maputo
pop: 19,607,000
area (sq. mi.): 303,769
lang: Portuguese, African
   languages
money: metical
gov: Republic

MYANMAR

cap: Yangon
pop: 42,238,000
area (sq. mi.): 261,789
lang: Burmese, Karen, Shan
money: kyat
gov: Military

NAMIBIA

cap: Windhoek
pop: 18,200,000
area (sq. mi.): 317,818
lang: Afrikaans, English,
   others
money: dollar
gov: Republic

NAURU

cap: Yaren
pop: 12,329
area (sq. mi.): 8
lang: Nauruan, English
money: dollar
gov: Republic

NEPAL

cap: Kathmandu
pop: 25,873,000
area (sq. mi.): 56,136
lang: Nepali, others
money: rupee
gov: Constitutional monarchy

NETHERLANDS

cap: Amsterdam
pop: 16,067,000
area (sq. mi.): 15,770
lang: Dutch
money: euro
gov: Parliamentary
   democracy under a
   constitutional monarch

NEW ZEALAND

cap: Wellington
pop: 3,908,000
area (sq. mi.): 103,736
lang: English, Maori
money: dollar
gov: Parliamentary
   democracy

NICARAGUA

cap: Managua
pop: 5,023,000
area (sq. mi.): 50,193
lang: Spanish, indigenous
   languages
money: córdoba
gov: Republic

NIGER

cap: Niamey
pop: 10,639,000
area (sq. mi.): 489,189
lang: French, Hausa, Djema
money: CFA franc
gov: Republic

NIGERIA

cap: Abuja
pop: 129,934,000
area (sq. mi.): 356,667
lang: English, Hausa, others
money: naira
gov: Republic

Countries of the World (cont.)

NORWAY

cap: Oslo
pop: 4,525,000
area (sq. mi.): 125,181
lang: Norwegian, Lapp, Finnish
money: krone
gov: Hereditary constitutional monarchy

OMAN

cap: Muscat
pop: 2,713,000
area (sq. mi.): 82,030
lang: Arabic, Balachi, others
money: rial omani
gov: Absolute monarchy

PAKISTAN

cap: Islamabad
pop: 147,663,000
area (sq. mi.): 310,403
lang: Urdu, English, others
money: rupee
gov: In transition

PALAU

cap: Koror
pop: 19,400
area (sq. mi.): 179
lang: English
money: dollar
gov: Republic

PANAMA

cap: Panama City
pop: 2,882,000
area (sq. mi.): 29,762
lang: Spanish, English
money: balboa
gov: Constitutional republic

PAPUA NEW GUINEA

cap: Port Moresby
pop: 5,172,000
area (sq. mi.): 178,260
lang: English, Melanesian, Papuan
money: kina
gov: Parliamentary democracy

PARAGUAY

cap: Asunción
pop: 5,882,000
area (sq. mi.): 157,047
lang: Spanish, Guarani
money: guarani
gov: Republic

PERU

cap: Lima
pop: 27,949,000
area (sq. mi.): 496,222
lang: Spanish, Quecha, Aymara
money: nuevo sol
gov: Republic

PHILIPPINES

cap: Manila
pop: 84,525,000
area (sq. mi.): 115,831
lang: Filipino, Tagalog, English, others
money: peso
gov: Republic

POLAND

cap: Warsaw
pop: 38,600,000
area (sq. mi.): 120,727
lang: Polish
money: zloty
gov: Republic

PORTUGAL

cap: Lisbon
pop: 10,084,000
area (sq. mi.): 36,390
lang: Portuguese
money: euro
gov: Republic

QATAR

cap: Doha
pop: 793,000
area (sq. mi.): 4,247
lang: Arabic, English
money: riyal
gov: Traditional monarchy

ROMANIA

cap: Bucharest
pop: 22,317,000
area (sq. mi.): 91,699
lang: Romanian, Hungarian, German
money: leu
gov: Republic

RUSSIA

cap: Moscow
pop: 144,978,000
area (sq. mi.): 6,592,800
lang: Russian, Ukrainian, others
money: ruble
gov: Federation

RWANDA

cap: Kigali
pop: 7,398,000
area (sq. mi.): 10,169
lang: French, Kinyarwanda, Bantu
money: franc
gov: Republic

ST. KITTS AND NEVIS

cap: Basseterre
pop: 38,700
area (sq. mi.): 101
lang: English
money: dollar
gov: Constitutional monarchy

Countries of the World (cont.)

ST. LUCIA

cap: Castries
pop: 160,000
area (sq. mi.): 238
lang: English, French patois
money: dollar
gov: Parliamentary
democracy

ST. VINCENT AND THE GRENADINES

cap: Kingstown
pop: 116,000
area (sq. mi.): 150
lang: English, French patois
money: dollar
gov: Constitutional monarchy

SAMOA

cap: Apia
pop: 178,000
area (sq. mi.): 1,133
lang: Samoan, English
money: tala
gov: Constitutional monarchy

SAN MARINO

cap: San Marino
pop: 27,700
area (sq. mi.): 24
lang: Italian
money: euro
gov: Republic

SÃO TOMÉ AND PRINCIPE

cap: São Tomé
pop: 170,300
area (sq. mi.): 372
lang: Portuguese
money: dobra
gov: Republic

SAUDI ARABIA

cap: Riyadh
pop: 23,513,000
area (sq. mi.): 839,996
lang: Arabic
money: riyal
gov: Monarch with council of
ministers

SENEGAL

cap: Dakar
pop: 10,589,000
area (sq. mi.): 75,750
lang: French, Wolof, others
money: CFA franc
gov: Republic

SERBIA AND MONTENEGRO

cap: Belgrade
pop: 9,979,000
area (sq. mi.): 26,940
lang: Serbo-Croatian,
Albanian
money: dinar
gov: Republic

SEYCHELLES

cap: Victoria
pop: 80,100
area (sq. mi.): 171
lang: English, French, Creole
money: rupee
gov: Republic

SIERRE LEONE

cap: Freetown
pop: 5,614,000
area (sq. mi.): 27,925
lang: English, Kiro, others
money: leone
gov: Republic

SINGAPORE

cap: Singapore
pop: 4,452,000
area (sq. mi.): 224
lang: Malay, Tamil, Chinese,
English
money: dollar
gov: Republic

SLOVAKIA

cap: Bratislava
pop: 5,422,000
area (sq. mi.): 18,932
lang: Slovak, Hungarian,
others
money: koruna
gov: Republic

SLOVENIA

cap: Ljubljana
pop: 1,932,000
area (sq. mi.): 7,819
lang: Slovenian, Serbo-
Croatian, others
money: tolar
gov: Republic

SOLOMON ISLANDS

cap: Honiara
pop: 494,700
area (sq. mi.): 10,640
lang: English, Papuan, others
money: dollar
gov: Parliamentary
democracy with the
Commonwealth of Nations

SOMALIA

cap: Mogadishu
pop: 7,753,000
area (sq. mi.): 246,300
lang: Somali, Arabic, others
money: shilling
gov: In transition

SOUTH AFRICA

cap: Pretoria, Cape Town,
and Bloemfontein
pop: 43,647,000
area (sq. mi.): 472,359
lang: Afrikaans, English,
Nguni, others
money: rand
gov: Federal republic with
bicameral parliament
and universal suffrage

Countries of the World (cont.)

SPAIN

cap: Madrid
pop: 40,077,000
area (sq. mi.): 194,896
lang: Spanish, Catalan, others
money: euro
gov: Constitutional monarchy

SRI LANKA

cap: Colombo
pop: 19,576,000
area (sq. mi.): 25,332
lang: Sinhalese, Tamil, English
money: rupee
gov: Republic

SUDAN

cap: Khartoum
pop: 37,090,000
area (sq. mi.): 966,757
lang: Arabic, Dinka, others
money: dinar
gov: Military

SURINAME

cap: Paramaribo
pop: 436,000
area (sq. mi.): 63,037
lang: Dutch, Sranan Tongo, English
money: guilder
gov: Republic

SWAZILAND

cap: Mlabane
pop: 1,123,000
area (sq. mi.): 6,704
lang: Siswati, English
money: lilangeni
gov: Constitutional monarchy

SWEDEN

cap: Stockholm
pop: 8,876,000
area (sq. mi.): 173,731
lang: Swedish, Lapp, Finnish
money: krona
gov: Constitutional monarchy

SWITZERLAND

cap: Bern
pop: 7,301,000
area (sq. mi.): 15,941
lang: French, German, Italian, Romansch
money: franc
gov: Federal republic

SYRIA

cap: Damascus
pop: 17,155,000
area (sq. mi.): 71,498
lang: Arabic, Kurdish, Armenian
money: pound
gov: Republic (under military regime)

TAJIKISTAN

cap: Dushanbe
pop: 6,719,000
area (sq. mi.): 54,019
lang: Tadzhik, Russian
money: ruble
gov: Republic

TANZANIA

cap: Dar-es-Salaam
pop: 37,187,000
area (sq. mi.): 364,886
lang: Swahili, English, others
money: shilling
gov: Republic

THAILAND

cap: Bangkok
pop: 62,354,000
area (sq. mi.): 198,456
lang: Thai, Chinese, others
money: baht
gov: Constitutional monarchy

TOGO

cap: Lomé
pop: 5,285,000
area (sq. mi.): 21,622
lang: French, Ewe, others
money: CFA franc
gov: Republic

TONGA

cap: Nuku'alofa
pop: 106,000
area (sq. mi.): 270
lang: Tongan, English
money: pa'anga
gov: Constitutional monarchy

TRINIDAD AND TOBAGO

cap: Port of Spain
pop: 1,163,000
area (sq. mi.): 1,980
lang: English, Hindi, others
money: dollar
gov: Parliamentary democracy

TUNISIA

cap: Tunis
pop: 9,815,000
area (sq. mi.): 63,170
lang: Arabic, French
money: dinar
gov: Republic

TURKEY

cap: Ankara
pop: 67,308,000
area (sq. mi.): 301,381
lang: Turkish, Kurdish, Arabic
money: lira
gov: Republic

Countries of the World (cont.)

TURKMENISTAN

cap: Ashgabad
pop: 4,688,000
area (sq. mi.): 188,417
lang: Turkmen, Russian,
   others
money: manat
gov: Republic

TUVALU

cap: Funafuti
pop: 11,100
area (sq. mi.): 10
lang: Tuvaluan, English
money: dollar
gov: Constitutional
   monarchy

UGANDA

cap: Kampala
pop: 24,699,000
area (sq. mi.): 93,354
lang: English, Luganda,
   Swahili
money: shilling
gov: Republic

UKRAINE

cap: Kyiv
pop: 48,396,000
area (sq. mi.): 23,100
lang: Ukrainian, Russian,
   others
money: hryvna
gov: Constitutional republic

UNITED ARAB EMIRATES

cap: Abu Dhabi
pop: 2,445,000
area (sq. mi.): 32,000
lang: Arabic, Persian, others
money: dirham
gov: Federation of emirates

UNITED KINGDOM

cap: London
pop: 59,778,000
area (sq. mi.): 94,226
lang: English, Welsh, Scottish,
   Gaelic
money: pound
gov: Constitutional monarchy

UNITED STATES

cap: Washington, DC
pop: 280,562,000
area (sq. mi.): 3,618,770
lang: English, Spanish
money: dollar
gov: Federal republic, strong
   democratic tradition

URUGUAY

cap: Montevideo
pop: 3,386,000
area (sq. mi.): 68,037
lang: Spanish
money: peso nuevo
gov: Republic

UZBEKISTAN

cap: Tashkent
pop: 25,563,000
area (sq. mi.): 172,700
lang: Uzbek, Russian, others
money: som
gov: Republic

VANUATU

cap: Port-Vila
pop: 196,000
area (sq. mi.): 5,700
lang: Bislama, English,
   French
money: vatu
gov: Republic

VATICAN CITY

cap: Vatican City
pop: 880
area (sq. mi.): 0.17
lang: Italian, Latin
money: lira

VENEZUELA

cap: Caracas
pop: 24,287,000
area (sq. mi.): 352,143
lang: Spanish, Indian
   languages
money: bolívar
gov: Federal republic

VIETNAM

cap: Hanoi
pop: 81,098,000
area (sq. mi.): 127,330
lang: Vietnamese, Chinese,
   others
money: dong
gov: Communist

YEMEN

cap: Sanaa
pop: 18,701,000
area (sq. mi.): 203,796
lang: Arabic
money: rial
gov: Republic

ZAMBIA

cap: Lusaka
pop: 9,958,000
area (sq. mi.): 290,586
lang: English, Bantu
   languages
money: kwacha
gov: Republic

ZIMBABWE

cap: Harare
pop: 11,300,000
area (sq. mi.): 150,803
lang: English, Shona, others
money: dollar
gov: Republic

Source: *CIA World Factbook*

World Population and Land Areas

Estimated Population, 2000

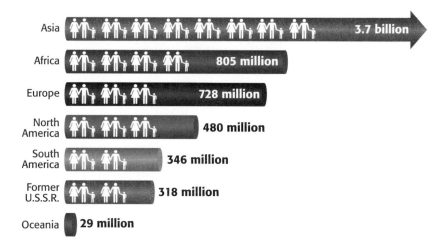

Asia	3.7 billion
Africa	805 million
Europe	728 million
North America	480 million
South America	346 million
Former U.S.S.R.	318 million
Oceania	29 million

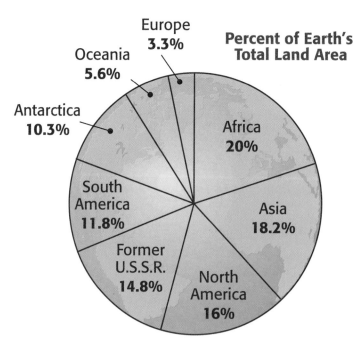

Percent of Earth's Total Land Area

Europe 3.3%
Oceania 5.6%
Antarctica 10.3%
South America 11.8%
Former U.S.S.R. 14.8%
North America 16%
Africa 20%
Asia 18.2%

Source: U.S. Census Bureau, International Data Base

Top 5 Highest Mountains in the World
(height of principal peak; lower peaks of same mountain excluded)

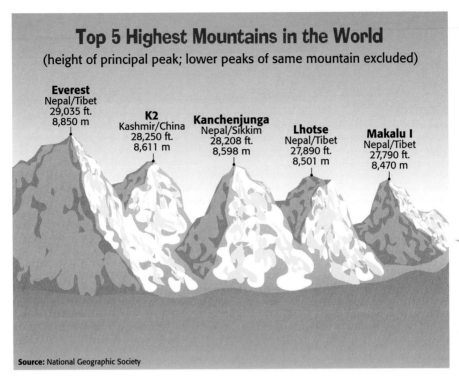

Everest
Nepal/Tibet
29,035 ft.
8,850 m

K2
Kashmir/China
28,250 ft.
8,611 m

Kanchenjunga
Nepal/Sikkim
28,208 ft.
8,598 m

Lhotse
Nepal/Tibet
27,890 ft.
8,501 m

Makalu I
Nepal/Tibet
27,790 ft.
8,470 m

Source: National Geographic Society

Top 5 Highest Waterfalls in the World

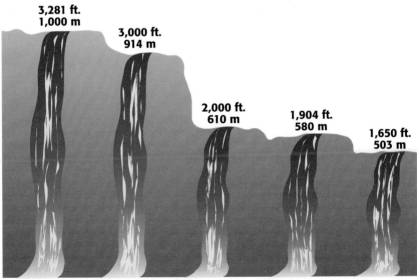

3,281 ft.
1,000 m

3,000 ft.
914 m

2,000 ft.
610 m

1,904 ft.
580 m

1,650 ft.
503 m

Angel
Venezuela
*Tributary of
Caroní River*

Tugela
Natal, South Africa
Tugela River

Cuquenán
Venezuela
Cuquenán River

Sutherland
South Island,
New Zealand
Arthur River

Takkakaw
British Columbia,
Canada
*Tributary of
Yoho River*

Source: Geological Survey, U.S. Department of the Interior

World's Top 5 Largest Oceans and Seas
(by area in square miles and millions of square kilometers [msk])

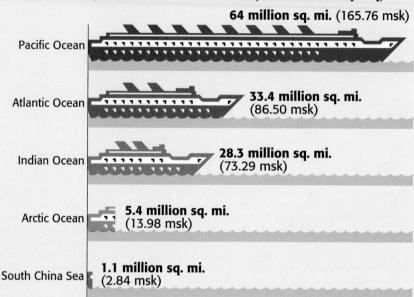

Pacific Ocean — **64 million sq. mi.** (165.76 msk)

Atlantic Ocean — **33.4 million sq. mi.** (86.50 msk)

Indian Ocean — **28.3 million sq. mi.** (73.29 msk)

Arctic Ocean — **5.4 million sq. mi.** (13.98 msk)

South China Sea — **1.1 million sq. mi.** (2.84 msk)

Source: Geological Survey, U.S. Department of the Interior

Top 5 Deepest Oceans and Seas in the World
(ranked by average depth)

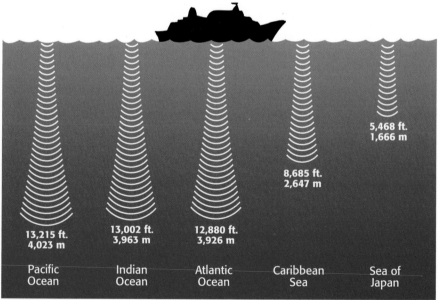

Pacific Ocean	Indian Ocean	Atlantic Ocean	Caribbean Sea	Sea of Japan
13,215 ft. 4,023 m	13,002 ft. 3,963 m	12,880 ft. 3,926 m	8,685 ft. 2,647 m	5,468 ft. 1,666 m

Source: U.S. Department of Defense; National Geographic Society

Top 5 Largest Lakes in the World
(ranked by approximate area in square miles/square kilometers)

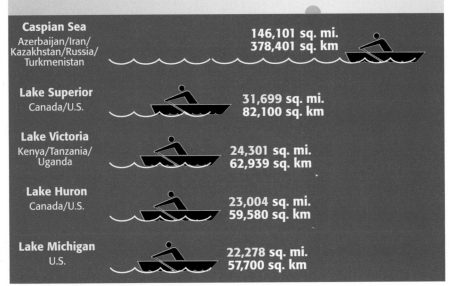

Caspian Sea
Azerbaijan/Iran/
Kazakhstan/Russia/
Turkmenistan
146,101 sq. mi.
378,401 sq. km

Lake Superior
Canada/U.S.
31,699 sq. mi.
82,100 sq. km

Lake Victoria
Kenya/Tanzania/
Uganda
24,301 sq. mi.
62,939 sq. km

Lake Huron
Canada/U.S.
23,004 sq. mi.
59,580 sq. km

Lake Michigan
U.S.
22,278 sq. mi.
57,700 sq. km

Source: Geological Survey, U.S. Department of the Interior

Top 5 Longest River Systems in the World

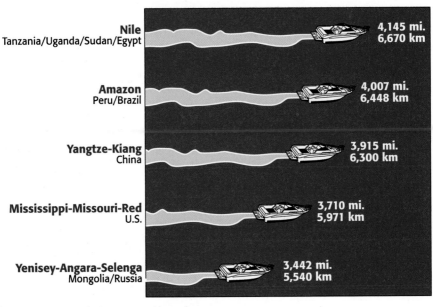

Nile
Tanzania/Uganda/Sudan/Egypt
4,145 mi.
6,670 km

Amazon
Peru/Brazil
4,007 mi.
6,448 km

Yangtze-Kiang
China
3,915 mi.
6,300 km

Mississippi-Missouri-Red
U.S.
3,710 mi.
5,971 km

Yenisey-Angara-Selenga
Mongolia/Russia
3,442 mi.
5,540 km

Source: Geological Survey, U.S. Department of the Interior

GOVERNMENT (U.S.)

History of the Pledge

The Pledge of Allegiance was published in 1892 to celebrate the 400th anniversary of the discovery of America. It was first recited in public schools to celebrate Columbus Day. The Pledge of Allegiance was officially recognized by Congress on June 22, 1942.

Flag Facts

The colors of our flag have specific meanings: white signifies purity and innocence; red signifies valor and bravery; and blue signifies vigilance, perseverance, and justice. The stars are considered a symbol of the heavens. The stripes are symbolic of the rays of light from the sun and the number of original colonies.

Symbolic Snack Swiper?

After six years of deliberation, the members of Congress decided in 1782 that the national emblem should be a bald eagle. It was chosen because it symbolized strength, courage, freedom, and immortality. However, Benjamin Franklin had originally argued for the symbol to be a turkey. He felt that the bald eagle was a dishonest bird because it sometimes stole its food from other birds.

Justices for All

The average tenure for Supreme Court justices is about 15 years. A new justice has typically been appointed to the Court about every 22 months. The presidents who appointed the most Supreme Court justices were George Washington, with 10 appointments, and Franklin D. Roosevelt, with 8 appointments. The longest-serving justice was John Marshall with a record 34 years.

The Branches of Government

EXECUTIVE
The President

- Symbol of our nation and head of state
- Shapes and conducts foreign policy and acts as chief diplomat
- Chief administrator of the federal government
- Commander-in-chief of armed forces
- Has authority to pass or veto congressional bills, plans, and programs
- Appoints and removes nonelected officials
- Leader of his or her political party

LEGISLATIVE
The Congress:
The Senate
The House of Representatives

- Chief lawmaking body
- Conducts investigations into matters of national importance
- Has power to impeach or remove any civil officer from office, including the president
- Can amend the Constitution
- The Senate is made up of 100 senators—2 from each state
- The House of Representatives is made up of 435 congressional representatives, apportioned to each state according to population

JUDICIAL
The Supreme Court

- Protects the Constitution
- Enforces commands of the executive and legislative branches
- Protects the rights of individuals and shields citizens from unfair laws
- Can declare laws unconstitutional
- Defines the laws of our nation

Highest Federal Salaries

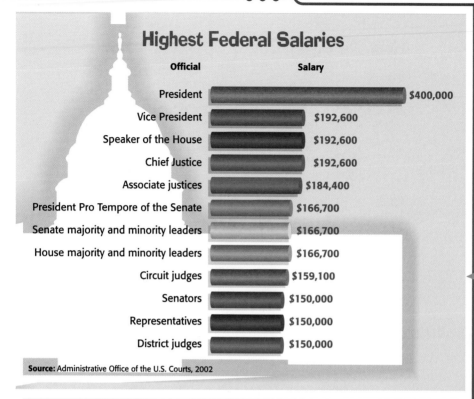

Official	Salary
President	$400,000
Vice President	$192,600
Speaker of the House	$192,600
Chief Justice	$192,600
Associate justices	$184,400
President Pro Tempore of the Senate	$166,700
Senate majority and minority leaders	$166,700
House majority and minority leaders	$166,700
Circuit judges	$159,100
Senators	$150,000
Representatives	$150,000
District judges	$150,000

Source: Administrative Office of the U.S. Courts, 2002

Where the U.S. Government Gets Its Money

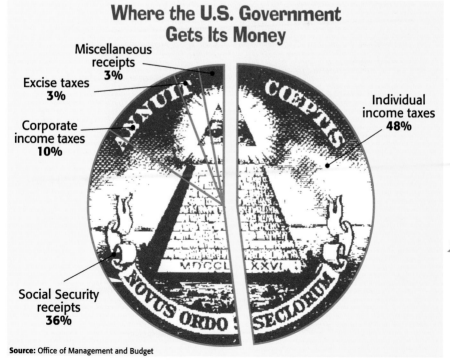

Miscellaneous receipts
3%

Excise taxes
3%

Corporate income taxes
10%

Individual income taxes
48%

Social Security receipts
36%

Source: Office of Management and Budget

173

How the Government Spends Its Money

(in billions, based on the 2002 budget)

Transportation
$62.1B
3.0%

Justice
$34.4B
1.7%

Natural resources,
environment
$30.2B
1.5%

Agriculture
$28.8B
1.4%

Veterans
$51.5B
2.5%

International
affairs $23.5B
1.2%

Science, space
technology
$21.8B
1.2%

Education
$71.7B
3.5%

Social
Security
$459.7B
22.4%

Interest
$178.4B
8.7%

E PLURIBUS UNUM

Health,
Medicare
$421.6B
20.5%

Other functions
$320.3B
15.5%

Defense
$348B
16.9%

Total: **$2,052B**
($2.052 trillion)

B=billion

Source: Office of Management and Budget

How a Bill Introduced in the House of Representatives Becomes a Law

(a similar procedure is followed for bills introduced in the Senate)

HOW BILLS ORIGINATE

The executive branch inspires much legislation. The president usually outlines broad objectives in the yearly State of the Union address.

Members of the president's staff may draft bills and ask congresspersons who are friendly to the legislation to introduce them.

Other bills originate independently of the administration, perhaps to fulfill a campaign pledge made by a congressperson.

HOW BILLS ARE INTRODUCED

Each bill must be introduced by a member of the House. The speaker then assigns the bill to the appropriate committee.

The committee conducts hearings during which members of the administration and others may testify for or against the bill.

If the committee votes to proceed, the bill goes to the Rules Committee, which decides whether to place it before the House.

THE HOUSE VOTES

A bill submitted to the House is voted on, with or without a debate. If a majority approves it, the bill is sent to the Senate.

SENATE PROCEDURE

The Senate assigns a bill to a Senate committee, which holds hearings and then approves, rejects, rewrites, or shelves the bill.

If the committee votes to proceed, it is submitted to the Senate for a vote, which may be taken with or without a debate.

RESULTS

If the Senate does not change the House version of the bill and a majority approves it, the bill goes to the president for signing.

If the bill the Senate approves differs from the House version, the bill is sent to a House-Senate conference for a compromise solution.

If the conference produces a compromise bill and it is approved by both the House and Senate, the bill goes to the president for signing.

WHEN A BILL BECOMES LAW

The bill becomes law if the president signs it. If the president vetoes it, two-thirds of both the House and Senate must approve it again before it can become law. If the bill comes to the president soon before Congress adjourns, the president may not do anything at all. If the bill is not signed before Congress adjourns, the bill dies. This is called the president's "pocket veto."

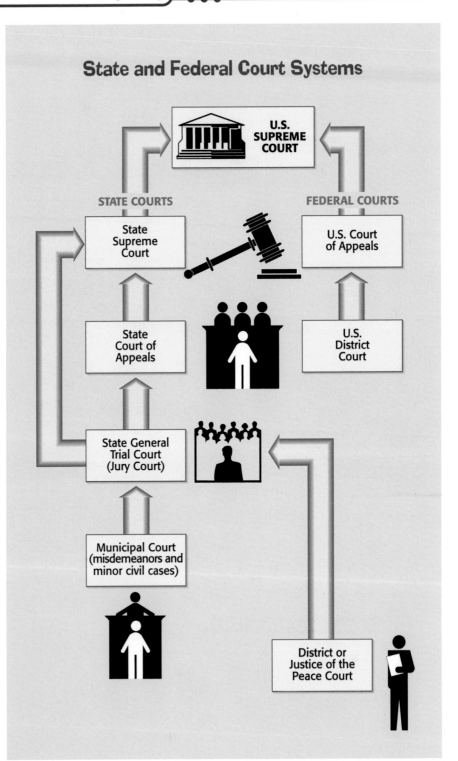

State and Federal Court Systems

The Sequence of Presidential Succession

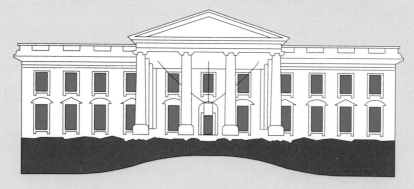

1. Vice President

2. Speaker of the House

3. President Pro Tempore of the Senate

4. Secretary of State

5. Secretary of the Treasury

6. Secretary of Defense

7. Attorney General

8. Secretary of the Interior

9. Secretary of Agriculture

10. Secretary of Commerce

11. Secretary of Labor

12. Secretary of Health and Human Services

13. Secretary of Housing and Urban Development

14. Secretary of Transportation

15. Secretary of Energy

16. Secretary of Education

Voting

Basic Laws and Requirements

- You must be 18 years of age or older before an election in order to vote in it.
- You must be an American citizen to vote.
- You must register before voting.
- You must show proof of residence in order to register.

How to Register

- Registering often only requires filling out a simple form.
- It does not cost anything to register.
- You need not be a member of any political party to register.
- To find out where to register, you can call your town hall or city board of elections.

- You can find out more information on voting and registering at:

http://www.fec.gov/pages/faqs.htm

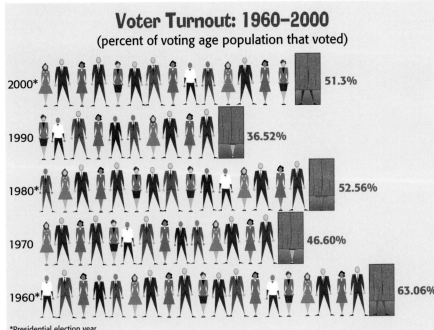

Voter Turnout: 1960–2000
(percent of voting age population that voted)

Year	Turnout
2000*	51.3%
1990	36.52%
1980*	52.56%
1970	46.60%
1960*	63.06%

*Presidential election year

Source: Congressional Research Service reports; Election Data Services, Inc.; State Election Offices

Voter Profile, by Selected Characteristics

(percent of eligible population that voted)

By Sex

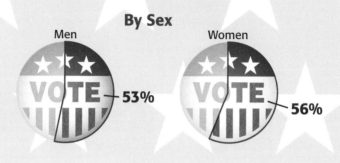

Men — 53%

Women — 56%

By Age

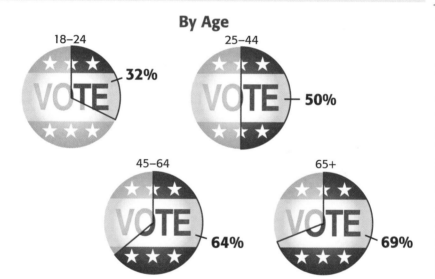

18–24 — 32%

25–44 — 50%

45–64 — 64%

65+ — 69%

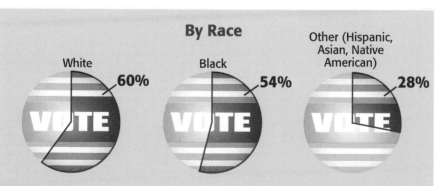

By Race

White — 60%

Black — 54%

Other (Hispanic, Asian, Native American) — 28%

Source: Based on data from the U.S. Census Bureau from the 2000 presidential election

The Electoral College

Although people go out on Election Day and cast their votes for president, the president and vice president are only indirectly elected by the American people. In fact, the president and vice president are the only elected federal officials not chosen by direct vote of the people. These two people are elected by the Electoral College, which was created by the framers of the Constitution.

Here is a simple outline of how the Electoral College works:

- There are 538 electoral votes.
- The votes are divided by the states and the District of Columbia. The number of votes that each state has is equal to the number of senators and representatives for that state. (California has 52 representatives and 2 senators; it has a total of 54 electoral votes.)
- During an election, the candidate who wins the majority of popular votes in a given state wins all the electoral votes from that state.
- A presidential candidate needs 270 electoral votes to win.

You may have heard that it is possible for a presidential candidate who has not won the most popular votes to win an election. This can happen if a candidate wins the popular vote in large states (ones with lots of electoral votes) by only a slim margin and loses the popular votes in smaller states by a wide margin.

Electoral Votes for President
(based on the 2000 Census)

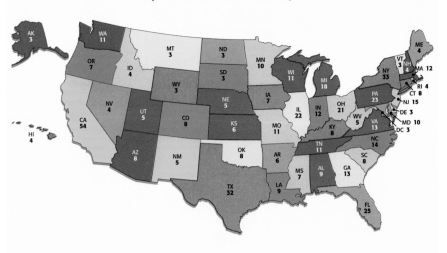

Source: Voter News Service; Federal Election Committee

U.S. Presidents With the Most Electoral Votes

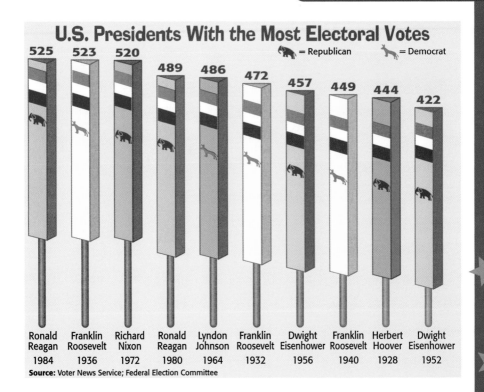

= Republican   = Democrat

Ronald Reagan 1984	Franklin Roosevelt 1936	Richard Nixon 1972	Ronald Reagan 1980	Lyndon Johnson 1964	Franklin Roosevelt 1932	Dwight Eisenhower 1956	Franklin Roosevelt 1940	Herbert Hoover 1928	Dwight Eisenhower 1952
525	523	520	489	486	472	457	449	444	422

Source: Voter News Service; Federal Election Committee

Top 5 U.S. Presidents With the Greatest Number of Popular Votes

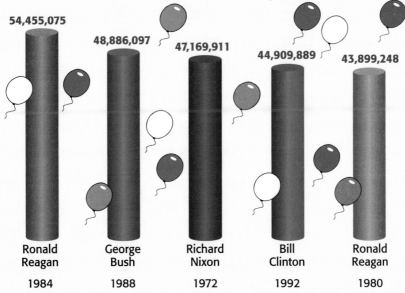

Ronald Reagan 1984	George Bush 1988	Richard Nixon 1972	Bill Clinton 1992	Ronald Reagan 1980
54,455,075	48,886,097	47,169,911	44,909,889	43,899,248

Source: Federal Election Commission

HEALTH

Sleep Stats

If people sleep eight hours each day, they sleep the equivalent of 122 days per year. Most people dream about five times during each eight-hour period of sleep—an average of 1,825 dreams every year!

A Baby Bone

The smallest bone in the adult human body is the stapes, which is located in the ear. It is only .10 to .13 inches (.25 to .33 cm) long and weighs only 1.9 to 4.3 milligrams.

Traffic Tragedies

About 42,000 people are killed in traffic accidents each year, and some 16,000 fatalities are alcohol-related. This represents an average of one alcohol-related death every 32 minutes.

Use Your Head!

Helmets really help protect heads from harm! Head injuries account for 62% of all bicycle-related deaths. Bicycle helmets reduce the risk for head injury by as much as 85% and reduce the risk for brain injury by as much as 88%.

Get a Move On!

Exercise isn't only fun, it helps your entire body. Getting a little physical exercise—just 30 minutes a day—will help build strong bones and muscles, reduce body fat and stress, and make you feel great!

The Six Systems of the Human Body

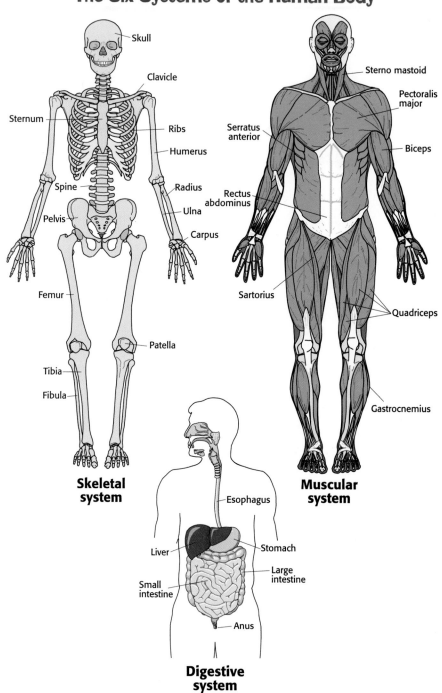

Skeletal system

- Skull
- Clavicle
- Sternum
- Ribs
- Humerus
- Spine
- Radius
- Pelvis
- Ulna
- Carpus
- Femur
- Patella
- Tibia
- Fibula

Muscular system

- Sterno mastoid
- Pectoralis major
- Serratus anterior
- Biceps
- Rectus abdominus
- Sartorius
- Quadriceps
- Gastrocnemius

Digestive system

- Esophagus
- Liver
- Stomach
- Small intestine
- Large intestine
- Anus

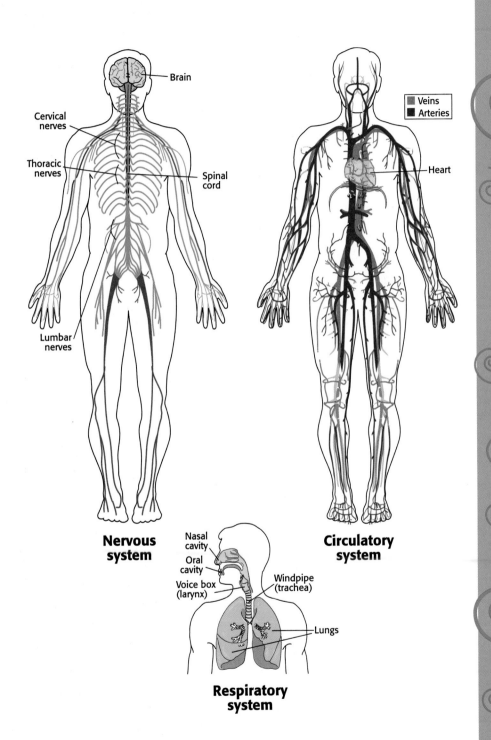

Nervous system

Brain

Cervical nerves

Thoracic nerves

Spinal cord

Lumbar nerves

Circulatory system

Veins
Arteries

Heart

Respiratory system

Nasal cavity

Oral cavity

Voice box (larynx)

Windpipe (trachea)

Lungs

The Food Pyramid

The U.S. Department of Agriculture (USDA) has recommended
this balance of food groups for good nutrition.

Fats, oils, & sweets
USE SPARINGLY

Meats, poultry, fish,
dry beans, eggs,
& nuts group
2–3 SERVINGS
DAILY

Milk, yogurt,
& cheese group
2–3 SERVINGS
DAILY

Vegetable group
3–5 SERVINGS
DAILY

Fruit group
2–4 SERVINGS
DAILY

Bread, cereal, rice, & pasta group 6–11 SERVINGS DAILY

Source: U.S. Department of Agriculture

Expanding Waistlines

More than 55% of the U.S. population is
considered to be overweight or obese.

Men

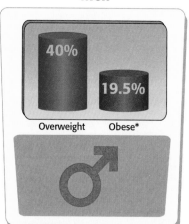

40%

19.5%

Overweight   Obese*

Women

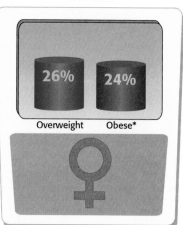

26%   24%

Overweight   Obese*

*Having a Body Mass Index (BMI) greater than or equal to 30.

Source: *Health,* National Institutes of Health, 2000

How Americans Keep Fit

About 54 million Americans ages six and over
participated in fitness activities in 2001.
Their top activities, in millions of participants:

Fitness walking  81.3M

Swimming  59.3M

Exercising with equipment  43.2M

Biking  42.5M

Aerobics  27.2M

Basketball  27.2M

Source: National Sporting Goods Association

Top 5 Reasons for Emergency Room Visits
(as given by patients)

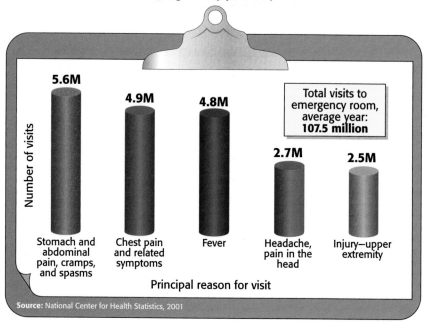

Number of visits

5.6M **4.9M** **4.8M** **2.7M** **2.5M**

Total visits to
emergency room,
average year:
107.5 million

| Stomach and abdominal pain, cramps, and spasms | Chest pain and related symptoms | Fever | Headache, pain in the head | Injury—upper extremity |

Principal reason for visit

Source: National Center for Health Statistics, 2001

Most Common Causes of Unnatural Death in the U.S.

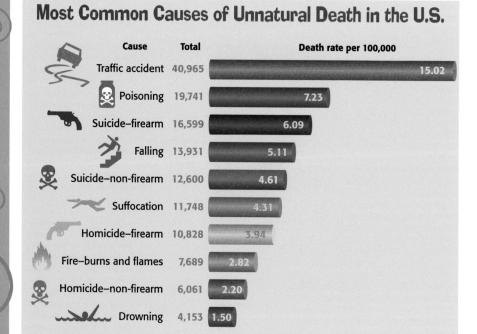

	Cause	Total	Death rate per 100,000
	Traffic accident	40,965	15.02
	Poisoning	19,741	7.23
	Suicide–firearm	16,599	6.09
	Falling	13,931	5.11
	Suicide–non-firearm	12,600	4.61
	Suffocation	11,748	4.31
	Homicide–firearm	10,828	3.94
	Fire–burns and flames	7,689	2.82
	Homicide–non-firearm	6,061	2.20
	Drowning	4,153	1.50

Source: National Center for Injury Prevention and Control, 2000

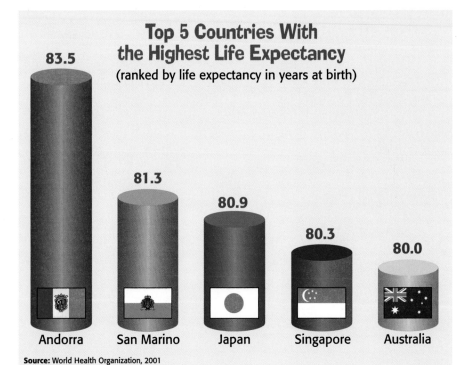

Top 5 Countries With the Highest Life Expectancy
(ranked by life expectancy in years at birth)

83.5 — Andorra
81.3 — San Marino
80.9 — Japan
80.3 — Singapore
80.0 — Australia

Source: World Health Organization, 2001

Top 5 Countries With the Lowest Life Expectancy
(ranked by life expectancy in years at birth)

35.3 — Botswana
35.5 — Mozambique
36.5 — Zimbabwe
36.6 — Malawi
37.0 — Swaziland

Source: World Health Organization, 2001

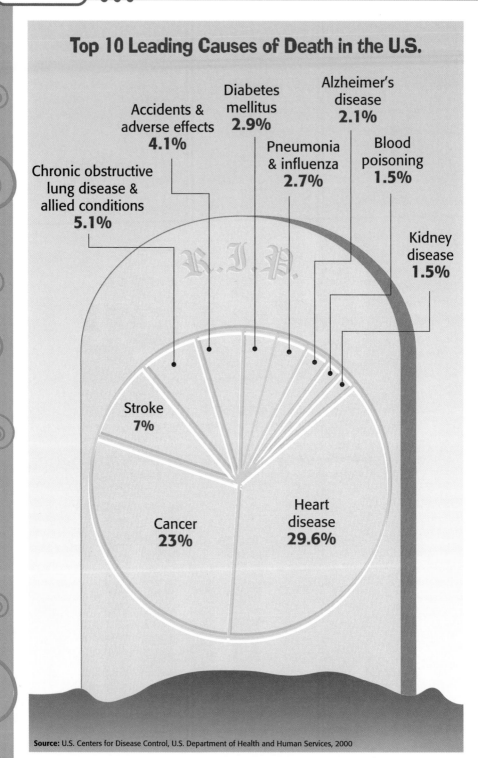

Top 10 Leading Causes of Death in the U.S.

Diabetes mellitus 2.9%

Alzheimer's disease 2.1%

Accidents & adverse effects 4.1%

Pneumonia & influenza 2.7%

Blood poisoning 1.5%

Chronic obstructive lung disease & allied conditions 5.1%

Kidney disease 1.5%

R.I.P.

Stroke 7%

Cancer 23%

Heart disease 29.6%

Source: U.S. Centers for Disease Control, U.S. Department of Health and Human Services, 2000

Risk in the Sun

Your chance of developing melanoma has increased more than 1,800% since the 1930s.

1935	1960	1980	1985	1992	1996	2002
1/1,500	1/600	1/250	1/150	1/105	1/87	1/51

Source: *Journal of the American Academy of Dermatology,* May 2002

Top 10 Most Common Phobias

Object of Phobia	Medical Term
1. Spiders	Arachnophobia
2. People and social situations	Anthropophobia
3. Flying	Aerophobia
4. Open spaces	Agoraphobia
5. Confined spaces	Claustrophobia
6. Heights	Acrophobia
7. Vomiting	Emetophobia
8. Cancer	Carcinomaphobia
9. Thunderstorms	Brontophobia
10. Death	Necrophobia

Accidental Deaths for Kids

(number of deaths, kids 5–14 years old, by types of accident per year)

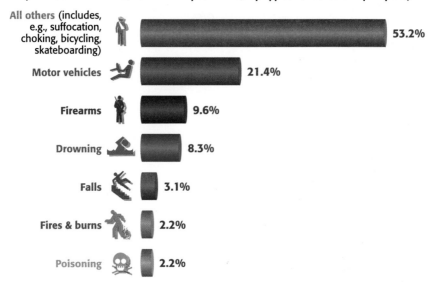

All others (includes, e.g., suffocation, choking, bicycling, skateboarding) **53.2%**

Motor vehicles **21.4%**

Firearms **9.6%**

Drowning **8.3%**

Falls **3.1%**

Fires & burns **2.2%**

Poisoning **2.2%**

Source: National Safety Council, 2001

Smokers' Profile

Among Americans ages 12 and over, 24.4% smoke.
Percentage of smokers by groups:

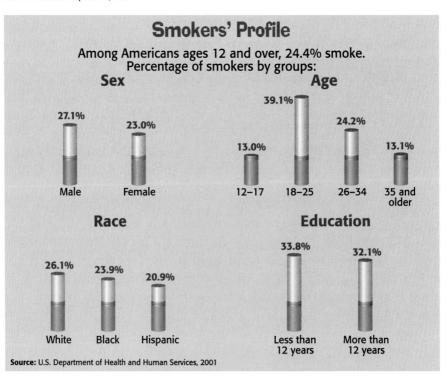

Sex

27.1% Male
23.0% Female

Age

13.0% 12–17
39.1% 18–25
24.2% 26–34
13.1% 35 and older

Race

26.1% White
23.9% Black
20.9% Hispanic

Education

33.8% Less than 12 years
32.1% More than 12 years

Source: U.S. Department of Health and Human Services, 2001

Profile: Cigarettes at School

Nearly one in five 12th graders reported daily cigarette smoking in a 30-day period.

Legend:
- 8th graders
- 10th graders
- 12th graders

ANY CIGARETTE USE
10.7% 17.7% 26.7%

DAILY USE
5.1% 10.1% 16.9%

HALF PACK OR MORE PER DAY
2.1% 4.4% 9.1%

SMOKELESS TOBACCO
3.3% 6.1% 6.5%

Cigarette use by grade level

Grade	Use
9	30.6%
10	32.4%
11	35.7%
12	32.5%
Average	**32.8%**

Teen cigarette use by race/ethnicity

Race	8th grade	12th grade
Whites	12.0%	32.5%
Blacks	7.7%	12.1%
Hispanics	12.7%	21.3%

Source: U.S. Centers for Disease Control and Prevention, 2002

World AIDS Cases

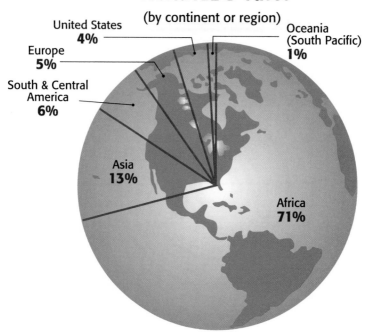

(by continent or region)

United States
4%

Oceania
(South Pacific)
1%

Europe
5%

South & Central
America
6%

Asia
13%

Africa
71%

Source: World Health Organization, 2000

Number of AIDS Cases Diagnosed in the United States Through December 2001

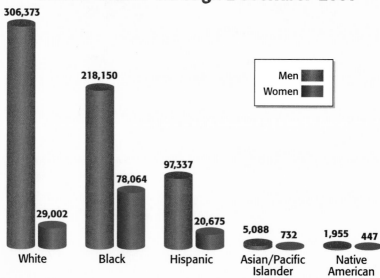

306,373

218,150

Men
Women

97,337

78,064

29,002

20,675

5,088   732

1,955   447

White   Black   Hispanic   Asian/Pacific   Native
                                            Islander   American

Source: U.S. Centers for Disease Control and Prevention

194

How Adults and Adolescents Contract AIDS in the U.S.

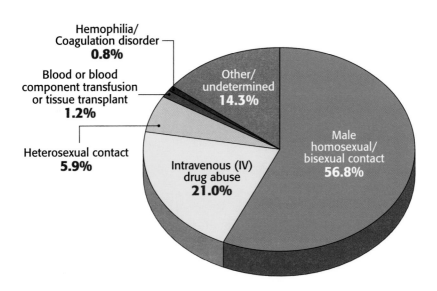

Hemophilia/
Coagulation disorder
0.8%

Blood or blood
component transfusion
or tissue transplant
1.2%

Heterosexual contact
5.9%

Other/
undetermined
14.3%

Intravenous (IV)
drug abuse
21.0%

Male
homosexual/
bisexual contact
56.8%

How Children Contract AIDS in the U.S.

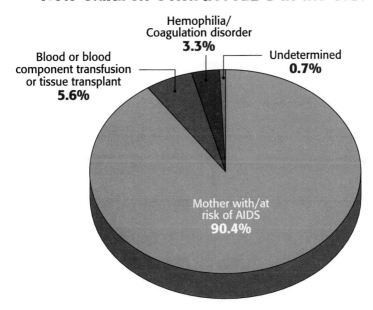

Hemophilia/
Coagulation disorder
3.3%

Blood or blood
component transfusion
or tissue transplant
5.6%

Undetermined
0.7%

Mother with/at
risk of AIDS
90.4%

Source: U.S. Department of Health and Human Services, U.S. Centers for Disease Control and Prevention, 2001

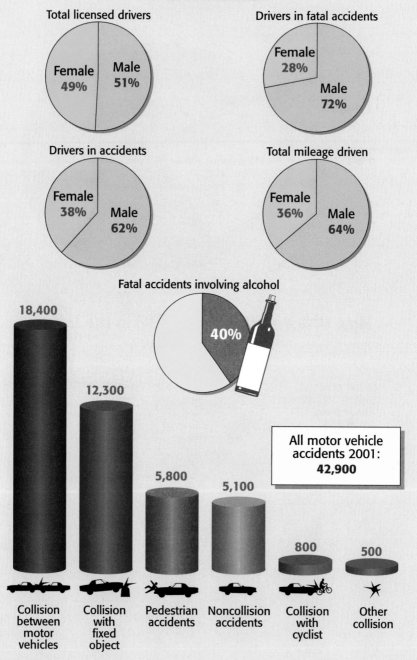

Profile: U.S. Motor Vehicle Drivers and Accidents

Total licensed drivers
- Female 49%
- Male 51%

Drivers in fatal accidents
- Female 28%
- Male 72%

Drivers in accidents
- Female 38%
- Male 62%

Total mileage driven
- Female 36%
- Male 64%

Fatal accidents involving alcohol
- 40%

All motor vehicle accidents 2001: **42,900**

Collision between motor vehicles	Collision with fixed object	Pedestrian accidents	Noncollision accidents	Collision with cyclist	Other collision
18,400	12,300	5,800	5,100	800	500

Source: National Safety Council, 2001

196

Top 10 Countries With the Most Smokers

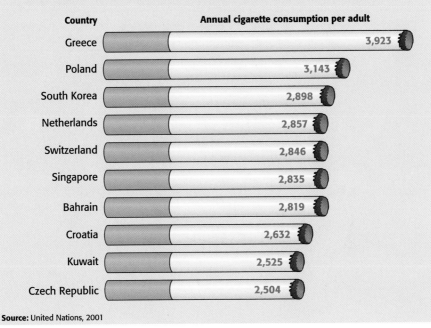

Country	Annual cigarette consumption per adult
Greece	3,923
Poland	3,143
South Korea	2,898
Netherlands	2,857
Switzerland	2,846
Singapore	2,835
Bahrain	2,819
Croatia	2,632
Kuwait	2,525
Czech Republic	2,504

Source: United Nations, 2001

Number of Drug-Related Deaths by Race and Sex in 2002

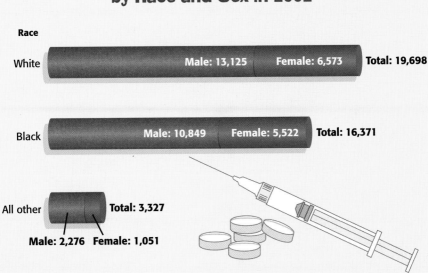

Race

White	Male: 13,125 Female: 6,573 Total: 19,698
Black	Male: 10,849 Female: 5,522 Total: 16,371
All other	Total: 3,327 Male: 2,276 Female: 1,051

Source: Bureau of Alcohol, Tobacco, and Firearms

HISTORY (U.S.)

In Mint Condition

The U.S. Mint produced its first circulating coins—11,178 copper cents—in March 1793. Before creation of a national mint, "currency" included foreign and colonial banknotes, livestock, produce, and wampum. Each year, the mint produces 4.18 billion pennies, 416 million nickels, 1.1 billion dimes, and 1.56 billion quarters.

Presidential Projects

Many presidents have remodeled or modernized the White House in some way while in office. Franklin Pierce ordered the first bathtub to be installed. Rutherford B. Hayes had the first telephone installed. Benjamin Harrison had the White House wired for electricity. Franklin D. Roosevelt had a swimming pool and movie theater built on the property.

Bragging Rights

President James Polk (1845–1849) was the first president to have his photograph taken. President Theodore Roosevelt (1901–1909) was not only the first president to ride in an automobile, but also the first president to travel outside the country, when he visited Panama. President Franklin Roosevelt (1933–1945) was the first president to ride in an airplane.

Presidential Résumés

Many U.S. Presidents did not start out as politicians. Before becoming president, Abraham Lincoln was a lawyer, Lyndon Johnson was a school teacher, James Garfield was a preacher, William Howard Taft was a judge, and both George Washington and Jimmy Carter were farmers.

History Timeline: 1000–1700

c. 1000 Viking explorer Leif Ericson explores North American coast and founds temporary colony called Vinland.

1497 John Cabot claims Newfoundland for King Henry VII of England.

1513 Juan Ponce de León discovers Florida. Vasco Núñez de Balboa crosses Panama and sights Pacific Ocean.

1519 Hernán Cortés lands in Mexico.

1522 Cortés captures Mexico City and conquers Aztec empire.

1541 Coronado discovers Mississippi River.

1492 On first voyage to America, Christopher Columbus lands at San Salvador island in the Bahamas.

1520 Ferdinand Magellan, first to sail around world, discovers South American straits, named after him.

1524 Giovanni de Verrazano, commissioned by King Francis I of France, discovers New York Harbor and Hudson River.

1540 Francisco Vásquez de Coronado explores Southwest, discovering Grand Canyon and introducing horses to North America.

1499 Florentine merchant Amerigo Vespucci visits New World and begins writing popular accounts of his voyages.

1603 Samuel de Champlain of France explores St. Lawrence River; later founds Quebec.

1534–1539 Jacques Cartier of France explores coast of Newfoundland and Gulf of St. Lawrence. Hernando de Soto conquers Florida and begins three-year trek across Southeast.

1608 Capt. John Smith imprisoned by Indians and saved by Pocahontas, daughter of Chief Powhatan.

1585 Raleigh establishes England's first American colony at Roanoke.

1607 First permanent English settlement in America established at Jamestown, VA. Only 32 of original 105 colonists survive the first winter.

1584 Sir Walter Raleigh discovers Roanoke Island and names land Virginia, after Queen Elizabeth I.

1572 Sir Francis Drake of England makes first voyage to America, landing in Panama.

1626 Dutch colony of New Amsterdam founded on Manhattan Island, bought from Native Americans for about $24.

1609 Henry Hudson sets out in search of Northwest Passage. Champlain sails into Great Lakes.

1676 Bacon's Rebellion overthrows government of Virginia and burns down Jamestown.

1620 Pilgrims and others board *Mayflower* and travel to Plymouth, MA. They draw up Mayflower Compact.

1675 Thousands die in King Philip's War between New Englanders and five Native American tribes.

1692 Witchcraft hysteria breaks out in Salem, MA, leading to 20 executions.

History Timeline: 1700s

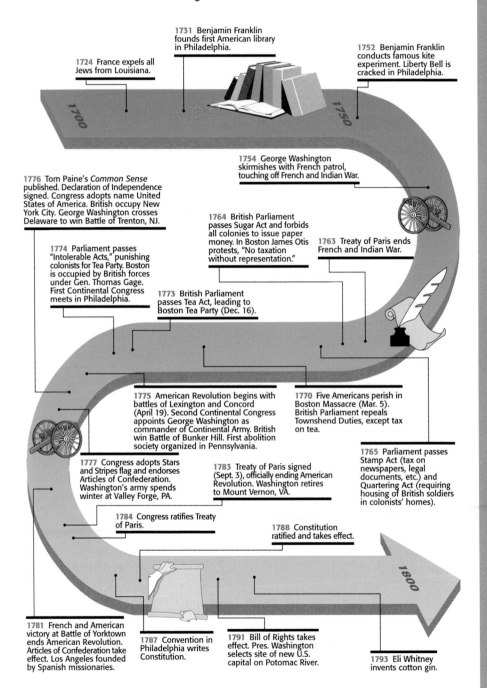

1724 France expels all Jews from Louisiana.

1731 Benjamin Franklin founds first American library in Philadelphia.

1752 Benjamin Franklin conducts famous kite experiment. Liberty Bell is cracked in Philadelphia.

1754 George Washington skirmishes with French patrol, touching off French and Indian War.

1776 Tom Paine's *Common Sense* published. Declaration of Independence signed. Congress adopts name United States of America. British occupy New York City. George Washington crosses Delaware to win Battle of Trenton, NJ.

1764 British Parliament passes Sugar Act and forbids all colonies to issue paper money. In Boston James Otis protests, "No taxation without representation."

1763 Treaty of Paris ends French and Indian War.

1774 Parliament passes "Intolerable Acts," punishing colonists for Tea Party. Boston is occupied by British forces under Gen. Thomas Gage. First Continental Congress meets in Philadelphia.

1773 British Parliament passes Tea Act, leading to Boston Tea Party (Dec. 16).

1775 American Revolution begins with battles of Lexington and Concord (April 19). Second Continental Congress appoints George Washington as commander of Continental Army. British win Battle of Bunker Hill. First abolition society organized in Pennsylvania.

1770 Five Americans perish in Boston Massacre (Mar. 5). British Parliament repeals Townshend Duties, except tax on tea.

1777 Congress adopts Stars and Stripes flag and endorses Articles of Confederation. Washington's army spends winter at Valley Forge, PA.

1783 Treaty of Paris signed (Sept. 3), officially ending American Revolution. Washington retires to Mount Vernon, VA.

1765 Parliament passes Stamp Act (tax on newspapers, legal documents, etc.) and Quartering Act (requiring housing of British soldiers in colonists' homes).

1784 Congress ratifies Treaty of Paris.

1788 Constitution ratified and takes effect.

1781 French and American victory at Battle of Yorktown ends American Revolution. Articles of Confederation take effect. Los Angeles founded by Spanish missionaries.

1787 Convention in Philadelphia writes Constitution.

1791 Bill of Rights takes effect. Pres. Washington selects site of new U.S. capital on Potomac River.

1793 Eli Whitney invents cotton gin.

History Timeline: 1800s

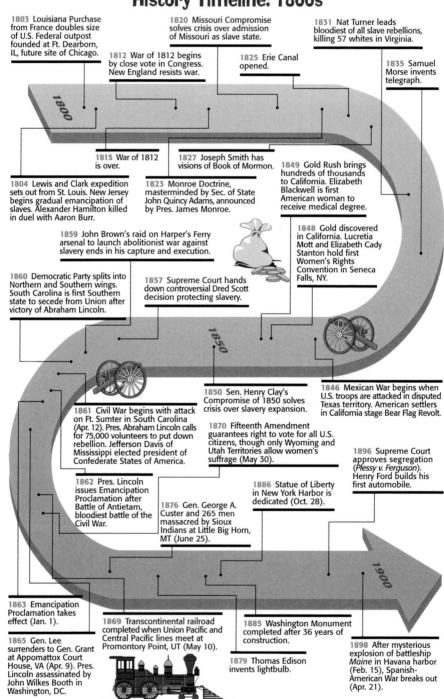

1803 Louisiana Purchase from France doubles size of U.S. Federal outpost founded at Ft. Dearborn, IL, future site of Chicago.

1820 Missouri Compromise solves crisis over admission of Missouri as slave state.

1831 Nat Turner leads bloodiest of all slave rebellions, killing 57 whites in Virginia.

1812 War of 1812 begins by close vote in Congress. New England resists war.

1825 Erie Canal opened.

1835 Samuel Morse invents telegraph.

1800

1815 War of 1812 is over.

1827 Joseph Smith has visions of Book of Mormon.

1849 Gold Rush brings hundreds of thousands to California. Elizabeth Blackwell is first American woman to receive medical degree.

1804 Lewis and Clark expedition sets out from St. Louis. New Jersey begins gradual emancipation of slaves. Alexander Hamilton killed in duel with Aaron Burr.

1823 Monroe Doctrine, masterminded by Sec. of State John Quincy Adams, announced by Pres. James Monroe.

1848 Gold discovered in California. Lucretia Mott and Elizabeth Cady Stanton hold first Women's Rights Convention in Seneca Falls, NY.

1859 John Brown's raid on Harper's Ferry arsenal to launch abolitionist war against slavery ends in his capture and execution.

1860 Democratic Party splits into Northern and Southern wings. South Carolina is first Southern state to secede from Union after victory of Abraham Lincoln.

1857 Supreme Court hands down controversial Dred Scott decision protecting slavery.

1850

1850 Sen. Henry Clay's Compromise of 1850 solves crisis over slavery expansion.

1846 Mexican War begins when U.S. troops are attacked in disputed Texas territory. American settlers in California stage Bear Flag Revolt.

1861 Civil War begins with attack on Ft. Sumter in South Carolina (Apr. 12). Pres. Abraham Lincoln calls for 75,000 volunteers to put down rebellion. Jefferson Davis of Mississippi elected president of Confederate States of America.

1870 Fifteenth Amendment guarantees right to vote for all U.S. citizens, though only Wyoming and Utah Territories allow women's suffrage (May 30).

1896 Supreme Court approves segregation (*Plessy v. Ferguson*). Henry Ford builds his first automobile.

1862 Pres. Lincoln issues Emancipation Proclamation after Battle of Antietam, bloodiest battle of the Civil War.

1886 Statue of Liberty in New York Harbor is dedicated (Oct. 28).

1876 Gen. George A. Custer and 265 men massacred by Sioux Indians at Little Big Horn, MT (June 25).

1863 Emancipation Proclamation takes effect (Jan. 1).

1869 Transcontinental railroad completed when Union Pacific and Central Pacific lines meet at Promontory Point, UT (May 10).

1885 Washington Monument completed after 36 years of construction.

1900

1865 Gen. Lee surrenders to Gen. Grant at Appomattox Court House, VA (Apr. 9). Pres. Lincoln assassinated by John Wilkes Booth in Washington, DC.

1879 Thomas Edison invents lightbulb.

1898 After mysterious explosion of battleship *Maine* in Havana harbor (Feb. 15), Spanish-American War breaks out (Apr. 21).

The Confederate States of America, 1860–1866

State	Seceded from Union	Readmitted to Union*
1. South Carolina	Dec. 20, 1860	July 9, 1868
2. Mississippi	Jan. 9, 1861	Feb. 23, 1870
3. Florida	Jan. 10, 1861	June 25, 1868
4. Alabama	Jan. 11, 1861	July 13, 1868
5. Georgia	Jan. 19, 1861	July 15, 1870**
6. Louisiana	Jan. 26, 1861	July 9, 1868
7. Texas	Mar. 2, 1861	Mar. 30, 1870
8. Virginia	April 17, 1861	Jan. 26, 1870
9. Arkansas	May 6, 1861	June 22, 1868
10. North Carolina	May 20, 1861	July 4, 1868
11. Tennessee	June 8, 1861	July 24, 1866

*Date of readmission to representation in U.S. House of Representatives.
**Second readmission date. First date was July 21, 1868, but the representatives were unseated March 5, 1869.
Note: Four other slave states—Delaware, Kentucky, Maryland, and Missouri—remained in the Union.

Source: National Archives

History Timeline: 1900s–2000s

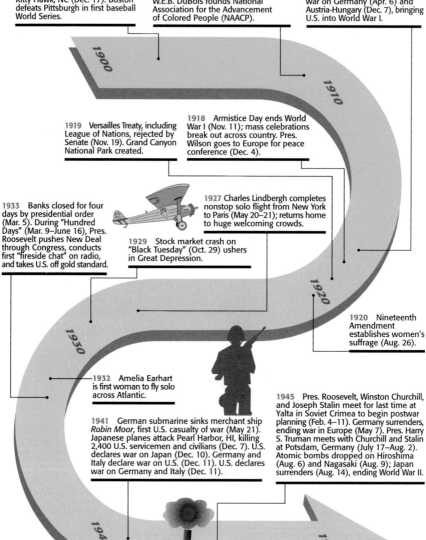

1903 Orville and Wilbur Wright conduct first powered flight near Kitty Hawk, NC (Dec. 17). Boston defeats Pittsburgh in first baseball World Series.

1909 Expedition team led by Robert E. Peary and Matthew Henson plants American flag at North Pole (Apr. 6). W.E.B. DuBois founds National Association for the Advancement of Colored People (NAACP).

1917 After Pres. Wilson proclaims "the world must be made safe for democracy," Congress declares war on Germany (Apr. 6) and Austria-Hungary (Dec. 7), bringing U.S. into World War I.

1919 Versailles Treaty, including League of Nations, rejected by Senate (Nov. 19). Grand Canyon National Park created.

1918 Armistice Day ends World War I (Nov. 11); mass celebrations break out across country. Pres. Wilson goes to Europe for peace conference (Dec. 4).

1933 Banks closed for four days by presidential order (Mar. 5). During "Hundred Days" (Mar. 9–June 16), Pres. Roosevelt pushes New Deal through Congress, conducts first "fireside chat" on radio, and takes U.S. off gold standard.

1927 Charles Lindbergh completes nonstop solo flight from New York to Paris (May 20–21); returns home to huge welcoming crowds.

1929 Stock market crash on "Black Tuesday" (Oct. 29) ushers in Great Depression.

1920 Nineteenth Amendment establishes women's suffrage (Aug. 26).

1932 Amelia Earhart is first woman to fly solo across Atlantic.

1945 Pres. Roosevelt, Winston Churchill, and Joseph Stalin meet for last time at Yalta in Soviet Crimea to begin postwar planning (Feb. 4–11). Germany surrenders, ending war in Europe (May 7). Pres. Harry S. Truman meets with Churchill and Stalin at Potsdam, Germany (July 17–Aug. 2). Atomic bombs dropped on Hiroshima (Aug. 6) and Nagasaki (Aug. 9); Japan surrenders (Aug. 14), ending World War II.

1941 German submarine sinks merchant ship *Robin Moor*, first U.S. casualty of war (May 21). Japanese planes attack Pearl Harbor, HI, killing 2,400 U.S. servicemen and civilians (Dec. 7). U.S. declares war on Japan (Dec. 10). Germany and Italy declare war on U.S. (Dec. 11). U.S. declares war on Germany and Italy (Dec. 11).

1950 North Korea invades South Korea, beginning Korean War (June 27). Truman obtains U.N. support (July 7), asks Congress for a $10 billion rearmament program (July 20), and calls up reserves (Aug. 4).

1900　1910　1920　1930　1940　1950

1954 Supreme Court orders school desegregation in *Brown v. Board of Education* decision (May 17).

1958 In response to Soviet launch of *Sputnik*, U.S. launches *Explorer I*, first American satellite.

1965 Black nationalist Malcolm X assassinated in New York City (Feb. 21). Pres. Johnson orders U.S. Marines into South Vietnam (Mar. 8) and into Santo Domingo (Apr. 28). U.S. troops authorized to undertake offensive operations in South Vietnam (June 8).

1955 Dr. Jonas Salk perfects polio vaccine. Civil rights leader Dr. Martin Luther King, Jr., leads bus boycott in Montgomery, AL.

1962 Lt. Col. John H. Glenn, Jr., is first American to orbit Earth.

1950

1960

1963 Civil rights movement reaches climax with mass demonstrations in Birmingham, AL, and epic March on Washington, where Martin Luther King, Jr., delivers his "I Have a Dream" speech (Aug. 28). Pres. Kennedy assassinated in Dallas, TX (Nov. 22).

1972 Congress debates Equal Rights Amendment.

1973 Supreme Court disallows state restrictions on abortions (*Roe v. Wade*). U.S. signs Paris peace accords ending Vietnam War (Jan. 27). Vice Pres. Spiro Agnew resigns after threat of indictment for tax evasion (Oct. 10).

1968 Pres. Johnson makes surprise announcement that he will not seek re-election (Mar. 31). Martin Luther King, Jr., is murdered by James Earl Ray in Memphis, TN (Apr. 4). After winning California primary, Sen. Robert F. Kennedy of New York is murdered by Sirhan Sirhan in Los Angeles (June 5).

1974 Pres. Nixon resigns (Aug. 8), elevating Vice Pres. Ford to presidency (Aug. 9). Pres. Ford shocks nation by pardoning Nixon for all crimes committed in office (Sept. 8).

1969 Neil Armstrong and Edwin "Buzz" Aldrin of *Apollo 11* are first men to walk on moon (July 20).

1970

1980

1981 *Columbia* completes first successful space shuttle mission (Apr. 12–14). Senate votes 99 to 0 to confirm Sandra Day O'Connor as first woman Justice of Supreme Court.

1993 Without warning, a powerful car bomb rips through the underground parking garage of one of the twin towers of New York's World Trade Center, killing seven, injuring about 1,000, and causing the evacuation of more than 50,000 workers (Feb. 26).

2001 On September 11, hijackers overtake four U.S. planes, crashing two of them into the World Trade Center in New York City. In all, 2,800 lives are lost.

1983 Sally Ride, aboard space shuttle *Challenger*, is first American woman astronaut. U.S. invades Grenada to overthrow Cuban-backed regime (Oct. 25).

2003 Suspecting possession of weapons of mass destruction in Iraq, U.S. declares war with Iraq and sends 242,000 troops to the Persian Gulf (Mar. 19). Official combat ends May 1.

1986 Space shuttle *Challenger* explodes in midair over Florida.

1990

2000

1990 After Iraq's invasion of Kuwait (Aug. 2), U.S. launches Operation Desert Shield: more than 200,000 U.S. troops move into Saudi Arabia, and the navy blockades all oil exports from Iraq and all imports except food.

1991 U.S. sends 400,000 troops, 1,500 aircraft, and 65 warships to the Persian Gulf to drive Iraq's armed forces from Kuwait in Operation Desert Storm (Jan. 17). The ground war begins six weeks later and lasts only 100 hours (Feb. 23–27).

Important U.S. Supreme Court Decisions

Marbury v. Madison (1803)   The Court struck down a law "repugnant to the constitution" for the first time and set the precedent for judicial review of acts of Congress. In a politically ingenious ruling on the Judiciary Act of 1789, Chief Justice John Marshall asserted the Supreme Court's power "to say what the law is," while avoiding a confrontation with President Thomas Jefferson. Not until the *Dred Scott* decision of 1857 would another federal law be ruled unconstitutional.

1800

Dred Scott v. Sanford (1857)   Dred Scott, a Missouri slave, sued for his liberty after his owner took him into free territory. The Court ruled that Congress could not bar slavery in the territories. Scott remained a slave because the Missouri Compromise of 1820, which prohibited slavery from part of the Louisiana Purchase, violated the Fifth Amendment by depriving slave owners of their right to enjoy property without due process of law. Scott himself could not even sue, for he was held to be property, not a citizen. This decision sharpened sectional conflict by sweeping away legal barriers to the expansion of slavery.

1850

Plessy v. Ferguson (1896)   The "separate but equal" doctrine supporting public segregation received the Court's approval in this ruling, which originated as a means to segregate railroad cars in Louisiana. The Court held that as long as equal accommodations were provided, segregation was not discrimination and did not deprive blacks of equal protection under the Fourteenth Amendment. This decision was overturned by *Brown v. Board of Education* (1954).

1900

Brown v. Board of Education (1954)   Chief Justice Earl Warren led the Court to decide unanimously that segregated schools violated the equal protection clause of the Fourteenth Amendment. The "separate but equal" doctrine of *Plessy v. Ferguson* (1896) was overruled after a series of cases dating back to *Missouri ex. rel. Gaines v. Canada* (1938) had already limited it. "Separate educational facilities are inherently unequal," held the Court. Efforts to desegregate Southern schools after the Brown decision met with massive resistance for many years.

Miranda v Arizona (1966)   Expanding on *Gideon v. Wainwright* (1963) and *Escobedo v. Illinois* (1964), the Court set forth stringent interrogation procedures for criminal suspects, to protect their Fifth Amendment freedom from self-incrimination. Miranda's confession to kidnapping and rape was obtained without counsel and without his having been advised of his right to silence, so it was ruled inadmissible as evidence. This decision obliged police to advise suspects of their rights upon taking them into custody.

1950

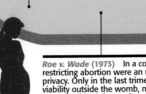

Roe v. Wade (1973)   In a controversial ruling, the Court held that state laws restricting abortion were an unconstitutional invasion of a woman's right to privacy. Only in the last trimester of pregnancy, when the fetus achieved viability outside the womb, might states regulate abortion—except when the life or health of the mother was at stake. Feelings ran high on both sides of the abortion issue. In *Planned Parenthood of Central Missouri v. Danforth* (1976), the Court added further that wives did not need their husbands' consent to obtain abortions.

U.S. Presidents and Their Parties

1.	Washington[1]	1789–1797	Federalist
2.	J. Adams	1797–1801	Federalist
3.	Jefferson	1801–1809	Democratic-Republican
4.	Madison	1809–1817	Democratic-Republican
5.	Monroe	1817–1825	Democratic-Republican
6.	J. Q. Adams	1825–1829	Democratic-Republican
7.	Jackson	1829–1837	Democratic
8.	Van Buren	1837–1841	Democratic
9.	W. H. Harrison[2]	1841	Whig
10.	Tyler	1841–1845	Whig
11.	Polk	1845–1849	Democratic
12.	Taylor	1849–1850	Whig
13.	Fillmore	1850–1853	Whig
14.	Pierce	1853–1857	Democratic
15.	Buchanan	1857–1861	Democratic
16.	Lincoln[3]	1861–1865	Republican
17.	A. Johnson[4]	1865–1869	Union
18.	Grant	1869–1877	Republican
19.	Hayes	1877–1881	Republican
20.	Garfield[3]	1881	Republican
21.	Arthur	1881–1885	Republican
22.	Cleveland	1885–1889	Democratic
23.	B. Harrison	1889–1893	Republican
24.	Cleveland[5]	1893–1897	Democratic
25.	McKinley[3]	1897–1901	Republican
26.	T. Roosevelt	1901–1909	Republican
27.	Taft	1909–1913	Republican
28.	Wilson	1913–1921	Democratic
29.	Harding[2]	1921–1923	Republican
30.	Coolidge	1923–1929	Republican
31.	Hoover	1929–1933	Republican
32.	F. D. Roosevelt[2]	1933–1945	Democratic
33.	Truman	1945–1953	Democratic
34.	Eisenhower	1953–1961	Republican
35.	Kennedy[3]	1961–1963	Democratic
36.	L. B. Johnson	1963–1969	Democratic
37.	Nixon[6]	1969–1974	Republican
38.	Ford	1974–1977	Republican
39.	Carter	1977–1981	Democratic
40.	Reagan	1981–1989	Republican
41.	G. Bush	1989–1993	Republican
42.	Clinton	1993–2001	Democratic
43.	G. W. Bush	2001–	Republican

Source: Library of Congress

1. No party for first election. The party system in the U.S. made its appearance during Washington's first term. 2. Died in office. 3. Assassinated in office. 4. The Republican National Convention of 1864 adopted the name Union Party. It renominated Lincoln for president; for vice president it nominated Johnson, a War Democrat. Although frequently listed as a Republican vice president and President, Johnson undoubtedly considered himself strictly a member of the Union Party. When that party broke apart after 1868, he returned to the Democratic Party. 5. Second nonconsecutive term. 6. Resigned Aug. 9, 1974

The Declaration of Independence

In Congress, July 4, 1776

The Unanimous Declaration of the Thirteen United States of America

When in the Course of human events, it becomes necessary for one people to dissolve the political bands which have connected them with another, and to assume among the powers of the earth, the separate and equal station to which the Laws of Nature and of Nature's God entitle them, a decent respect to the opinions of mankind requires that they should declare the causes which impel them to the separation.

We hold these truths to be self-evident, that all men are created equal, that they are endowed by their Creator with certain unalienable Rights, that among these are Life, Liberty and the pursuit of Happiness. That to secure these rights, Governments are instituted among Men, deriving their just powers from the consent of the governed, That whenever any Form of Government becomes destructive of these ends, it is the Right of the People to alter or to abolish it, and to institute new Government, laying its foundation on such principles and organizing its powers in such form, as to them shall seem most likely to effect their Safety and Happiness. Prudence, indeed, will dictate that Governments long established should not be changed for light and transient causes; and accordingly all experience hath shown, that mankind are more disposed to suffer, while evils are sufferable, than to right themselves by abolishing the forms to which they are accustomed. But when a long train of abuses and usurpations, pursuing invariably the same Object evinces a design to reduce them under absolute Despotism, it is their right, it is their duty, to throw off such Government, and to provide new Guards for their future security. Such has been the patient sufferance of these Colonies; and such is now the necessity which constrains them to alter their former Systems of Government. The history of the present King of Great Britain is a history of repeated injuries and usurpations, all having in direct object the establishment of an absolute Tyranny over these States. To prove this, let Facts be submitted to a candid world.

He has refused his Assent to Laws, the most wholesome and necessary for the public good.

He has forbidden his Governors to pass Laws of immediate and pressing importance, unless suspended in their operation till his Assent should be obtained; and when so suspended, he has utterly neglected to attend to them.

He has refused to pass other Laws for the accommodation of large districts of people, unless those people would relinquish the right of Representation in the Legislature, a right inestimable to them and formidable to tyrants only.

He has called together legislative bodies at places unusual, uncomfortable, and distant from the depository of their public Records, for the sole purpose of fatiguing them into compliance with his measures.

He has dissolved Representative Houses repeatedly, for opposing with manly firmness his invasions on the rights of the people.

He has refused for a long time, after such dissolutions, to cause others to be elected; whereby the Legislative powers, incapable of Annihilation, have returned to the People at large for their exercise; the State remaining in the mean time exposed to all the dangers of invasion from without, and convulsions within.

He has endeavored to prevent the population of these States; for that purpose obstructing the Laws for Naturalization of Foreigners; refusing to pass others to encourage their migrations hither, and raising the conditions of new Appropriations of Lands.

He has obstructed the Administration of Justice, by refusing his Assent to Laws for establishing Judiciary powers.

He has made Judges dependent on his Will alone, for the tenure of their offices, and the amount and payment of their salaries.

He has erected a multitude of New Offices, and sent hither swarms of Officers to harrass our people, and eat out their substance.

He has kept among us, in times of peace, Standing Armies without the Consent of our legislatures.

He has affected to render the Military independent of and superior to the Civil power.

Note: Phrases in red are key ideas.

He has combined with others to subject us to a jurisdiction foreign to our constitution, and unacknowledged by our laws; giving his Assent to their Acts of pretended Legislation:

For Quartering large bodies of armed troops among us:

For protecting them, by a mock Trial, from punishment for any Murders which they should commit on the Inhabitants of these States:

For cutting off our Trade with all parts of the world:

For imposing Taxes on us without our Consent:

For depriving us in many cases, of the benefits of Trial by Jury:

For transporting us beyond Seas to be tried for pretended offences:

For abolishing the free System of English Laws in a neighbouring Province, establishing therein an Arbitrary government, and enlarging its Boundaries so as to render it at once an example and fit instrument for introducing the same absolute rule into these Colonies:

For taking away our Charters, abolishing our most valuable Laws, and altering fundamentally the Forms of our Governments:

For suspending our own Legislatures, and declaring themselves invested with power to legislate for us in all cases whatsoever.

He has abdicated Government here, by declaring us out of his Protection and waging War against us.

He has plundered our seas, ravaged our Coasts, burnt our towns, and destroyed the lives of our people.

He is at this time transporting large Armies of foreign Mercenaries to compleat the works of death, desolation and tyranny, already begun with circumstances of Cruelty & perfidy scarcely paralleled in the most barbarous ages, and totally unworthy the Head of a civilized nation.

He has constrained our fellow Citizens taken Captive on the high Seas to bear Arms against their Country, to become the executioners of their friends and Brethren, or to fall themselves by their Hands.

He has excited domestic insurrections amongst us, and has endeavoured to bring on the inhabitants of our frontiers, the merciless Indian Savages, whose known rule of warfare, is an undistinguished destruction of all ages, sexes and conditions.

In every stage of these Oppressions We have Petitioned for Redress in the most humble terms: Our repeated Petitions have been answered only by repeated injury. A Prince whose character is thus marked by every act which may define a Tyrant, is unfit to be the ruler of a free people.

Nor have We been wanting in attentions to our British brethren. We have warned them from time to time of attempts by their legislature to extend an unwarrantable jurisdiction over us. We have reminded them of the circumstances of our emigration and settlement here. We have appealed to their native justice and magnanimity, and we have conjured them by the ties of our common kindred to disavow these usurpations, which, would inevitably interrupt our connections and correspondence. They too have been deaf to the voice of justice and of consanguinity. We must, therefore, acquiesce in the necessity, which denounces our Separation, and hold them, as we hold the rest of mankind, Enemies in War, in Peace Friends.

We, therefore, the Representatives of the United States of America, in General Congress, Assembled, appealing to the Supreme Judge of the world for the rectitude of our intentions, do, in the Name, and by Authority of the good People of these Colonies, solemnly publish and declare, That these United Colonies are, and of Right ought to be Free and Independent States; that they are Absolved from all Allegiance to the British Crown, and that all political connection between them and the State of Great Britain, is and ought to be totally dissolved; and that as Free and Independent States, they have full Power to levy War, conclude Peace, contract Alliances, establish Commerce, and to do all other Acts and Things which Independent States may of right do. And for the support of this Declaration, with a firm reliance on the protection of divine Providence, we mutually pledge to each other our Lives, our Fortunes and our sacred Honor.

Source: National Archives and Records Administration

The Bill of Rights

THE FIRST 10 AMENDMENTS TO THE CONSTITUTION
[The first 10 amendments, known collectively as
the Bill of Rights, were adopted in 1791.]

Amendment I
Congress shall make no law respecting an establishment of religion, or prohibiting the free exercise thereof; or abridging the freedom of speech, or of the press; or the right of the people peaceably to assemble, and to petition the Government for a redress of grievances.

Amendment II
A well regulated Militia, being necessary to the security of a free State, the right of the people to keep and bear Arms, shall not be infringed.

Amendment III
No Soldier shall, in time of peace be quartered in any house, without the consent of the Owner, nor in time of war, but in a manner to be prescribed by law.

Amendment IV
The right of the people to be secure in their persons, houses, papers, and effects, against unreasonable searches and seizures, shall not be violated, and no Warrants shall issue, but upon probable cause, supported by Oath or affirmation, and particularly describing the place to be searched, and the persons or things to be seized.

Amendment V
No person shall be held to answer for a capital, or otherwise infamous crime, unless on a presentment or indictment of a Grand Jury, except in cases arising in the land or naval forces, or in the Militia, when in actual service in time of War or public danger; nor shall any person be subject for the same offence to be twice put in jeopardy of life or limb; nor shall be compelled in any criminal case to be a witness against himself, nor be deprived of life, liberty, or property, without due process of law; nor shall private property be taken for public use, without just compensation.

Amendment VI
In all criminal prosecutions, the accused shall enjoy the right to a speedy and public trial, by an impartial jury of the State and district wherein the crime shall have been committed, which district shall have been previously ascertained by law, and to be informed of the nature and cause of the accusation; to be confronted with the witnesses against him; to have compulsory process for obtaining witnesses in his favor, and to have the Assistance of Counsel for his defence.

Amendment VII
In suits at common law, where the value in controversy shall exceed twenty dollars, the right of trial by jury shall be preserved, and no fact tried by a jury, shall be otherwise re-examined in any Court of the United States, than according to the rules of the common law.

Amendment VIII
Excessive bail shall not be required, nor excessive fines imposed, nor cruel and unusual punishments inflicted.

Amendment IX
The enumeration in the Constitution, of certain rights, shall not be construed to deny or disparage others retained by the people.

Amendment X
The powers not delegated to the United States by the Constitution, nor prohibited by it to the States, are reserved to the States respectively, or to the people.

Source: National Archives and Records Administration   **Note:** Phrases in red are key ideas.

Chief Justices of the United States Supreme Court

Chief Justice	Tenure	Appointed By
John Jay	1789-1795	George Washington
John Rutledge	1795	George Washington
Oliver Ellsworth	1796-1800	George Washington
John Marshall	1801-1835	John Adams
Roger B. Taney	1836-1864	Andrew Jackson
Salmon P. Chase	1864-1873	Abraham Lincoln
Morrison R. Waite	1874-1888	Ulysses S. Grant
Melville W. Fuller	1888-1910	Grover Cleveland
Edward D. White	1910-1921	William H. Taft
William Howard Taft	1921-1930	Warren G. Harding
Charles Evans Hughes	1930-1941	Herbert Hoover
Harlan F. Stone	1941-1946	Franklin D. Roosevelt
Fred M. Vinson	1946-1953	Harry S Truman
Earl Warren	1953-1969	Dwight Eisenhower
Warren E. Burger	1969-1987	Richard Nixon
William H. Rehnquist	1987-	Ronald Reagan

Source: The White House

HISTORY (WORLD)

Women and Children Last?

Women were not allowed on Christopher Columbus's first two voyages to the New World. On the third trip, Columbus was only allowed to take one woman for every ten male emigrants.

Loony Laws

In some parts of the world, people have to be careful not to break some unusual laws. It's unlawful to kiss in a movie theater in London, England. In Finland, people must be able to read in order to get married. In Greece, if you are poorly dressed while driving on the public roads of Athens, you may have your license taken away. In Iceland, seeing-eye dogs are the only canines allowed in the country. In Japan, it's against the law to buy or eat rice grown in another country.

Rich Royalty

Prince Alwaheed Bin Talal Alsaud of Saudi Arabia is the wealthiest member of royalty in the world with $17.7 billion.

Nations United

There are currently 191 members of the United Nations. The headquarters is in New York City, but the land and buildings are considered international territory. The United Nations has its own flag, its own post office, and its own postage stamps. Six official languages are used at the United Nations—Arabic, Chinese, English, French, Russian, and Spanish.

Timeline
Prehistory: Before Common Era* (B.C.)

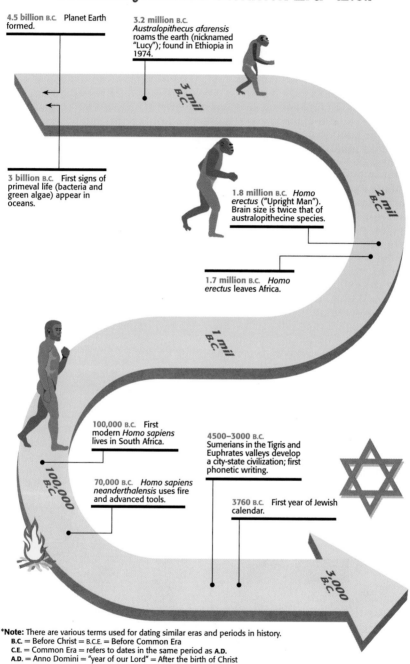

4.5 billion B.C. Planet Earth formed.

3.2 million B.C. *Australopithecus afarensis* roams the earth (nicknamed "Lucy"); found in Ethiopia in 1974.

3 mil B.C.

3 billion B.C. First signs of primeval life (bacteria and green algae) appear in oceans.

1.8 million B.C. *Homo erectus* ("Upright Man"). Brain size is twice that of australopithecine species.

2 mil B.C.

1.7 million B.C. *Homo erectus* leaves Africa.

1 mil B.C.

100,000 B.C. First modern *Homo sapiens* lives in South Africa.

4500–3000 B.C. Sumerians in the Tigris and Euphrates valleys develop a city-state civilization; first phonetic writing.

100,000 B.C.

70,000 B.C. *Homo sapiens neanderthalensis* uses fire and advanced tools.

3760 B.C. First year of Jewish calendar.

3,000 B.C.

*Note: There are various terms used for dating similar eras and periods in history.
B.C. = Before Christ = B.C.E. = Before Common Era
C.E. = Common Era = refers to dates in the same period as **A.D.**
A.D. = Anno Domini = "year of our Lord" = After the birth of Christ

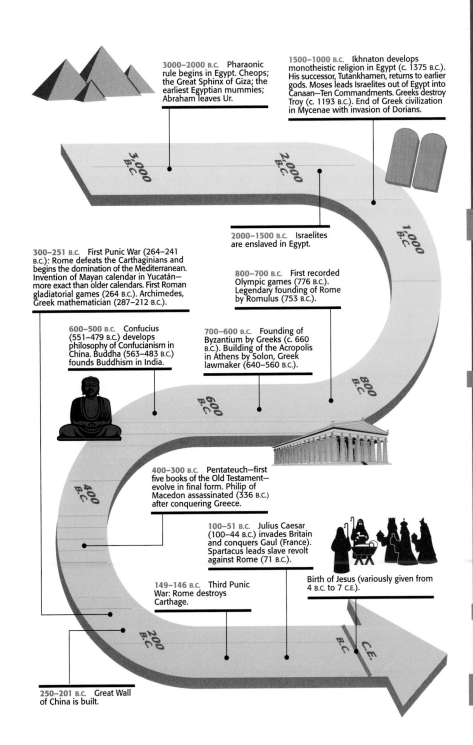

3000–2000 B.C. Pharaonic rule begins in Egypt. Cheops; the Great Sphinx of Giza; the earliest Egyptian mummies; Abraham leaves Ur.

1500–1000 B.C. Ikhnaton develops monotheistic religion in Egypt (c. 1375 B.C.). His successor, Tutankhamen, returns to earlier gods. Moses leads Israelites out of Egypt into Canaan—Ten Commandments. Greeks destroy Troy (c. 1193 B.C.). End of Greek civilization in Mycenae with invasion of Dorians.

2000–1500 B.C. Israelites are enslaved in Egypt.

300–251 B.C. First Punic War (264–241 B.C.): Rome defeats the Carthaginians and begins the domination of the Mediterranean. Invention of Mayan calendar in Yucatán—more exact than older calendars. First Roman gladiatorial games (264 B.C.). Archimedes, Greek mathematician (287–212 B.C.).

800–700 B.C. First recorded Olympic games (776 B.C.). Legendary founding of Rome by Romulus (753 B.C.).

600–500 B.C. Confucius (551–479 B.C.) develops philosophy of Confucianism in China. Buddha (563–483 B.C.) founds Buddhism in India.

700–600 B.C. Founding of Byzantium by Greeks (c. 660 B.C.). Building of the Acropolis in Athens by Solon, Greek lawmaker (640–560 B.C.).

400–300 B.C. Pentateuch—first five books of the Old Testament—evolve in final form. Philip of Macedon assassinated (336 B.C.) after conquering Greece.

100–51 B.C. Julius Caesar (100–44 B.C.) invades Britain and conquers Gaul (France). Spartacus leads slave revolt against Rome (71 B.C.).

149–146 B.C. Third Punic War: Rome destroys Carthage.

Birth of Jesus (variously given from 4 B.C. to 7 C.E.).

250–201 B.C. Great Wall of China is built.

Timeline:
Common Era: 1 c.e.–Fifteenth Century

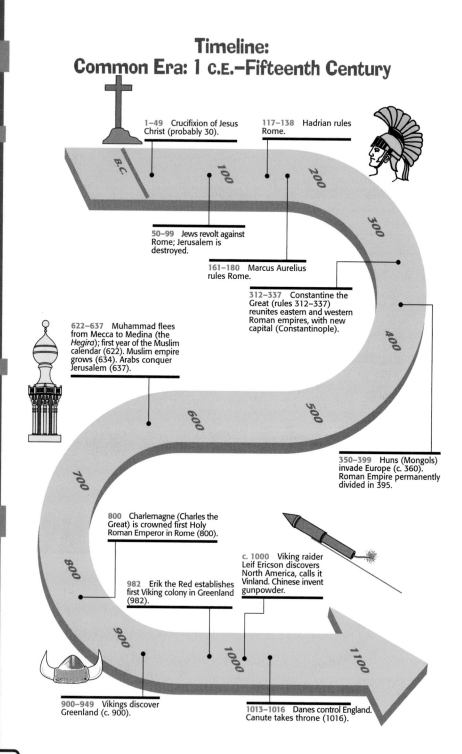

1–49 Crucifixion of Jesus Christ (probably 30).

117–138 Hadrian rules Rome.

50–99 Jews revolt against Rome; Jerusalem is destroyed.

161–180 Marcus Aurelius rules Rome.

312–337 Constantine the Great (rules 312–337) reunites eastern and western Roman empires, with new capital (Constantinople).

622–637 Muhammad flees from Mecca to Medina (the *Hegira*); first year of the Muslim calendar (622). Muslim empire grows (634). Arabs conquer Jerusalem (637).

350–399 Huns (Mongols) invade Europe (c. 360). Roman Empire permanently divided in 395.

800 Charlemagne (Charles the Great) is crowned first Holy Roman Emperor in Rome (800).

c. 1000 Viking raider Leif Ericson discovers North America, calls it Vinland. Chinese invent gunpowder.

982 Erik the Red establishes first Viking colony in Greenland (982).

900–949 Vikings discover Greenland (c. 900).

1013–1016 Danes control England. Canute takes throne (1016).

B.C 100 200 300 400 500 600 700 800 900 1000 1100

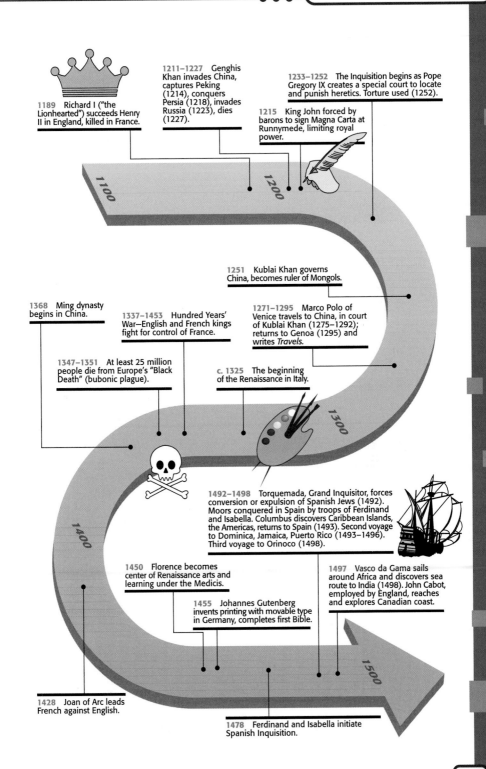

1189 Richard I ("the Lionhearted") succeeds Henry II in England, killed in France.

1211–1227 Genghis Khan invades China, captures Peking (1214), conquers Persia (1218), invades Russia (1223), dies (1227).

1233–1252 The Inquisition begins as Pope Gregory IX creates a special court to locate and punish heretics. Torture used (1252).

1215 King John forced by barons to sign Magna Carta at Runnymede, limiting royal power.

1100

1200

1251 Kublai Khan governs China, becomes ruler of Mongols.

1368 Ming dynasty begins in China.

1337–1453 Hundred Years' War—English and French kings fight for control of France.

1271–1295 Marco Polo of Venice travels to China, in court of Kublai Khan (1275–1292); returns to Genoa (1295) and writes *Travels.*

1347–1351 At least 25 million people die from Europe's "Black Death" (bubonic plague).

c. 1325 The beginning of the Renaissance in Italy.

1300

1492–1498 Torquemada, Grand Inquisitor, forces conversion or expulsion of Spanish Jews (1492). Moors conquered in Spain by troops of Ferdinand and Isabella. Columbus discovers Caribbean Islands, the Americas, returns to Spain (1493). Second voyage to Dominica, Jamaica, Puerto Rico (1493–1496). Third voyage to Orinoco (1498).

1400

1450 Florence becomes center of Renaissance arts and learning under the Medicis.

1497 Vasco da Gama sails around Africa and discovers sea route to India (1498). John Cabot, employed by England, reaches and explores Canadian coast.

1455 Johannes Gutenberg invents printing with movable type in Germany, completes first Bible.

1500

1428 Joan of Arc leads French against English.

1478 Ferdinand and Isabella initiate Spanish Inquisition.

Timeline:
Early Exploration: 1492–1800

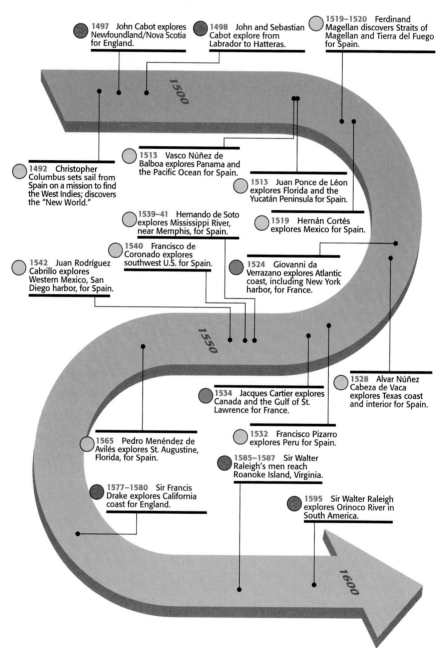

1497 John Cabot explores Newfoundland/Nova Scotia for England.

1498 John and Sebastian Cabot explore from Labrador to Hatteras.

1519–1520 Ferdinand Magellan discovers Straits of Magellan and Tierra del Fuego for Spain.

1492 Christopher Columbus sets sail from Spain on a mission to find the West Indies; discovers the "New World."

1513 Vasco Núñez de Balboa explores Panama and the Pacific Ocean for Spain.

1513 Juan Ponce de Léon explores Florida and the Yucatán Peninsula for Spain.

1539–41 Hernando de Soto explores Mississippi River, near Memphis, for Spain.

1519 Hernán Cortés explores Mexico for Spain.

1540 Francisco de Coronado explores southwest U.S. for Spain.

1542 Juan Rodríguez Cabrillo explores Western Mexico, San Diego harbor, for Spain.

1524 Giovanni da Verrazano explores Atlantic coast, including New York harbor, for France.

1528 Alvar Núñez Cabeza de Vaca explores Texas coast and interior for Spain.

1534 Jacques Cartier explores Canada and the Gulf of St. Lawrence for France.

1565 Pedro Menéndez de Avilés explores St. Augustine, Florida, for Spain.

1532 Francisco Pizarro explores Peru for Spain.

1585–1587 Sir Walter Raleigh's men reach Roanoke Island, Virginia.

1577–1580 Sir Francis Drake explores California coast for England.

1595 Sir Walter Raleigh explores Orinoco River in South America.

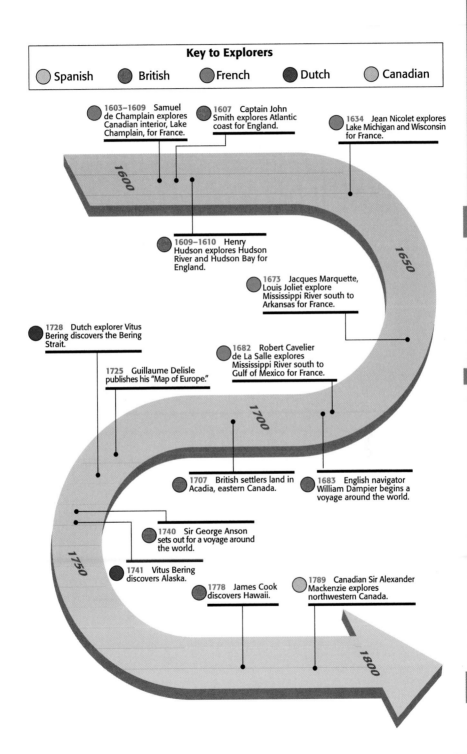

Key to Explorers

◯ Spanish ● British ● French ● Dutch ◯ Canadian

1603–1609 Samuel de Champlain explores Canadian interior, Lake Champlain, for France.

1607 Captain John Smith explores Atlantic coast for England.

1634 Jean Nicolet explores Lake Michigan and Wisconsin for France.

1609–1610 Henry Hudson explores Hudson River and Hudson Bay for England.

1673 Jacques Marquette, Louis Joliet explore Mississippi River south to Arkansas for France.

1728 Dutch explorer Vitus Bering discovers the Bering Strait.

1682 Robert Cavelier de La Salle explores Mississippi River south to Gulf of Mexico for France.

1725 Guillaume Delisle publishes his "Map of Europe."

1707 British settlers land in Acadia, eastern Canada.

1683 English navigator William Dampier begins a voyage around the world.

1740 Sir George Anson sets out for a voyage around the world.

1741 Vitus Bering discovers Alaska.

1778 James Cook discovers Hawaii.

1789 Canadian Sir Alexander Mackenzie explores northwestern Canada.

1600
1650
1700
1750
1800

Timeline:
Modern Exploration: 1800–Today

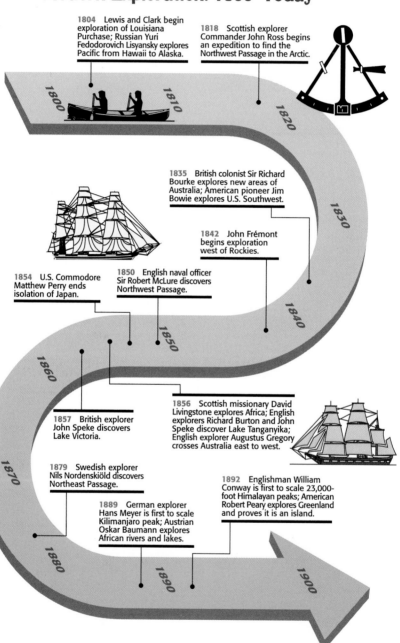

1804 Lewis and Clark begin exploration of Louisiana Purchase; Russian Yuri Fedodorovich Lisyansky explores Pacific from Hawaii to Alaska.

1818 Scottish explorer Commander John Ross begins an expedition to find the Northwest Passage in the Arctic.

1835 British colonist Sir Richard Bourke explores new areas of Australia; American pioneer Jim Bowie explores U.S. Southwest.

1842 John Frémont begins exploration west of Rockies.

1854 U.S. Commodore Matthew Perry ends isolation of Japan.

1850 English naval officer Sir Robert McLure discovers Northwest Passage.

1857 British explorer John Speke discovers Lake Victoria.

1856 Scottish missionary David Livingstone explores Africa; English explorers Richard Burton and John Speke discover Lake Tanganyika; English explorer Augustus Gregory crosses Australia east to west.

1879 Swedish explorer Nils Nordenskiöld discovers Northeast Passage.

1889 German explorer Hans Meyer is first to scale Kilimanjaro peak; Austrian Oskar Baumann explores African rivers and lakes.

1892 Englishman William Conway is first to scale 23,000-foot Himalayan peaks; American Robert Peary explores Greenland and proves it is an island.

1800 1810 1820 1830 1840 1850 1860 1870 1880 1890 1900

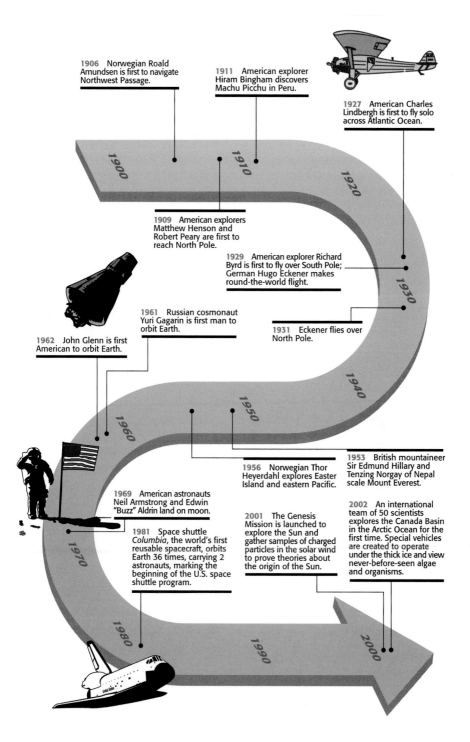

1906 Norwegian Roald Amundsen is first to navigate Northwest Passage.

1911 American explorer Hiram Bingham discovers Machu Picchu in Peru.

1927 American Charles Lindbergh is first to fly solo across Atlantic Ocean.

1900

1910

1920

1909 American explorers Matthew Henson and Robert Peary are first to reach North Pole.

1929 American explorer Richard Byrd is first to fly over South Pole; German Hugo Eckener makes round-the-world flight.

1930

1961 Russian cosmonaut Yuri Gagarin is first man to orbit Earth.

1962 John Glenn is first American to orbit Earth.

1931 Eckener flies over North Pole.

1940

1950

1960

1953 British mountaineer Sir Edmund Hillary and Tenzing Norgay of Nepal scale Mount Everest.

1956 Norwegian Thor Heyerdahl explores Easter Island and eastern Pacific.

1969 American astronauts Neil Armstrong and Edwin "Buzz" Aldrin land on moon.

2001 The Genesis Mission is launched to explore the Sun and gather samples of charged particles in the solar wind to prove theories about the origin of the Sun.

2002 An international team of 50 scientists explores the Canada Basin in the Arctic Ocean for the first time. Special vehicles are created to operate under the thick ice and view never-before-seen algae and organisms.

1981 Space shuttle *Columbia*, the world's first reusable spacecraft, orbits Earth 36 times, carrying 2 astronauts, marking the beginning of the U.S. space shuttle program.

1970

1980

1990

2000

Armed Forces and Vehicles by Nation

Active Forces

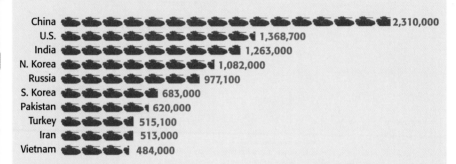

China	2,310,000
U.S.	1,368,700
India	1,263,000
N. Korea	1,082,000
Russia	977,100
S. Korea	683,000
Pakistan	620,000
Turkey	515,100
Iran	513,000
Vietnam	484,000

Submarines

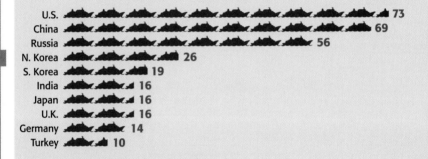

U.S.	73
China	69
Russia	56
N. Korea	26
S. Korea	19
India	16
Japan	16
U.K.	16
Germany	14
Turkey	10

Fighter Aircraft

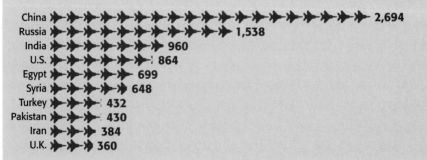

China	2,694
Russia	1,538
India	960
U.S.	864
Egypt	699
Syria	648
Turkey	432
Pakistan	430
Iran	384
U.K.	360

Source: *The Military Balance*, 2001–2002, International Institute for Strategic Studies

Top 5 Highest Death Counts in World War II

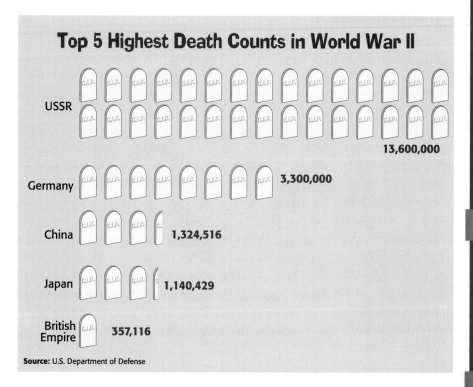

USSR — 13,600,000

Germany — 3,300,000

China — 1,324,516

Japan — 1,140,429

British Empire — 357,116

Source: U.S. Department of Defense

World Population Growth

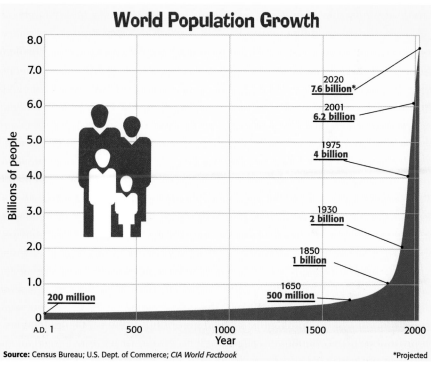

2020
7.6 billion*

2001
6.2 billion

1975
4 billion

1930
2 billion

1850
1 billion

1650
500 million

200 million

Billions of people

Year

A.D. 1   500   1000   1500   2000

Source: Census Bureau; U.S. Dept. of Commerce; *CIA World Factbook*

*Projected

INVENTORS AND INVENTIONS

Puttering Around

James Wright was an engineer for General Electric when he invented Silly Putty. He mixed silicone oil with boric acid and found it had a bouncing ability almost 25% higher than a normal rubber ball. In 1949, the material was sold as Silly Putty, selling faster than any other toy in history with more than $6 million in sales for the year.

Summer Candy Creations

Chocolate manufacturer Clarence Crane invented Life Savers in 1912. He called them a summer candy because they withstood the heat better than chocolate. Pep-O-Mint was the first Life Savers flavor. The five-flavor roll first appeared in 1935.

One Crafty Lady

Beulah Henry of Memphis, Tennessee, is considered to be the "Lady Edison" of inventions. She created more than 100 inventions and held 49 patents. Some of her inventions included the bobbinless sewing machine (1940), the vacuum ice cream freezer (1912), and the Dolly Dips soap sponges for children (1929).

Temporary Talk Time

After almost throwing out her unreliable cell phone in frustration, Randice-Lisa Altschul created the world's first disposable cell phone in 1999. It is called the Phone-Card-Phone and is the thickness of just three credit cards. It has 60 minutes of airtime, and then the user can toss it in the trash.

Ferris Wheel Facts

Bridge builder George W. Ferris built the first Ferris wheel for the 1893 World's Fair in Chicago. Two 140-foot (42.7-m) steel towers supported the wheel, and they were connected by a 45-foot (13.7-m) axle. It was, at the time, the largest single piece of forged steel ever made. The wheel section had a diameter of 250 feet (76.3 m) and a circumference of 825 feet (251.6 m). The ride cost 50 cents and made $726,805.50 during the World's Fair.

Timeline of Major Inventions
3500 B.C. to 1450 A.D.

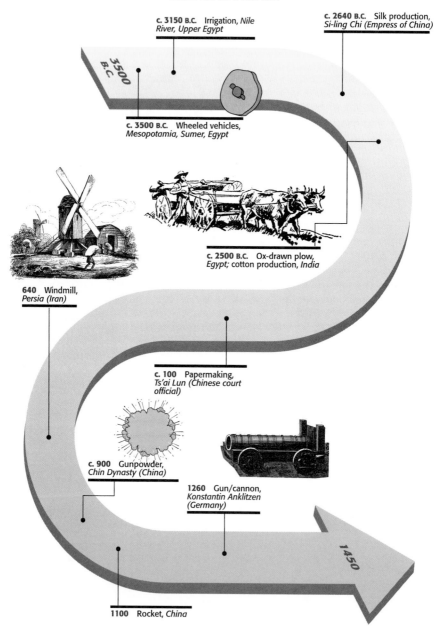

c. 3150 B.C. Irrigation, *Nile River, Upper Egypt*

c. 2640 B.C. Silk production, *Si-ling Chi (Empress of China)*

3500 B.C.

c. 3500 B.C. Wheeled vehicles, *Mesopotamia, Sumer, Egypt*

c. 2500 B.C. Ox-drawn plow, *Egypt;* cotton production, *India*

640 Windmill, *Persia (Iran)*

c. 100 Papermaking, *Ts'ai Lun (Chinese court official)*

c. 900 Gunpowder, *Chin Dynasty (China)*

1260 Gun/cannon, *Konstantin Anklitzen (Germany)*

1100 Rocket, *China*

1450

1450 to 1800

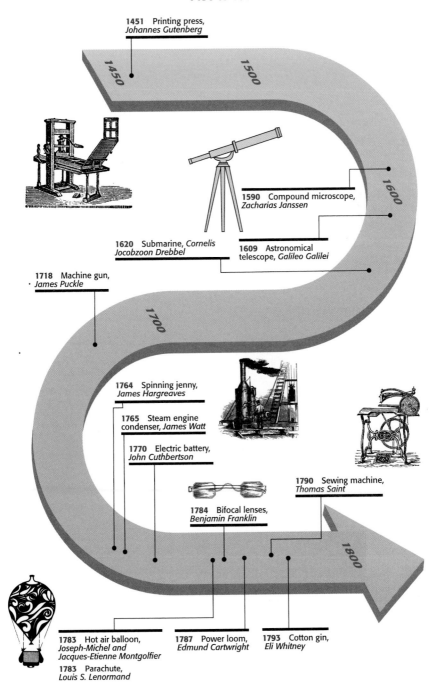

1451   Printing press, *Johannes Gutenberg*

1450

1500

1590   Compound microscope, *Zacharias Janssen*

1600

1620   Submarine, *Cornelis Jocobzoon Drebbel*

1609   Astronomical telescope, *Galileo Galilei*

1718   Machine gun, *James Puckle*

1700

1764   Spinning jenny, *James Hargreaves*

1765   Steam engine condenser, *James Watt*

1770   Electric battery, *John Cuthbertson*

1790   Sewing machine, *Thomas Saint*

1784   Bifocal lenses, *Benjamin Franklin*

1800

1783   Hot air balloon, *Joseph-Michel and Jacques-Etienne Montgolfier*

1783   Parachute, *Louis S. Lenormand*

1787   Power loom, *Edmund Cartwright*

1793   Cotton gin, *Eli Whitney*

Major Inventions and Their Inventors

Air brake   George Westinghouse, U.S., 1869

Air conditioning   Willis Carrier, U.S., 1911

Airplane   Orville and Wilbur Wright, U.S., 1903

Airship   (nonrigid) Henri Giffard, France, 1852; (rigid) Ferdinand von Zeppelin, Germany, 1900

Antibiotics   Discovery of penicillin, first antibiotic, Alexander Fleming, 1928; (penicillin's infection-fighting properties) Howard Florey, Ernst Chain, England, 1940

Antiseptic   (surgery) Joseph Lister, England, 1867

Antitoxin, diphtheria   Emil von Behring, Germany, 1890

Aqua-Lung (oxygen tank)   Jacques-Yves Cousteau, Emile Gagnan, France, 1943

Aspirin   Dr. Felix Hoffman, Germany, 1899

Automobile   (first with internal combustion engine, 250 rpm) Karl Benz, Germany, 1885

Braille   Louis Braille, France, 1829

Camera   (hand-held) George Eastman, U.S., 1888; (Polaroid Land) Edwin Land, U.S., 1948

Cellular phone   Marty Cooper, U.S., 1973

Chewing gum   (spruce-based) John Curtis, U.S., 1848; (chicle-based) Thomas Adams, U.S., 1870

Clock, pendulum   Christian Huygens, Netherlands, 1656

Coca-Cola   John Pemberton, U.S., 1886

Compact disc   RCA, U.S., 1972

Computer   (Mark 1, first information-processing digital computer) Howard Aiken, U.S., 1944; (ENIAC, Electronic Numerical Integrator and Calculator, first all-electronic) J. Presper Eckert, John W. Mauchly, U.S., 1946

Cotton gin   Eli Whitney, U.S., 1793

Digital video disc (DVD)   Hitachi, JVC, Matsushita, Mitsubishi, Philips, Pioneer, Sony, Thomson, Time Warner, and Toshiba, 1995

Dynamite   Alfred Nobel, Sweden, 1867

Elevator, passenger   (safety device permitting use by passengers) Elisha G. Otis, U.S., 1852; (elevator utilizing safety device) 1857

Fiber optics   Narinder Kapany, England, 1955

Gunpowder   China, c. 900

Helicopter   (double rotor) Heinrich Focke, Germany, 1936; (single rotor) Igor I. Sikorsky, U.S., 1939

Insulin   Sir Frederick C. Banting, J. J. R. MacLeod, Canada, 1922

Laser   (theoretical work on) Charles H. Townes, Arthur L. Schawlow, U.S.; N. Basov, A. Prokhorov, U.S.S.R., 1958; (first working model) T. H. Maiman, U.S., 1960

Lens, bifocal   Benjamin Franklin, U.S., 1784

Lightning rod   Benjamin Franklin, U.S., 1752

Locomotive   (steam powered) Richard Trevithick, England, 1804

Microphone   Charles Wheatstone, England, 1827; Emile Berliner, U.S., 1877

Microscope   (compound) Zacharias Janssen, Netherlands, 1590; (electron) Vladimir Zworykin et al., U.S., Canada, Germany, 1932–1939

Microwave oven   Percy Spencer, U.S., 1957

Motion pictures   Thomas Edison, U.S., 1893

Motor, electric   Michael Faraday, England, 1822; (alternating current) Nikola Tesla, U.S., 1892

Motorcycle   (motor tricycle) Edward Butler, England, 1884; (gasoline-engine motorcycle) Gottlieb Daimler, Germany, 1885

Paper   China, c.100

Parachute   Louis S. Lenormand, France, 1783

Pen   (fountain) Lewis E. Waterman, U.S., 1884; (ballpoint, for marking on rough surfaces) John H. Loud, U.S., 1888; (ballpoint, for handwriting) Lazlo Biro, Argentina, 1944

Source: U.S. Department of Commerce; U.S. Patent and Trademark Office

Phonograph   Thomas Edison, U.S., 1877

Photography   (first paper negative, first photograph, on metal) Joseph Nicéphore Niepce, France, 1816–1827; (first direct positive image on silver plate, the daguerreotype) Louis Daguerre, based on work with Niepce, France, 1839; (first color images) Alexandre Becquerel, Claude Niepce de Saint-Victor, France, 1848–1850; (commercial color film with three emulsion layers, Kodachrome) U.S., 1935

Piano (Hammerklavier) Bartolommeo Cristofori, Italy, 1709; (pianoforte with sustaining and damper pedals) John Broadwood, England, 1873

Polio, vaccine against   (vaccine made from dead virus strains) Jonas E. Salk, U.S., 1954; (vaccine made from live virus strains) Albert Sabin, U.S., 1960

Printing   (block) Japan, c. 700; (movable type) Korea, c.1400; Johannes Gutenberg, Germany, 1451

Radar   (limited to 1-mile range) Christian Hulsmeyer, Germany, 1904

Radio   (electromagnetism, theory of) James Clerk Maxwell, England, 1873; (first practical system of wireless telegraphy) Guglielmo Marconi, Italy, 1895; (vacuum electron tube, basis for radio telephony) Sir John Fleming, England, 1904

Refrigerator   Alexander Twining, U.S., James Harrison, Australia, 1850

Revolver   Samuel Colt, U.S., 1835

Rifle   (muzzle-loaded) Italy, Germany, c. 1475; (breech-loaded) England, France, Germany, U.S., c. 1866; (bolt-action) Paul von Mauser, Germany, 1889; (automatic) John Browning, U.S., 1918

Rocket   (liquid-fueled) Robert Goddard, U.S., 1926

Rubber   (vulcanization process) Charles Goodyear, U.S., 1839

Steam engine   (first commercial version based on principles of French physicist Denis Papin) Thomas Savery, England, 1639; (modern condensing, double acting) James Watt, England, 1765

Steamship   Claude de Jouffroy d'Abbans, France, 1783; James Rumsey, U.S., 1787; John Fitch, U.S., 1790; all preceded Robert Fulton, U.S., credited with launching first commercially successful steamship in 1807

Tank, military   Sir Ernest Swinton, England, 1914

Tape recorder   (magnetic steel tape) Valdemar Poulsen, Denmark, 1899

Telegraph   Samuel F. B. Morse, U.S., 1837

Telephone   Alexander Graham Bell, U.S., 1876

Telescope   Hans Lippershey, Netherlands, 1608; (astronomical) Galileo Galilei, Italy, 1609; (reflecting) Isaac Newton, England, 1668

Television   (mechanical disk-scanning method) successfully demonstrated by J. K. Baird, England, C. F. Jenkins, U.S., 1926; (electronic scanning method) Vladimir K. Zworykin, U.S., 1928

Thermometer   (open-column) Galileo Galilei, Italy, c. 1593; (clinical) Santorio Santorio, Padua, c.1615; (mercury, also Fahrenheit scale) Daniel G. Fahrenheit, Germany, 1714; (centigrade scale) Anders Celsius, Sweden, 1742; (absolute-temperature, or Kelvin, scale) William Thompson, Lord Kelvin, England, 1848

Tractor   Benjamin Holt, U.S., 1900

Transistor   John Bardeen, William Shockley, Walter Brittain, U.S., 1948

Videodisc   Philips Co., Netherlands, 1972

Wheel   (cart, solid wood) Mesopotamia, c. 3800–3500 B.C.

Xerography   Chester Carlson, U.S., 1938

Profiles of Major Inventors

Alexander Graham Bell
(Scottish American, 1847–1922)
TELEGRAPHY Despite the title of this patent, the invention here was the telephone.

Emile Berliner (German American, 1851–1929)
MICROPHONE AND GRAMOPHONE Berliner's microphone made it possible to use Alexander Graham Bell's telephone over long distances. With the $50,000 patent rights payment he received from the Bell Telephone Company, Berliner developed the gramophone, the forerunner of the record player .

William Seward Burroughs
(American, 1857–1898)
CALCULATING MACHINE Although the calculating machine dates from the 17th century, Burroughs's was the first that could be mass produced and easily used.

Chester F. Carlson
(American, 1906–1968)
ELECTROPHOTOGRAPHY Carlson invented the dry copying method called xerography. Although patented in 1940, the dry copier was not marketed until 1958, by which time Carlson had patented many improvements to it.

George Washington Carver
(American, 1864–1943)
PRODUCTS USING PEANUTS AND SWEET POTATOES A successful African-American scientist in Iowa who later taught at the prestigious Tuskegee Institute, Carver developed more than 300 uses for the peanut and 118 sweet potato by-products as an incentive for farmers to plant regenerative crops rather than the traditional soil-destroying cotton and tobacco.

John Deere (American, 1804–1886)
PLOW Anyone who grew up near a farm knows the name John Deere. His vastly improved plow was the start of his commercial success, and the company he founded still makes farm tools.

Rudolph Diesel (German, 1858–1913)
INTERNAL COMBUSTION ENGINE The pressure-ignited heat engine is still called the diesel engine.

George Eastman (American, 1854–1932)
METHOD AND APPARATUS FOR COATING PLATES FOR USE IN PHOTOGRAPHY Eastman developed the dry plate negative and transparent roll film for still cameras and a motion picture film for the newly invented movie camera.

Thomas Alva Edison
(American, 1847–1931)
ELECTRIC LAMP One of the world's greatest and most prolific inventors. In addition to the carbon-filament electric lamp, Edison patented a phonograph, the mimeograph, the fluoroscope, and motion picture cameras and projectors.

Philo Taylor Farnsworth
(American,1906–1971)
TELEVISION SYSTEM Farnsworth patented many components of all-electronic television. He also worked on an electron microscope, radar, the use of ultraviolet light for seeing in the dark, and nuclear fusion.

Source: U.S. Department of Commerce; *Webster's Biographical Dictionary*

Enrico Fermi (Italian American, 1901–1954) NEUTRONIC REACTOR Fermi's nuclear reactor is the basis of nuclear power today. His many contributions to modern physics include basic theoretical work as well as experimental physics.

Henry Ford (American, 1863–1947) TRANSMISSION MECHANISM Best remembered for his innovative business practices, Ford also invented and patented numerous mechanisms used in automobiles, including a moving assembly line.

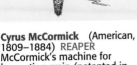

Guglielmo Marconi (Italian, 1874–1937) TRANSMITTING ELECTRICAL SIGNALS Marconi's patent for using radio waves to carry coded messages is best known as wireless telegraphy.

Cyrus McCormick (American, 1809–1884) REAPER McCormick's machine for harvesting grain (patented in 1834) and his other inventions revolutionized American agriculture.

Samuel F. B. Morse (American, 1791–1872) TELEGRAPH SIGNALS Morse developed the first commercially successful telegraph. Joseph

Henry was the genius behind the electronics, but Morse and his dot-dash code made instantaneous long-distance communications possible.

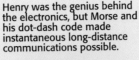

Louis Pasteur (French, 1822–1895) PASTEURIZATION Pasteur's work on beer and ale is generally considered unsuccessful, but he invented several vaccines, and he developed pasteurization, the heating process that protects beverages and food from microbe contamination.

Igor I. Sikorsky (Russian American, 1889–1972) HELICOPTER CONTROLS Sikorsky designed and built many successful airplanes, but in 1931 he made a critical breakthrough in helicopter design. His continued developments led to the helicopter of today.

An Wang (Chinese American, 1920–1990) MAGNETIC PULSE CONTROLLING DEVICE Although best known for his state-of-the-art word processor of the 1960s and 1970s, Wang contributed many fundamental ideas to the development of

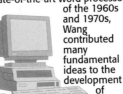

electronic computers, including the principle on which magnetic core memory is built.

George Westinghouse (American, 1846–1914) STEAM-POWERED BRAKE DEVICES In 1869 Westinghouse patented an air brake for locomotives, his most important contribution to railroad safety. His later work on signals and switches led him to form the Westinghouse Electric Co. in 1884.

Eli Whitney (American, 1765–1825) COTTON GIN By making it possible to remove seeds from cotton mechanically, the gin made large-scale cotton farming possible. Whitney also introduced interchangeable parts, the beginning of mass production.

Orville Wright (American, 1871–1948) and **Wilbur Wright** (American, 1867–1912) FLYING MACHINE The Wright brothers not only invented the first airplane in 1903, they also popularized, manufactured, and sold the new machines.

JOBS AND UNEMPLOYMENT

The World's Workers

Employment rates vary greatly by country. In 1997, just 2.7% of Liechtenstein's labor force was unemployed. In 1996, Bosnia-Herzegovina had the highest rate of unemployment, with 75% of the labor force not in paid work. The United States, by comparison, had an average unemployment rate of 4.8% in 2001.

Value of Volunteering

Not all jobs in the United States are based on salary. Each year about 84 million Americans, or 44% of the adult population, spend time doing volunteer work. All of their efforts combined equal about 9 million full-time employees at a value of $239 billion.

Computer Careers

Network know-how will really pay off in the next few years. The jobs that are projected to grow the most between 2000 and 2010 all involve computers—computer software engineers, computer support specialists, network administrators, and network analysts. Each of these fields is expected to grow at least 100%.

Jobs for Juniors

Grown-ups aren't the only ones cashing paychecks. Each year an average of 2.9 million young people ages 15 to 17 worked during school months, and 4 million worked during the summer months. About 62% of youths ages 15 to 17 work in retail trades, specifically in eating and drinking places.

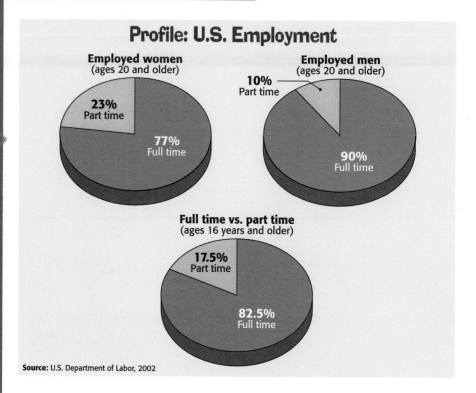

Profile: U.S. Employment

Employed women
(ages 20 and older)

23%
Part time

77%
Full time

Employed men
(ages 20 and older)

10%
Part time

90%
Full time

Full time vs. part time
(ages 16 years and older)

17.5%
Part time

82.5%
Full time

Source: U.S. Department of Labor, 2002

Profile: U.S. Unemployment

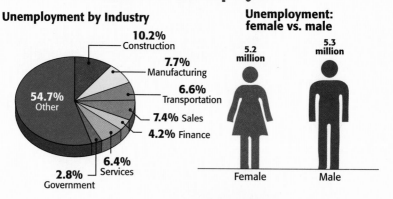

Unemployment by Industry

10.2%
Construction

7.7%
Manufacturing

6.6%
Transportation

7.4% Sales

4.2% Finance

54.7%
Other

6.4% Services

2.8%
Government

Unemployment: female vs. male

5.2 million

5.3 million

Female

Male

Note: Unemployment statistics vary from month to month. Percentages based on averages.

Unemployment by race

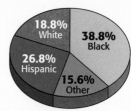

18.8%
White

38.8%
Black

26.8%
Hispanic

15.6%
Other

Source: U.S. Department of Labor, 2002

Top 5 Most Common Types of Jobs in the U.S.
(number of people employed per profession)

21,765,000
20,506,000
18,656,000
16,201,000
15,138,000

| Professional specialty occupations | Executive and administrative positions | Service occupations | Sales occupations | Construction, craft, and repair occupations |

Source: U.S. Department of Labor, 2002

Average Salaries by Job Type
(average weekly salaries, before taxes)

$891 $884 $675 $609 $602 $581 $551 $476 $385 $364

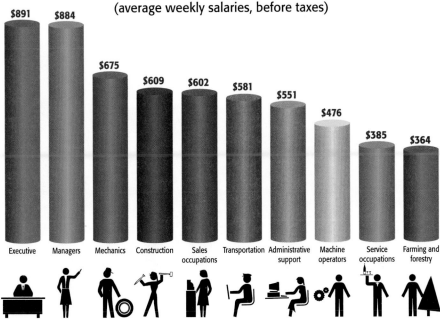

| Executive | Managers | Mechanics | Construction | Sales occupations | Transportation | Administrative support | Machine operators | Service occupations | Farming and forestry |

Source: U.S. Department of Labor, 2002

Labor Force by Sex

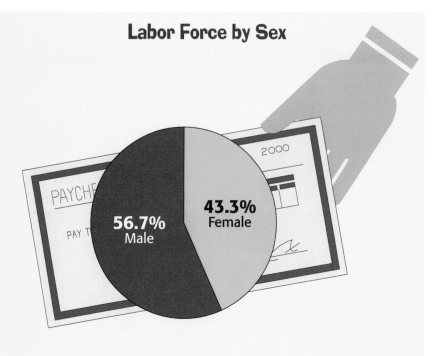

56.7% Male

43.3% Female

2000

PAYCHE

PAY T

Source: U.S. Department of Labor, Bureau of Labor Statistics, 2002

Growth of Working Mothers in U.S. Labor Force
(percentage of all women in labor force)

27.0% — 1955
47.4% — 1975
62.1% — 1985
70.0% — 1996
72.1% — 2001

Source: U.S. Department of Labor, Bureau of Labor Statistics, 2001

Top 5 Top-Paying Occupations
(estimated yearly salaries*)

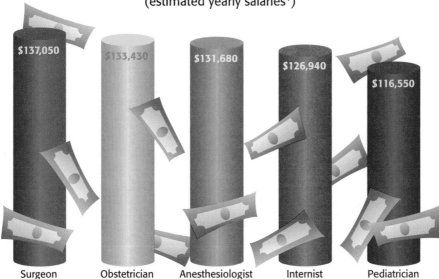

| Surgeon | Obstetrician | Anesthesiologist | Internist | Pediatrician |
| $137,050 | $133,430 | $131,680 | $126,940 | $116,550 |

Source: Department of Labor, 2001   *not based on hourly rate

Home Office Use in the United States
About 40 million people had home offices in 2001.
More than half of home office users are college
graduates with incomes above $40,000.

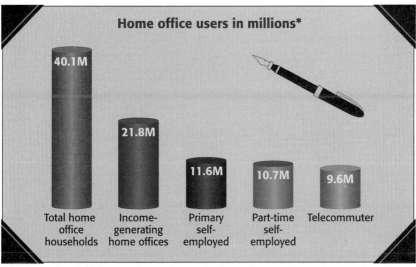

Home office users in millions*

| Total home office households | Income-generating home offices | Primary self-employed | Part-time self-employed | Telecommuter |
| 40.1M | 21.8M | 11.6M | 10.7M | 9.6M |

*Because some households have more than one homeworker, they can be counted in more than one category.
Source: *Home Business Magazine*, 2001

LANGUAGES

Losing the Language

Although there are more than 7,000 dialects spoken throughout the world, about 12 disappear each year. Some reasons they die out include war, lack of speakers, depopulation, or the appearance of a more dominant language.

Language Lowdown

There are more than 2,700 languages throughout the world and more than 7,000 dialects.

Now That's Cooperation

There's no need for translators here. Somalia is the only African country in which the entire population speaks the same language, Somali. This is quite amazing, considering there are more than 1,000 languages spoken on the continent.

Webster's Words

Once a year, *Merriam-Webster's Collegiate Dictionary* updates its entry list to include words that have become popular in the English language. Some new entries for 2002 include treehugger (an environmentalist), hottie (an attractive person), and roadrage (a motorist's uncontrolled anger).

Body Language

Sometimes people can say things without actually speaking. In India, grasping your ear means "I'm sorry." In Spain, snapping your fingers is a form of applause. In Sri Lanka, moving your head from side to side means "yes" and nodding your head up and down means "no." In Taiwan, extending your palm forward and waving your hand from side to side means "no."

Mother Tongues of the World

NORTH
AMERICA

SOUTH
AMERICA

**Proportion of the World's Population
Speaking One of These Languages
as Their Mother Tongue**

French	Spanish	Portuguese	English	German	Russian	Italian	Turkish	Malay	Arabic	Chinese	Japanese	Hindi	Swahili	Other
2%	6%	3%	10%	2%	6%	1%	1%	4%	3%	21%	3%	4%	2%	32%

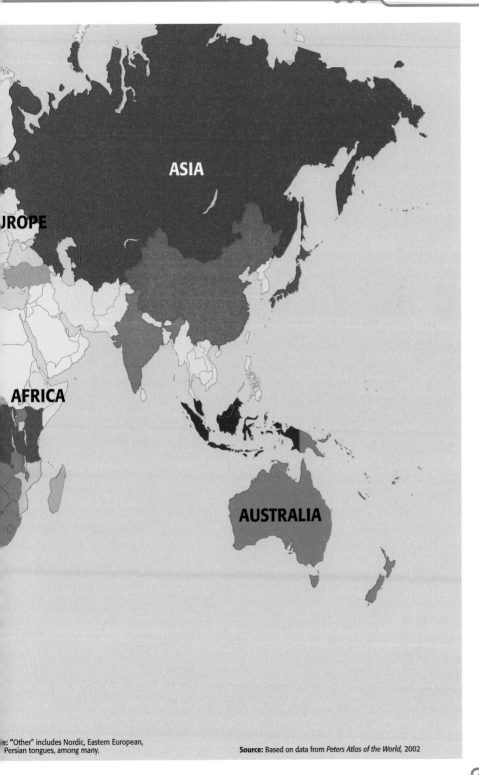

ASIA

EUROPE

AFRICA

AUSTRALIA

e: "Other" includes Nordic, Eastern European, Persian tongues, among many.

Source: Based on data from *Peters Atlas of the World,* 2002

Common Words and Phrases: Selected World Languages

GERMAN

Hello	*Guten Tag* (GOO-tn TAHK)
Good-bye	*Auf Wiedersehen* (ahf VEE-dehr-zeh-hehn)
Good morning	*Guten Morgen* (GOO-tn mor-gun)
Yes	*Ja* (yah)
No	*Nein* (nain)
Please	*Bitte* (BIH-teh)
Thank you	*Danke* (DAHN-keh)
One	*Ein* (ain)
Sunday	*Sonntag* (ZOHN-tahk)

ITALIAN

Hello, or so long	*Ciao* (chow)
Good-bye	*Arrivederci* (ah-ree-vay-DEHR-chee)
Good morning, good afternoon, or a general hello	*Buon giorno* (bwohn-JOOR-noh)
Good evening	*Buona sera* (BWOHN-ah SAY-rah)
Good night	*Buona notte* (BWOHN-ah NOHT-tay)
Yes	*Si* (SEE)
No	*No* (NOH)
Please	*Per favore* (purr fa-VO-ray)
Thank you	*Grazie* (GRAH-tsyay)
How are you?	*Come sta?* (KOH-may STAH)
Fine, very well	*Molto bene* (MOHL-toh BAY-nay)
Excuse me	*Scusi* (SKOO-zee)

UKRAINIAN

Hello	(prih-VEET)
Good morning	(DOH-bray RAH-nok)
Good afternoon	(DOH-bray dehn)
Good evening	(DOH-bray VEH-cheer)
Yes	(yah)
No	(nee-yet)
How are you?	(yak zhi-VESH)
Very well	(DOO-zheh DO-breh)
What's new?	(shcho no-VO-ho)

MANDARIN CHINESE

Hello	*Hao* (how)
Good-bye	*Zaijian* (zay-GEE-en)
Yes	*Shide* (SURE-duh)
No	*Bu shi* (BOO sure)
Have you eaten? (How are you?)	*Ni chiguo fan mei you?* (nee CHUR-gwaw FAHN may yo)
I've eaten (I'm fine)	*Chiguo le* (CHUR-gwaw leh)
Are you hungry?	*Ni e le ma?* (nee UH leh ma)

SPANISH

Hi, hello	*Hola* (OH-lah)
Good-bye	*Adiós* (ah-dee-OS)
Good morning	*Buenas días* (BWAY-nahs DEE-ahs)
Good afternoon	*Buenas tardes* (BWAY-nahs TAHR-dehs)
Good evening	*Buenas noches* (BWAY-nahs NOH-chehs)
Yes	*Sí* (SEE)
No	*No* (NOH)
Please	*Por favor* (por fa-VOHR)
Thank you	*Gracias* (GRAH-see-ahs)
What's going on?	*¿Qué pasa?* (kay PAH-sah)
How are you?	*¿Cómo está Usted?* (COH-mo es-TAH oo-STEHD)
I'm well	*Estoy bien* (ehs-TOY bee-EHN)
My name is . . .	*Me llamo . . .* (may YAH-mo . . .)

EGYPTIAN ARABIC

Good-bye	*Ma salama* (MA sa-LA-ma)
Good morning	*Sabah el khair* (sa-BAH el KHAIR)
Yes	*Aiwa* (AI-wa)
No	*La* (la)
Please	*Min fadlek* (min FAD-lek)
Thank you	*Shukran* (SHU-kran)
How are you?	*Izzayak* (iz-ZAY-ak)
My name is . . .	*Ismi . . .* (IS-mi . . .)
I speak English	*Ana bahki Ingleezi* (Ana BAH-ki in-GLEEZ-i)
What is your name?	*Ismak ay?* (IS-mak AY)
No problem	*Ma feesh mushkila* (ma FEESH mush-KI-la)

NIGERIAN (four of the major Nigerian language groups)

English	Fulani	Hausa	Ibo	Yoruba
I'm fine	*Jam tan* (JAM-taan)	*Kalau* (KA-lay-U)	*Adimnma* (ah-DEE-mm-NMAA)	*A dupe* (ah DEW-pay)
one	*goqo* (GO-quo)	*daya* (DA-ya)	*otu* (o-TOO)	*eni* (EE-nee)
two	*didi* (DEE-dee)	*biyu* (BEE-you)	*abua* (ah-BOO-ah)	*eji* (EE-gee)
three	*tati* (TA-tea)	*uku* (OO-coo)	*ato* (ah-TOE)	*eta* (EE-ta)
nine	*jeenayi* (gee-NA-yee)	*tara* (TAA-ra)	*iteghete* (IT-egg-HE-tee)	*esan* (EE-san)
ten	*sappo* (SAP-poe)	*goma* (GO-ma)	*iri* (EE-ree)	*ewa* (EE-wa)

LIFE SCIENCE

Please Take a Number

Scientists estimate that there are probably between 13 to 14 million living species in the world today. Amazingly, two-thirds of them are insects. And, only about 15% of all species have been studied and given scientific names. Scientists fear that they may never know the exact number of species because many will become extinct before they are counted.

Fishy Facts

There are more than 30,000 different species of fish. That's more than all other species of vertebrates, or animals with backbones. In fact, there are more fish in the ocean than the world's entire population of birds, mammals, amphibians, and reptiles combined.

Lots of Little Life-Forms

Humans and other large members of the animal kingdom are actually quite rare. Almost 99% of all known animal species are smaller than bumblebees.

Coding Manual

Thousands of scientists have worked on The Human Genome Project during the last decade to piece together the sequence of 3 billion letters in the human genetic code. Although some researchers originally predicted that humans have about 100,000 genes, it's now estimated that we have somewhere between 30,000 to 40,000.

Egg-cellent Discovery

The largest dinosaur egg fossils ever found by scientists belong to the *Hypselosaurus priscus*. This 40-foot-long (12-m) titanosaurid had eggs that would have measured 12 inches (30 cm) in length. Samples of these eggs were found in France during the fall of 1961.

The 5 Kingdoms of Life

Scientists classify all living things into one of five kingdoms.
Here is how they are organized.

ANIMAL KINGDOM		Includes (among others) sponges, flatworms, roundworms, mollusks, true worms, arthropods, crustaceans, vertebrates, jellyfish, corals, sea anemones, echinoderms
PLANT KINGDOM		Includes (among others) ferns, mosses, ginkgos, horsetails, conifers, flowering plants, liverworts, hornworts
FUNGI KINGDOM		Includes (among others) molds, mildews, blights, smuts, rusts, mushrooms, puffballs, stinkhorns, penicillia, lichens, black molds, dung fungi, yeasts, morels, truffles
PROTISTA KINGDOM		Includes (among others) yellow-green algae, golden algae, protozoa, green algae, brown algae, red algae
MONERA KINGDOM		Includes bacteria, blue-green algae

Source: Discovery.com, 2002

The Order of Scientific Classification

	CATEGORY	EXAMPLE: Human Being
Most general ↑	Kingdom	Animal
	Phylum	Chordate (Chordata)
	Subphylum	Vertebrate (Animals with backbones) (Vertebrata)
	Superclass	Vertebrate with jaws (Gnathostomata)
	Class	Mammal (Mammalia)
	Subclass	Advanced mammal (Theria)
	Infraclass	Placental mammal (Eutheria)
	Order	Primate (Prosimians)
	Family	Hominid
	Genus	Homo
Most specific ↓	Species	Homo sapiens

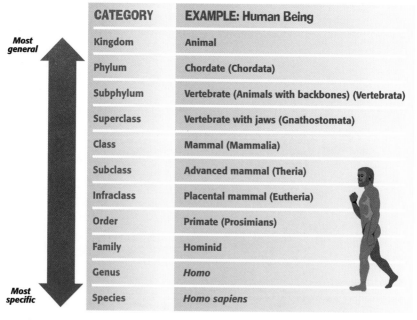

Source: Discovery.com, 2002

Major Discoveries of Human Ancestors

Years Ago	Species	Major Discovery	Details
c. 4.4 million	*Ardipithecus ramidus*	1994 in Ethiopia	Oldest known human ancestor. Chimpanzee-like skull.
c. 4.2 million	*Australopithecus anamensis*	1995, two sites at Lake Turkana, Kanapoi, and Allia Bay, Kenya	Possible ancestor of *A. afarensis* ("Lucy"). Walked upright.
c. 3.2 million	*Australopithecus afarensis*	1974 at Hadar in the Afar triangle of eastern Ethiopia	Nicknamed "Lucy." Her skeleton is 3.5 feet (100 cm) tall. Ape-like skull. Walked fully upright. Lived in family groups throughout eastern Africa.
c. 2.5 million	*Australopithecus africanus*	1924 at Taung, northern Cape Province, South Africa	Descendant of Lucy. Lived in social groups.
c. 2 million	*Australopithecus robustus*	1938 in Kromdraai, South Africa	Was related to *A. africanus.*
c. 2 million	*Homo habilis* (skillful man)	1960 in Olduvai Gorge, Tanzania	First brain expansion; is believed to have used stone tools.
c. 1.8 million	*Homo erectus* (upright man)	1891 at Trinil, Java	Brain size twice that of australopithecine species. Regarded as ancestor of *Homo sapiens*. Invented the hand ax. Could probably make fires. Was first to migrate out of Africa.
c. 100,000 (?)	*Homo sapiens* (knowing or wise man)	1868, Cro-Magnon, France	Anatomically modern humans.

About 60 million years back to last dinosaurs

Present

Source: Smithsonian Institution (www.mnh.si.edu)

Paleontology: The History of Life

(All dates are approximate and are subject to change based on new fossil finds or new dating techniques; but the sequence of events is generally accepted. Dates are in billions and millions of years before the present.)

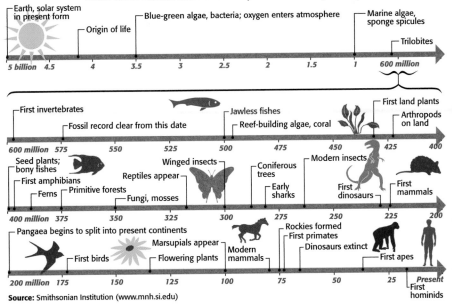

Source: Smithsonian Institution (www.mnh.si.edu)

Major Discoveries in Life Sciences

c. 400 B.C. Hippocrates establishes the profession of physician.

c. 400 B.C. Aristotle classifies 500 species of animals into eight classes.

1628 William Harvey discovers how blood circulates in the human body.

1665 Robert Hooke describes cells for the first time, viewed in pieces of cork.

1735 Carolus Linnaeus introduces the system for the classification of living things that is still in use today.

1673 Anton van Leeuwenhoek announces the first discoveries made with a simple microscope.

1737 Linnaeus explains classification in botany and classifies 18,000 species of plants.

1675 Marcello Malpighi publishes the first important work on plant anatomy.

1794 Erasmus Darwin publishes a book that contains the basis of a theory of evolution.

1801 Jean-Baptiste Lamarck publishes a classification system for invertebrates and proposes a preliminary theory of evolution.

1683 Leeuwenhoek observes bacteria, which will not be seen by other scientists until more than 100 years later.

1859 Charles Darwin publishes *On the Origin of Species,* which explains his evolutionary principle of natural selection.

1953 James D. Watson and Francis H. Crick develop the double-helix model of DNA, which explains how hereditary information is transmitted.

1988 The U.S. Patent Office issues Harvard Medical School a patent for a mouse genetically engineered by Philip Leder and Timothy Stewart. It is the first patent issued for a vertebrate.

1882 Walther Flemming announces discovery of chromosomes and mitosis.

1944 Oswald Theodore Avery, Colin MacLeod, and Maclyn McCarthy determine that DNA is the hereditary material for every living thing.

1981 Chinese scientists are the first to successfully clone an animal: a golden carp.

1860 After working with peas and fruit flies, Gregor Mendel discovers the laws of heredity.

2002 Scientists in the United States, Canada, and England map almost all of the genetic material, or genomes, of a mouse.

Source: Data from *Timetables of Science,* Touchstone, 1988, and *Nature,* 2002

Biology: Who Studies What?

Scientists who study living things are called biologists. Biology, however, can be broken down into many different categories. Each category is a special science unto itself. Here are some categories of biologists and what they study.

Botanists specialize in *botany*, the study of plants.

Zoologists specialize in *zoology*, the study of animals.

Microbiologists specialize in *microbiology*, the study of microscopic (very tiny) plants and animals.

Cytologists specialize in *cytology*, the study of cells.

Ecologists specialize in *ecology*, the study of the interrelationships of organisms and their environment.

Entomologists specialize in *entomology*, the study of insects.

Herpetologists specialize in *herpetology*, the study of reptiles and amphibians.

Ichthyologists specialize in *ichthyology*, the study of fish.

Mammalogists specialize in *mammalogy*, the study of mammals.

Marine biologists specialize in *marine biology*, the study of plants and animals in seas and oceans.

Ornithologists specialize in *ornithology*, the study of birds.

MATH

Summing Up Sports

Math plays a very big role in almost all professional sporting events. For instance, in basketball the circumference of the ball cannot be greater than 30 inches (76.2 cm) and not less than 29.5 inches (74.9 cm). In baseball, home plate must measure 127 feet 3.375 inches (38.8 m) from second base. And, in hockey, the rink must measure 200 feet (61 m) long by 85 feet (25.9 m) wide.

Decimals Through the Decades

Decimals were first used by the Chinese in 400 B.C. The decimal system was first introduced into Europe in the 14th century and is still widely used today. In fact, the entire metric system is based on decimal units.

Medieval Measurements

Before there were rulers and tape measures, people in ancient times had to measure things with the tools available. An inch was the width of a man's thumb. A foot was just over 11 inches (28 cm)—the average length of a man's foot. A yard was originally the length of a man's belt.

Modern Modem Math

Modern computers actually run on an ancient mathematical formula. The Hindus used a binary measuring system that divided things into halves, quarters, and eighths. Today computers run on programs that follow the binary code.

$$(-3x^{-3}y^2)(4x^2y^{-5})$$

$$5s^5t^{-5}$$

$$\left[\left(\frac{2x^2}{4y}\right)^{-3}\right]\left(\frac{32^{-2}}{50t^{-1}}\right)$$

$$\frac{x^4}{x^{-2}}$$

$$\left(\frac{4}{y}\right)^3\left(\frac{3}{y}\right)^4 \quad (2x^2)^{-2} \quad x^4y^6$$

$$\left[(x^4y^6)^{-2}\right]^6$$

Continual Counting

It's a good thing teachers don't practice counting past one hundred. It would take about 12 days to count to one million and about 32 years to count to one billion, if each count were about 1 second long.

Multiplication Table

X	1	2	3	4	5	6	7	8	9	10	11	12
1	1	2	3	4	5	6	7	8	9	10	11	12
2	2	4	6	8	10	12	14	16	18	20	22	24
3	3	6	9	12	15	18	21	24	27	30	33	36
4	4	8	12	16	20	24	28	32	36	40	44	48
5	5	10	15	20	25	30	35	40	45	50	55	60
6	6	12	18	24	30	36	42	48	54	60	66	72
7	7	14	21	28	35	42	49	56	63	70	77	84
8	8	16	24	32	40	48	56	64	72	80	88	96
9	9	18	27	36	45	54	63	72	81	90	99	108
10	10	20	30	40	50	60	70	80	90	100	110	120
11	11	22	33	44	55	66	77	88	99	110	121	132
12	12	24	36	48	60	72	84	96	108	120	132	144

Squares and Square Roots

Raising a number to its second power is also called squaring it; 3 squared (3^2), for example, is 9. By the same token, the square root of 9 is 3.

The symbol for square root is called a *radical sign*  .

Examples of squaring

2 squared: $2^2 = 2 \times 2 = 4$

3 squared: $3^2 = 3 \times 3 = 9$

4 squared: $4^2 = 4 \times 4 = 16$

Examples of square roots

Square root of 16: $\sqrt{16} = 4$

Square root of 9: $\sqrt{9} = 3$

Square root of 4: $\sqrt{4} = 2$

Square Roots to 40

$\sqrt{1}$	1	$\sqrt{121}$	11	$\sqrt{441}$	21	$\sqrt{961}$	31
$\sqrt{4}$	2	$\sqrt{144}$	12	$\sqrt{484}$	22	$\sqrt{1,024}$	32
$\sqrt{9}$	3	$\sqrt{169}$	13	$\sqrt{529}$	23	$\sqrt{1,089}$	33
$\sqrt{16}$	4	$\sqrt{196}$	14	$\sqrt{576}$	24	$\sqrt{1,156}$	34
$\sqrt{25}$	5	$\sqrt{225}$	15	$\sqrt{625}$	25	$\sqrt{1,225}$	35
$\sqrt{36}$	6	$\sqrt{256}$	16	$\sqrt{676}$	26	$\sqrt{1,296}$	36
$\sqrt{49}$	7	$\sqrt{289}$	17	$\sqrt{729}$	27	$\sqrt{1,369}$	37
$\sqrt{64}$	8	$\sqrt{324}$	18	$\sqrt{784}$	28	$\sqrt{1,444}$	38
$\sqrt{81}$	9	$\sqrt{361}$	19	$\sqrt{841}$	29	$\sqrt{1,521}$	39
$\sqrt{100}$	10	$\sqrt{400}$	20	$\sqrt{900}$	30	$\sqrt{1,600}$	40

Numbers Glossary

COMPOSITE NUMBERS

Composite numbers are all counting numbers that are not prime numbers. In other words, composite numbers are numbers that have more than two *factors*. The number *1*, because it has only one factor (itself), is **not** a composite number.

Examples of composite numbers 4 to 100
4, 6, 8, 9, 10, 12, 14, 15, 16, 18, 20, 21, 22, 24, 25, 26, 27, 28, 30, 32, 33, 34, 35, 36, 38, 39, 40, 42, 44, 45, 46, 48, 49, 50, 51, 52, 54, 55, 56, 57, 58, 60, 62, 63, 64, 65, 66, 68, 69, 70, 72, 74, 75, 76, 77, 78, 80, 81, 82, 84, 85, 86, 87, 88, 90, 91, 92, 93, 94, 95, 96, 98, 99, 100

COUNTING NUMBERS

Counting numbers, or *natural numbers*, begin with the number *1* and continue into infinity.

{1, 2, 3, 4, 5, 6, 7, 8, 9, 10 . . .}

INTEGERS

Integers include *0*, all counting numbers (called *positive* whole numbers), and all whole numbers less than *0* (called *negative* whole numbers).

PRIME NUMBERS

Prime numbers are counting numbers that can be divided by only two numbers: *1* and themselves.

Prime numbers between 1 and 1,000									
	2	3	5	7	11	13	17	19	23
29	31	37	41	43	47	53	59	61	67
71	73	79	83	89	97	101	103	107	109
113	127	131	137	139	149	151	157	163	167
173	179	181	191	193	197	199	211	223	227
229	233	239	241	251	257	263	269	271	277
281	283	293	307	311	313	317	331	337	347
349	353	359	367	373	379	383	389	397	401
409	419	421	431	433	439	443	449	457	461
463	467	479	487	491	499	503	509	521	523
541	547	557	563	569	571	577	587	593	599
601	607	613	617	619	631	641	643	647	653
659	661	673	677	683	691	701	709	719	727
733	739	743	751	757	761	769	773	787	797
809	811	821	823	827	829	839	853	857	859
863	877	881	883	887	907	911	919	929	937
941	947	953	967	971	977	983	991	997	(1,009)

RATIONAL NUMBERS

Rational numbers include any number that can be written in the form of a *fraction* (or a *ratio*), as long as the *denominator* (the bottom number of the fraction) is not equal to *0*.

All counting numbers and whole numbers can be written as fractions with a denominator equal to *1*. That means all counting numbers and whole numbers are also rational numbers.

WHOLE NUMBERS

Whole numbers are the same as counting numbers, except that the set of whole numbers begins with *0*.

{0, 1, 2, 3, 4, 5, 6, 7, 8, 9, 10 . . .}

A Selection of Mathematical Formulas

To find the CIRCUMFERENCE of a:

Circle—Multiply the diameter by 3.1416

To find the AREA of a:

Circle—Multiply the square of the radius by 3.1416

Rectangle—Multiply the base by the height

Sphere (surface)—Multiply the square of the radius by 3.1416 and multiply by 4

Square—Square the length of one side

Trapezoid—Add the two parallel sides, multiply by the height, and divide by 2

Triangle—Multiply the base by the height and divide by 2

To find the VOLUME of a:

Cone—Multiply the square of the radius of the base by 3.1416, multiply by the height, and divide by 3

Cube—Cube (raise to the third power) the length of one edge

Cylinder—Multiply the square of the radius of the base by 3.1416 and multiply by the height

Pyramid—Multiply the area of the base by the height and divide by 3

Rectangular prism—Multiply the length by the width by the height

Sphere—Multiply the cube of the radius by 3.1416, multiply by 4, and divide by 3

Large Numbers and How Many Zeros They Contain

million	6	1,000,000
billion	9	1,000,000,000
trillion	12	1,000,000,000,000
quadrillion	15	1,000,000,000,000,000
quintillion	18	1,000,000,000,000,000,000
sextillion	21	1,000,000,000,000,000,000,000
septillion	24	1,000,000,000,000,000,000,000,000
octillion	27	1,000,000,000,000,000,000,000,000,000
nonillion	30	1,000,000,000,000,000,000,000,000,000,000
decillion	33	1,000,000,000,000,000,000,000,000,000,000,000

Roman Numerals

I	1	XI	11	CD	400
II	2	XIX	19	D	500
III	3	XX	20	CM	900
IV	4	XXX	30	M	1,000
V	5	XL	40	$\bar{V}$	5,000
VI	6	L	50	$\bar{X}$	10,000
VII	7	LX	60	$\bar{L}$	50,000
VIII	8	XC	90	$\bar{C}$	100,000
IX	9	C	100	$\bar{D}$	500,000
X	10	CC	200	$\bar{M}$	1,000,000

Fractions, Decimals, and Percents

To find the equivalent of a fraction in decimal form, divide the numerator (top number) by the denominator (bottom number). To change from a decimal to a percent, multiply by 100. To change from a percent to a decimal, divide by 100.

Fraction	Decimal	Percent
1/16 (= 2/32)	0.0625	6.25
1/8 (= 2/16)	0.125	12.5
3/16 (= 6/32)	0.1875	18.75
1/4 (= 2/8; = 4/16)	0.25	25.0
5/16 (= 10/32)	0.3125	31.25
1/3 (= 2/6, = 4/12)	$0.\overline{3}$	$33.\overline{3}$
3/8 (= 6/16)	0.375	37.5
7/16 (= 14/32)	0.4375	43.75
1/2 (= 2/4; = 4/8; = 8/16)	0.5	50.0
9/16 (= 18/32)	0.5625	56.25
5/8 (= 10/16)	0.625	62.5
2/3 (= 4/6, = 8/12)	$0.\overline{6}$	$66.\overline{6}$
11/16 (= 22/32)	0.6875	68.75
3/4 (= 6/8; = 12/16)	0.75	75.0
13/16 (= 26/32)	0.8125	81.25
7/8 (= 14/16)	0.875	87.5
15/16 (= 30/32)	0.9375	93.75
1 (= 2/2; = 4/4; = 8/8; = 16/16)	1.0	100.0

Geometry Glossary

Acute angle   any angle that measures less than 90°

Angle   two rays that have the same endpoint form an angle

Area   the amount of surface inside a closed figure

Chord   a line segment whose endpoints are on a circle

Circumference   the distance around a circle

Congruent figures   geometric figures that are the same size and shape

Degree (angle)   a unit for measuring angles

Diameter   a chord that passes through the center of a circle

Endpoint   the end of a line segment

Line of symmetry   a line that divides a figure into two equal parts if the figure is folded along the line

Obtuse angle   any angle that measures greater than 90°

Perimeter   the distance around the outside of a plane figure

Pi (π)   the ratio of the circumference of a circle to its diameter. When rounded to the nearest hundredth, pi equals 3.14

Polygon   a simple closed figure whose sides are straight lines

Protractor   an instrument used to measure angles

Quadrilateral   a polygon with four sides

Radius   a straight line that connects the center of a circle to any point on the circumference of the circle

Ray   a straight line with one endpoint

Rectangle   a four-sided figure with four right angles

Right angle   an angle that measures 90°

Square   a rectangle with congruent sides and 90° angles in all four corners

Surface area   the total outside area of an object

Symmetrical figure   a figure that, when folded along a line of symmetry, has two halves that superimpose exactly on each other

Triangle   a three-sided figure on one plane

Vertex   the common endpoint of two or more rays that form angles

Geometric Glossary Shapes and Names

POLYGONS

Polygons are two-dimensional or flat shapes, formed from three or more line segments that lie within one plane.

Examples

TRIANGLES

Triangles are polygons that have three sides and three vertices, the common endpoints of two or more rays form angles.

Right triangles are formed when two of three line segments meet in 90° angles. In a right triangle, the longest side has a special name: the *hypotenuse*.

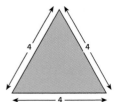

Isosceles triangles have two sides of equal length.

Scalene triangles have no sides of equal length.

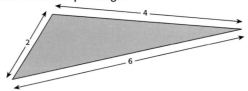

Equilateral triangles have three sides of equal length.

QUADRILATERALS

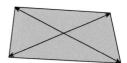

Quadrilaterals are polygons that have four sides and four vertices.

Parallelograms are quadrilaterals that have parallel line segments in both pairs of opposite sides.

Trapezoids are quadrilaterals that have one pair of parallel sides.

Squares are rectangles that have sides of equal length and four 90° angles.

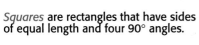

Rectangles are parallelograms formed by line segments that meet at right angles. A rectangle always has four right angles.

Rhombuses are parallelograms that have sides of equal length but don't meet at right angles.

CIRCLES

A *circle* is a set of points within a plane. Each point on the circle is at an equal distance from a common point inside the circle called the *center*.

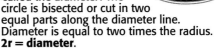

The distance from the center of the circle to any point on the circle is called the *radius*. **r = radius**.

A line segment drawn through the center of the circle to points on either side of the circle is called the *diameter*. The circle is bisected or cut in two equal parts along the diameter line. Diameter is equal to two times the radius. **2r = diameter**.

The distance around the circle is called the *circumference*. **πd** or **π2r = circumference**.

PHYSICS

Clue in to Curve Balls

For many years, scientists said curve balls were just optical illusions. In 1852, German physicist Gustav Magnus showed that a spinning sphere moving through a fluid experiences a sideways force. This is the fundamental principle behind the curved flight of any spinning ball, including the curve balls you see in baseball games!

Science of Smoke

When you blow out the candles on your birthday cake, you probably aren't thinking of the physics behind it. Once the candles are extinguished, the wicks will still smoke for a minute or two. This is because the hot wick is still vaporizing the candle wax. But without the heat of the flame it doesn't burn properly and only releases smoke.

The Color of Air

If it weren't for the air particles in our atmosphere, our sky would not appear blue. The sky would be jet black except for the stars and Sun. But, when sunlight tries to pass through the air particles on its way to Earth, some of its bluish light is redirected into our eyes at many different angles. This makes the sky appear to be blue.

Frisbee Flying Facts

There's more to a Frisbee than meets the eye. The main purpose of the rim on a Frisbee is to create an airfoil. When you throw a Frisbee, the edge comes in contact with the air. As the air flows over the top of the Frisbee, it speeds up and the pressure drops. This creates lift. A Frisbee without a rim will not be very stable in flight.

Coasting on Energy

The laws of physics are the real driving force behind roller coasters. A roller coaster has no engine. The cars are pulled by a pulley system to the top of a hill at the beginning of the ride, but after that the coaster must complete the ride on its own. The conversion of potential energy to kinetic energy drives the coaster, and all of the energy needed for the ride is accumulated after the drop on the first hill.

Timeline: Major Discoveries in Physics

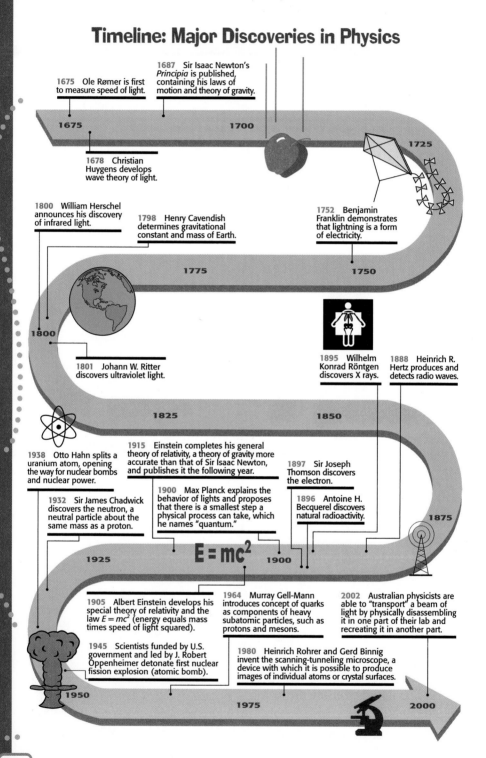

1675 Ole Rømer is first to measure speed of light.

1687 Sir Isaac Newton's *Principia* is published, containing his laws of motion and theory of gravity.

1678 Christian Huygens develops wave theory of light.

1800 William Herschel announces his discovery of infrared light.

1798 Henry Cavendish determines gravitational constant and mass of Earth.

1752 Benjamin Franklin demonstrates that lightning is a form of electricity.

1801 Johann W. Ritter discovers ultraviolet light.

1895 Wilhelm Konrad Röntgen discovers X rays.

1888 Heinrich R. Hertz produces and detects radio waves.

1938 Otto Hahn splits a uranium atom, opening the way for nuclear bombs and nuclear power.

1915 Einstein completes his general theory of relativity, a theory of gravity more accurate than that of Sir Isaac Newton, and publishes it the following year.

1897 Sir Joseph Thomson discovers the electron.

1932 Sir James Chadwick discovers the neutron, a neutral particle about the same mass as a proton.

1900 Max Planck explains the behavior of lights and proposes that there is a smallest step a physical process can take, which he names "quantum."

1896 Antoine H. Becquerel discovers natural radioactivity.

$$E = mc^2$$

1905 Albert Einstein develops his special theory of relativity and the law $E = mc^2$ (energy equals mass times speed of light squared).

1964 Murray Gell-Mann introduces concept of quarks as components of heavy subatomic particles, such as protons and mesons.

2002 Australian physicists are able to "transport" a beam of light by physically disassembling it in one part of their lab and recreating it in another part.

1945 Scientists funded by U.S. government and led by J. Robert Oppenheimer detonate first nuclear fission explosion (atomic bomb).

1980 Heinrich Rohrer and Gerd Binnig invent the scanning-tunneling microscope, a device with which it is possible to produce images of individual atoms or crystal surfaces.

1675   1700   1725   1750   1775   1800   1825   1850   1875   1900   1925   1950   1975   2000

The Basic Laws of Physics

LAW OF GRAVITY

The gravitational force between any two objects is proportional to the product of their masses and inversely proportional to the square of the distance between them.

NEWTON'S LAWS OF MOTION

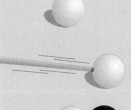

1. Any object at rest tends to stay at rest. A body in motion moves at the same velocity in a straight line unless acted upon by a force.

2. The acceleration of an object is directly proportional to the force acting on it and inversely proportional to the mass of the object.

3. For every action there is an equal and opposite reaction.

CONSERVATION LAWS

Conservation of momentum
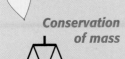

- In a closed system, momentum stays the same. This is equivalent to Newton's third law.

Conservation of angular momentum

- An object moving in a circle has a special kind of momentum, called angular momentum. In a closed system, angular momentum is conserved.

Conservation of mass
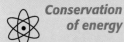

- In a closed system, the total amount of mass appears to be conserved in all but nuclear reactions and other extreme conditions.

Conservation of energy

- In a closed system, energy appears to be conserved in all but nuclear reactions and other extreme conditions.

Conservation of mass-energy

- The total amount of energy must be conserved: $E = mc^2$. In this equation, E is the amount of energy, m is the mass, and c is the speed of light in a vacuum.

$$E = mc^2$$

The Basic Symbols of Physics

α	alpha particle		e	electronic charge of electron
Å	angstrom unit		E	electric field
β	beta ray		G	conductance; weight
γ	gamma radiation		h	Planck's constant
ε	electromotive force		H	enthalpy
h	efficiency		L	inductance
L	equivalent conductivity; permeance		n	index of refraction
l	wavelength		P	momentum of a particle
m	magnetic moment		R	universal gas constant
u	frequency		S	entropy
r	density; specific resistance		T	absolute temperature; period
s	conductivity; cross section; surface tension		V	electrical potential; frequency
f	luminous flux; magnetic flux		W	energy
j	fluidity		X	magnification; reactance
Ω	ohm		Y	admittance
B	magnetic induction; magnetic field		Z	impedance
c	speed of light			

Timeline: Notable Nobel Prize Winners in Physics

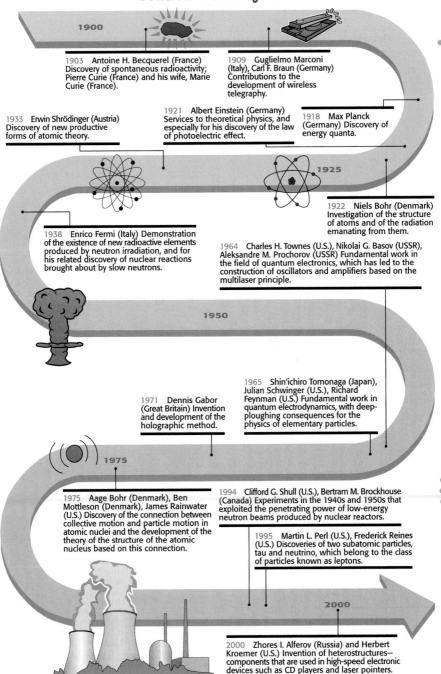

1900

1903   Antoine H. Becquerel (France) Discovery of spontaneous radioactivity; Pierre Curie (France) and his wife, Marie Curie (France).

1909   Guglielmo Marconi (Italy), Carl F. Braun (Germany) Contributions to the development of wireless telegraphy.

1933   Erwin Shrödinger (Austria) Discovery of new productive forms of atomic theory.

1921   Albert Einstein (Germany) Services to theoretical physics, and especially for his discovery of the law of photoelectric effect.

1918   Max Planck (Germany) Discovery of energy quanta.

1925

1922   Niels Bohr (Denmark) Investigation of the structure of atoms and of the radiation emanating from them.

1938   Enrico Fermi (Italy) Demonstration of the existence of new radioactive elements produced by neutron irradiation, and for his related discovery of nuclear reactions brought about by slow neutrons.

1964   Charles H. Townes (U.S.), Nikolai G. Basov (USSR), Aleksandre M. Prochorov (USSR) Fundamental work in the field of quantum electronics, which has led to the construction of oscillators and amplifiers based on the multilaser principle.

1950

1971   Dennis Gabor (Great Britain) Invention and development of the holographic method.

1965   Shin'ichiro Tomonaga (Japan), Julian Schwinger (U.S.), Richard Feynman (U.S.) Fundamental work in quantum electrodynamics, with deep-ploughing consequences for the physics of elementary particles.

1975

1975   Aage Bohr (Denmark), Ben Mottleson (Denmark), James Rainwater (U.S.) Discovery of the connection between collective motion and particle motion in atomic nuclei and the development of the theory of the structure of the atomic nucleus based on this connection.

1994   Clifford G. Shull (U.S.), Bertram M. Brockhouse (Canada) Experiments in the 1940s and 1950s that exploited the penetrating power of low-energy neutron beams produced by nuclear reactors.

1995   Martin L. Perl (U.S.), Frederick Reines (U.S.) Discoveries of two subatomic particles, tau and neutrino, which belong to the class of particles known as leptons.

2000

2000   Zhores I. Alferov (Russia) and Herbert Kroemer (U.S.) Invention of heterostructures— components that are used in high-speed electronic devices such as CD players and laser pointers.

PLANTS

Funky Fungus Facts

Plants come in all shapes and sizes. The Honey Mushroom in the Malheur National Forest in Oregon lives about 3 feet (90 cm) underground and spreads for 3.5 miles (5.6 km).

Meat-Eating Plants

Some plants are carnivorous. Pitcher plants and Sundew plants have hairs that trap insects inside the leaves. Then the plants' digestive juices help the plants consume their victims. Venus's-flytraps have leaves shaped like bear traps. When an insect wanders inside, the leaves quickly close, trapping the insect.

Frightening Flowers

The rafflesia plant in Southeast Asia has the largest flowers in the world. It has a reddish-brown blossom that can measure up to 3 feet wide and weigh up to 24 pounds.

Plentiful Plants

There are about 300,000 plant species in the world today. They can be found on land, in oceans, and in fresh water.

Prehistoric Pines

Bristlecone pinetrees are the oldest living trees known to scientists. Some of these trees in California, Nevada, and Utah date back more than 4,500 years.

Biological Classification of Plants

PROTISTA KINGDOM

Dinoflagellata DINOFLAGELLATES	*Chrysophyta* GOLDEN ALGAE
Xanthophyta YELLOW-GREEN ALGAE	*Bacillariophyta* DIATOMS
Phaeophyta BROWN ALGAE	*Rhodophyta* RED ALGAE

FUNGI KINGDOM

Euglenophyta EUGLENOID FLAGELLATES	*Cryptophyta* CRYPTOMONADS
Oomycota DOWNY MILDEW, POTATO BLIGHT	
Gamophyta CONJUGATING GREEN ALGAE	*Chlorophyta* GREEN ALGAE

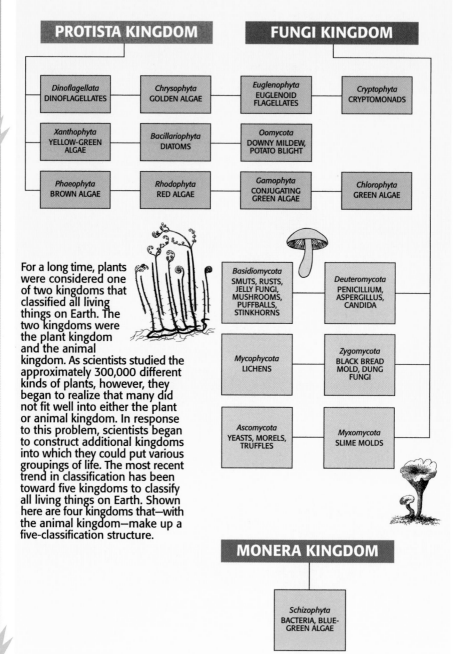

For a long time, plants were considered one of two kingdoms that classified all living things on Earth. The two kingdoms were the plant kingdom and the animal kingdom. As scientists studied the approximately 300,000 different kinds of plants, however, they began to realize that many did not fit well into either the plant or animal kingdom. In response to this problem, scientists began to construct additional kingdoms into which they could put various groupings of life. The most recent trend in classification has been toward five kingdoms to classify all living things on Earth. Shown here are four kingdoms that—with the animal kingdom—make up a five-classification structure.

Basidiomycota SMUTS, RUSTS, JELLY FUNGI, MUSHROOMS, PUFFBALLS, STINKHORNS	*Deuteromycota* PENICILLIUM, ASPERGILLUS, CANDIDA
Mycophycota LICHENS	*Zygomycota* BLACK BREAD MOLD, DUNG FUNGI
Ascomycota YEASTS, MORELS, TRUFFLES	*Myxomycota* SLIME MOLDS

MONERA KINGDOM

Schizophyta BACTERIA, BLUE-GREEN ALGAE

Source: Plants Database, United States Dept. of Agriculture, 2003

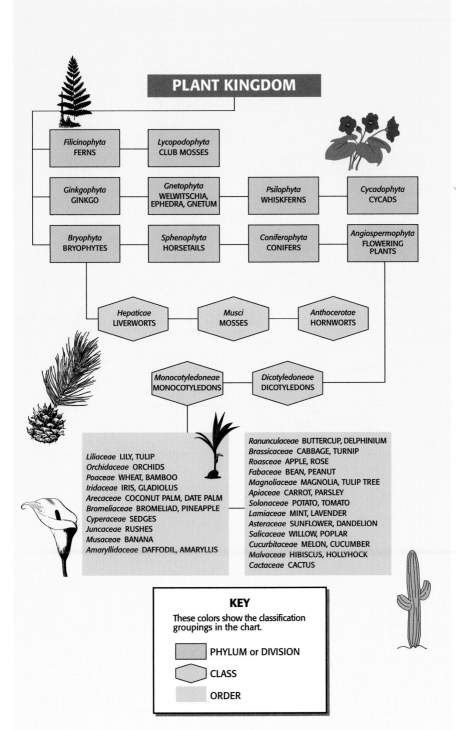

PLANT KINGDOM

Filicinophyta FERNS

Lycopodophyta CLUB MOSSES

Ginkgophyta GINKGO

Gnetophyta WELWITSCHIA, EPHEDRA, GNETUM

Psilophyta WHISKFERNS

Cycadophyta CYCADS

Bryophyta BRYOPHYTES

Sphenophyta HORSETAILS

Coniferophyta CONIFERS

Angiospermophyta FLOWERING PLANTS

Hepaticae LIVERWORTS

Musci MOSSES

Anthocerotae HORNWORTS

Monocotyledoneae MONOCOTYLEDONS

Dicotyledoneae DICOTYLEDONS

Liliaceae LILY, TULIP
Orchidaceae ORCHIDS
Poaceae WHEAT, BAMBOO
Iridaceae IRIS, GLADIOLUS
Arecaceae COCONUT PALM, DATE PALM
Bromeliaceae BROMELIAD, PINEAPPLE
Cyperaceae SEDGES
Juncaceae RUSHES
Musaceae BANANA
Amaryllidaceae DAFFODIL, AMARYLLIS

Ranunculaceae BUTTERCUP, DELPHINIUM
Brassicaceae CABBAGE, TURNIP
Roasceae APPLE, ROSE
Fabaceae BEAN, PEANUT
Magnoliaceae MAGNOLIA, TULIP TREE
Apiaceae CARROT, PARSLEY
Solonaceae POTATO, TOMATO
Lamiaceae MINT, LAVENDER
Asteraceae SUNFLOWER, DANDELION
Salicaceae WILLOW, POPLAR
Cucurbitaceae MELON, CUCUMBER
Malvaceae HIBISCUS, HOLLYHOCK
Cactaceae CACTUS

KEY

These colors show the classification groupings in the chart.

PHYLUM or DIVISION

CLASS

ORDER

The Plant Kingdom

There are more than 300,000 different plant species that have been scientifically identified. Some grow on land, others grow in the sea. Most life on Earth would not exist without plants. They are food for many animals, and they give off the oxygen that both humans and animals need to breathe.

	Plant	Description	Examples
Seed plants	**Angiosperms (Flowering plants)** Monocot	Plants produce seeds with one food part (cotyledon), leaves have parallel veins	Grasses, palms, lilies, and orchids
	Dicot	Plants produce seeds with two food parts (cotyledons), leaves have branching veins	Oak trees, roses, broccoli, tomatoes, and many others
	Gymnosperms (Naked seed plants) Conifers and others	Plants produce exposed seeds, usually on cones, and have no flowers. Most have needlelike leaves and are evergreen	Pines, spruces, junipers, firs, and other conifers, yews, and ginkgos
Some plants that don't make seeds	Moss	Produces spores, tiny green plants, no true roots, stems, or leaves, needs moist place to live	
	Liverwort	Produces spores, tiny green plants, no true roots, stems, or leaves, needs moist place to live	
	Horsetail	Produces spores, no true roots, stems, or leaves, needs moist place to live	
	Fern	Produces spores, green leafed, needs moist place to live	

Source: Plant Database, United States Dept. of Agriculture, 2003

Biomes of the World

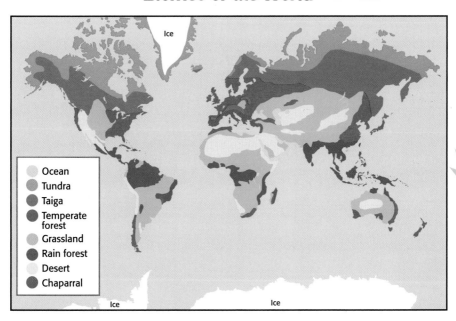

TUNDRA Found in far northern climates, too cold for trees to grow. Tundra lies on top of a layer of ice that never melts, called permafrost.

TAIGA Found mostly in far northern regions where summer is short and winter is long; pines, spruce, hemlock, and fir trees thrive here.

TEMPERATE FOREST Grows in mild climates, usually along coastlines and a bit inland. The giant sequoias of the Pacific Northwest grow here.

GRASSLAND Farming and grazing biomes; also known as prairies, savannahs, steppes, and pampas. Primarily grows thick grasses and, where cultivated, produces wheat, barley, oats, rye, and other grains.

RAIN FOREST Warm, wet biomes near or at the equator; lush vegetation of many kinds, often broken into three levels by scientists: the floor, the understory (10 to 50 feet [3 to 15 m] up), and the canopy (75 to 100 feet [23 to 30 m] above the floor).

DESERT This growing area usually receives less than 10 inches (25 cm) of rain a year; is only home to succulents, which are plants such as cacti that store water inside their thick, waxy leaves.

CHAPARRAL Also known as scrubland; a coastal biome that supports hearty evergreen shrubs.

Plants That Can Kill

The following chart lists a selection
of deadly plants and describes symptoms
of the illnesses they cause in humans.

Plants	Toxic portions	Symptoms of illness that can precede death:
Azalea	All parts	Nausea, vomiting, depression, breathing difficulty, prostration, coma
Belladonna	Young plants, seeds	Nausea, twitching muscles, paralysis
Castor bean	Seeds, foliage	Burning in mouth, convulsions
Daphne	Berries (red or yellow)	Severe burns to digestive tract followed by coma
Delphinium	Young plants, seeds	Nausea, twitching muscles, paralysis
Larkspur	Young plants, seeds	Nausea, twitching muscles, paralysis
Laurel	All parts	Nausea, vomiting, depression, breathing difficulty, prostration, coma
Mistletoe	All parts, especially berries	Weakness, blurred vision, vomiting, convulsions
Mushrooms, wild	All parts of many varieties	Diarrhea, abdominal cramps, nausea, vomiting
Oleander	All parts	Severe digestive upset, heart trouble, contact dermatitis
Poinsettia	All parts	Severe digestive upset
Rhododendron	All parts	Nausea, vomiting, depression, breathing difficulty, prostration, coma
Rhubarb	Leaf blade	Kidney disorder, convulsions, coma
Rosary pea	Seeds, foliage	Burning in mouth, convulsions

Source: www.calpoison.org; Cornell University Poisonous Plants Information Database 2003; U.S. Food and Drug Administration database

Amazing Plant Facts

World's oldest plant	A creosote plant found growing in southern California was in 1980 estimated to be 11,700 years old.
World's fastest growing plant	*Hesperoyucca whipplei*, a member of the lily family, grew 12 feet in 14 days in 1978 in Great Britain.
World's slowest flowering plant	A rare Bolivian herb, *Puya raimondii*, grows for 80–150 years, blooms once, then dies.
World's deadliest plant	The castor bean plant produces seeds that contain an extremely poisonous protein called ricin. Ricin is 6,000 times more poisonous than cyanide.

World Records for Vegetables

Biggest pumpkin: 1,131 lbs. (513 kg)

Biggest cucumber: 20 lbs., 1 oz. (9.1 kg)

Biggest zucchini: 64 lbs., 8 oz. (29.26 kg)

Biggest carrot: 18 lbs., 13 oz. (8.6 kg)

Medicines from Plants

An African plant called *Strophanthus* contains a chemical that was initially used in cortisone, a medicine that helps people suffering from arthritis.

A drug called reerpine, which calms people and lowers blood pressure, was originally found in snakeroot, a plant that grows on mountainsides.

Opium, which is used to make morphine, a painkiller, comes from the poppy flower.

Bark of the cinchora tree, which grows in Peru, was used for many years as the source of quinine, the only known treatment for the dangerous fever of malaria.

Clothes from Plants

- Linen comes from the flax plant.
- Cotton provides cotton clothes, fabrics.
- Rope and twine are made from hemp and other plants.

Fuel from Plants

- Decayed plants, when mixed with soil and water and compressed for many thousands of years, form coal, oil, and natural gas.

Wood and Paper from Trees

Millions of tons of lumber are produced every year in the United States. This wood is used in the construction of homes, offices, and countless other projects. Paper is made from the ground-up pulp of wood fibers. Paper products include everything from newspapers to magazines to your mail, and even the page you're reading right now!

Source: *Information Please Almanac*, *Encyclopedia Britannica*, and *Plants* (Our Living World series), Blackbirch Press

POPULATION (U.S.)

Wonder Women

The numbers of men and women ages 20 to 29 in the United States are about equal. However, the sex ratio drops gradually with age, to 92 men per 100 women for the 55-to-64 age group. For the older population, the sex ratio declines rapidly. There are 84 men per 100 women age 65 to 74. There are just 46 men per 100 women ages 85 years old and over.

Divorcing Data

Currently, the divorced population is the fastest growing marital status category. The number of divorced people has more than quadrupled in the last 25 years. They represent more than 10% of adults age 18 and over.

All in the Family

The number of extended families in the United States is on the rise. Some 5.7 million grandparents live with at least one of their grandchildren under the age of 18. About 2.4 million grandparents are solely responsible for most of the basic needs of one or more of the grandchildren they live with. Of these caregivers, 1.5 million are grandmothers and 900,000 are grandfathers.

Older Occupants on the Increase

As health care improves, many Americans are living longer. About 40,000 centenarians—or people who have reached their 100th birthday—currently live in the United States. More than 15% of them have celebrated their 105th birthday. Four out of five centenarians are women. Some researchers project there could be as many as 850,000 centenarians by the year 2050.

The Name Game

The most popular boys' names in 2002 were Jacob, Michael, Joshua, Matthew, Ethan, Joseph, Andrew, Christopher, Daniel, and Nicholas. The most popular girls' names of that same year were Emily, Madison, Hannah, Emma, Alexis, Ashley, Abigail, Sarah, Samantha, and Olivia.

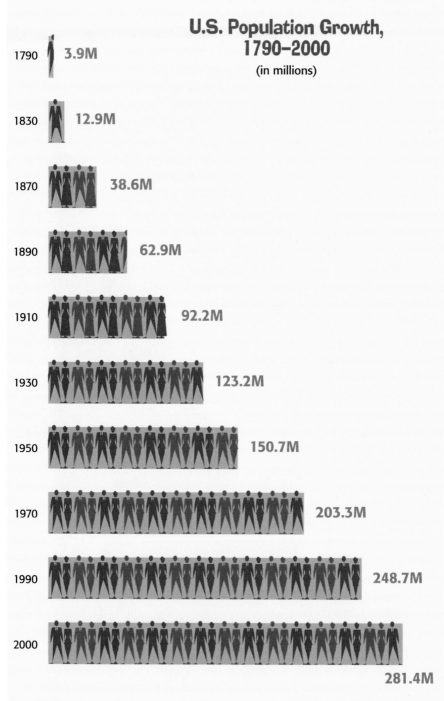

U.S. Population Growth, 1790–2000
(in millions)

Year	Population
1790	3.9M
1830	12.9M
1870	38.6M
1890	62.9M
1910	92.2M
1930	123.2M
1950	150.7M
1970	203.3M
1990	248.7M
2000	281.4M

Source: U.S. Census Bureau, 2000

U.S. Population Profile

Racial and ethnic composition, 2000

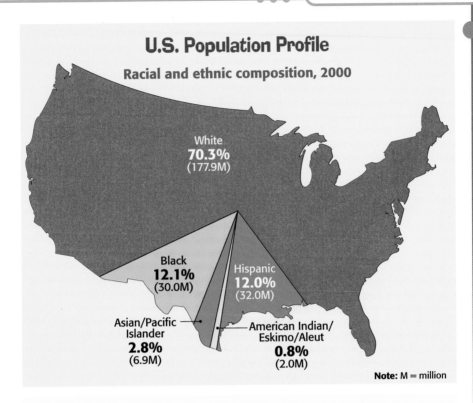

White
70.3%
(177.9M)

Black
12.1%
(30.0M)

Hispanic
12.0%
(32.0M)

Asian/Pacific
Islander
2.8%
(6.9M)

American Indian/
Eskimo/Aleut
0.8%
(2.0M)

Note: M = million

Population by Age

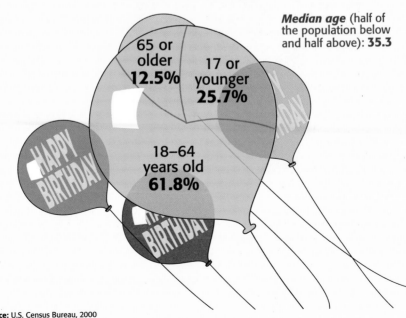

Median age (half of
the population below
and half above): **35.3**

65 or
older
12.5%

17 or
younger
25.7%

18–64
years old
61.8%

Source: U.S. Census Bureau, 2000

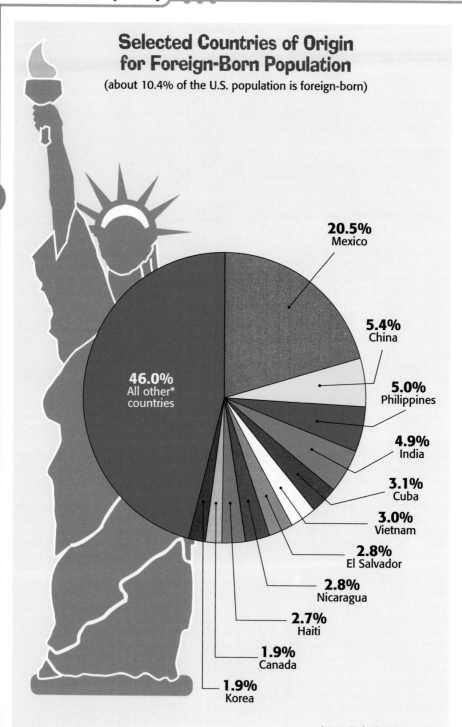

Selected Countries of Origin for Foreign-Born Population

(about 10.4% of the U.S. population is foreign-born)

20.5%
Mexico

5.4%
China

5.0%
Philippines

4.9%
India

3.1%
Cuba

3.0%
Vietnam

2.8%
El Salvador

2.8%
Nicaragua

2.7%
Haiti

1.9%
Canada

1.9%
Korea

46.0%
All other*
countries

*Note: "Other" nations each account for less than 1%.

Source: U.S. Census Bureau, 2000

U.S. Population Profile
Population projections, 2000–2050

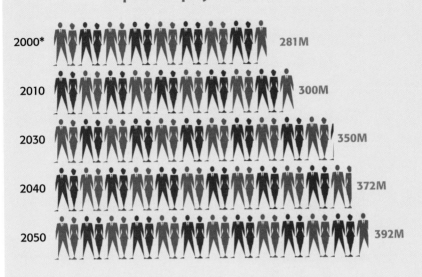

2000*   281M

2010   300M

2030   350M

2040   372M

2050   392M

Source: U.S. Census Bureau, 2000

*Census 2000 data   **Note:** M = million

U.S. Family Profile

Households with Families*, 2000

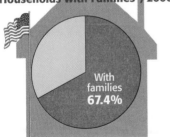

With families
67.4%

Families with Children, 2000

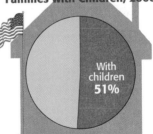

With children
51%

Who Heads Families?

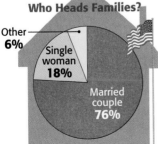

Other
6%

Single woman
18%

Married couple
76%

Who Heads Families with Children?

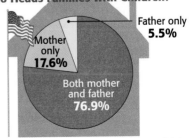

Father only
5.5%

Mother only
17.6%

Both mother and father
76.9%

Source: U.S. Census Bureau, 2000

*Families = any group of inhabitants who are related.

U.S. Population Profile

U.S. Population by Gender, 2001

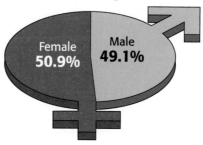

Female **50.9%**

Male **49.1%**

Population by Marriage Status, 2000

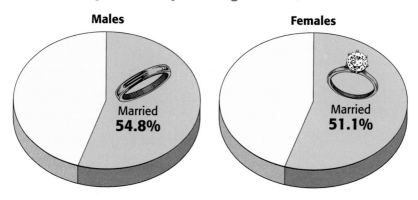

Males

Married **54.8%**

Females

Married **51.1%**

Divorce Rates, 1970–2000
(number of divorces per 1,000 people)

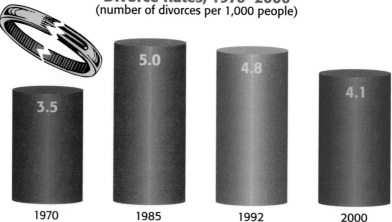

3.5	5.0	4.8	4.1
1970	1985	1992	2000

Source: U.S. Census Bureau

U.S. Birth Rate, 1960–2000
(number of births per 1,000 people)

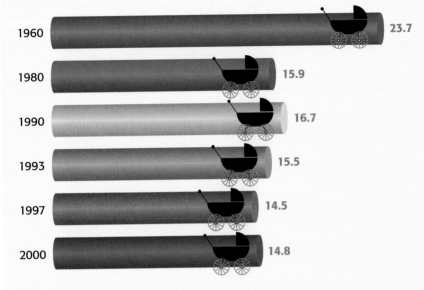

Year	Births per 1,000
1960	23.7
1980	15.9
1990	16.7
1993	15.5
1997	14.5
2000	14.8

Source: National Center for Health Statistics, U.S. Department of Health and Human Services, 2002

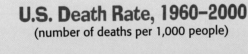

U.S. Death Rate, 1960–2000
(number of deaths per 1,000 people)

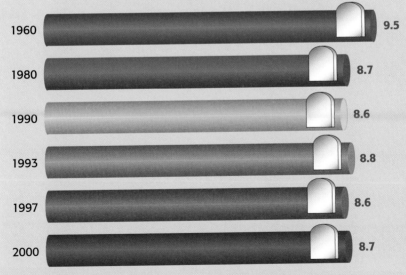

Year	Deaths per 1,000
1960	9.5
1980	8.7
1990	8.6
1993	8.8
1997	8.6
2000	8.7

Source: National Center for Health Statistics, U.S. Department of Health and Human Services, 2002

PRIZES AND AWARDS

MTV Movie Masters

The MTV Movie Awards are a hit with both actors and fans because of the laid-back atmosphere and unusual award categories. The actor with the most MTV Movie awards is Jim Carrey with nine. The actress with the most MTV Movie Awards is Alicia Silverstone with four.

Emmy Excitement

The television show with the most Emmy Awards® in a single season is *The West Wing*. The political drama won nine awards in September of 2000. The following year the show won eight awards, the second most Emmy Awards in a single season.

Best on Broadway

There is no greater honor for a Broadway show than to win a Tony Award. In 2001, *The Producers* became the first Broadway show in history to get nominated for 15 Tony Awards. Later that year the musical won 12 of the awards, making *The Producers* the show with the most Tony Award wins.

Grammy Grabbers

Two men share the record for the most Grammys won by a single recording artist in one year. Carlos Santana took home eight Grammys for his 1999 album *Supernatural*. In 1983, Michael Jackson won eight awards for his album *Thriller*.

All About Oscar

An Oscar® Award is a 13.5-inch (34-cm), 8.5-pound (3.9-kg) statuette made of alloy britannium, plated in copper, nickel silver, and 24-karat gold. During World War II, however, the Academy used plaster figurines due to metal shortages.

Major Prizes and Awards

Prize/Award	Background	Notable facts
Academy Award® (Oscar)	First given in 1928; members of the Academy of Motion Picture Arts and Sciences vote (3,000 members); members nominate in area of expertise but vote on all categories.	Films with most nominations: *Titanic* and *All About Eve* (14). Films with most awards: *Titanic* and *Ben-Hur* (11).
Emmy®	First presented in 1949; members of the National Academy of Television Arts and Sciences vote in approximately 70 categories.	TV show with most nominations: *Cheers* (117). TV show with most awards: *Mary Tyler Moore Show* (29). Top Emmy-winning actor: Ed Asner (7). Top Emmy-winning actresses: Dinah Shore and Mary Tyler Moore (8). Most consecutive wins: *Frasier* (5).
Tony®	First presented in 1947; members of the American Theater Wing vote for distinguished achievement in Broadway Theater.	Multiple Tony-winning playwrights include: Arthur Miller, Tom Stoppard, Peter Shaffer, Neil Simon, and Terrence McNally.
Grammy®	First presented in 1959; voted by members of the National Academy of Recording Arts and Sciences.	Recording artists and technicians with the most Grammys: Sir Georg Solti (31), Quincy Jones (26), and Vladimir Horowitz (25).

Prize/Award	Background	Notable facts
Pulitzer Prize	First awarded in 1917; Hungarian-born journalist Joseph Pulitzer endowed the Columbia School of Journalism, whose trustees award prizes.	Prizes awarded per year: journalism (14), literature and drama (6), and musical composition (1).
Nobel Prize	First awarded in 1901; established by gift of $9.2 million from Alfred Nobel, a Swedish chemical engineer who invented dynamite and other explosives.	Six prizes awarded for outstanding achievement in: chemistry, physics, physiology or medicine, peace, literature, and economic sciences.
Newbery Medal	First awarded in 1922; presented by the American Library Association for outstanding children's writing; named after John Newbery, the first English publisher of children's books.	Recent winners: Avi (*Crispin: The Cross of Lead*), Linda Sue Park (*A Single Shard*), and Richard Peck (*A Year Down Yonder*).
Caldecott Medal 	First awarded in 1938; presented by the American Library Association for outstanding children's picture-book illustration; named in honor of English illustrator Randolph Caldecott.	Recent winners: Eric Rohmann (*My Friend Rabbit*), David Wiesner (*The Three Pigs*), and David Small (*So You Want to Be President?*).

RELIGION

Buddhist Beliefs

The monks and nuns in the Buddhist religion use colored robes to signify their region and their tradition. Many times both nuns and monks who practice Buddhism also shave their heads.

Sizable Synagogue

Temple Emanu-El is the world's largest synagogue with an area of 37,921.2 square feet (3,523 sq. m). Built in 1929, it is located on Fifth Avenue and 65th Street in New York City. Its library houses more than 12,000 books on Jewish life, as well as its Judaica Collection—about 500 objects relating to the history of its congregation.

Plenty of Elbow Room

The world's largest church is the Basilica of Our Lady of Peace—also known as Nôtre Dame de la Paix. It is located in Côte d'Ivoire (the Ivory Coast) in Africa. Built in 1989, the church is 518 feet (158 m) high and has an area of 322,917 square feet (30,000 square m)— the same area as 5.5 football fields!

Sacred Spots

Most religions have certain locations that are considered to be most holy. Christians, Jews, and Muslims may make a pilgrimage to the Holy Land, the collective name for Egypt, Israel, and Jordan. Hindus sprinkle the ashes of their dead relatives in the Ganges River. And members of the Buddhist and Shinto religions consider Mount Fuji, in Japan, to be sacred.

Title-Holding Temple

The world's largest Buddhist temple is Borobudur in Indonesia. The massive structure was built between 750 and 842 A.D. and measures 113 feet (34.5 m) tall—higher than a 10-story building! Its base measures 403 feet by 403 feet (123 m x 123 m). It has recently been restored, which involved removing about a million stone blocks, cataloging them on a computer, cleaning them, and finally putting them back together.

Religions of the World

Key

- Roman Catholic
- Eastern Orthodox
- Protestant
- Mormon
- Mixed Christian
- Jewish
- Sunni Muslim[1]
- Shiite Muslim[1]
- Hindu[2]
- Buddhist
- Buddhist and Shintoist
- Buddhist, Confucianist, Taoist
- Native
- Information unavailable

Source: Based on information from *Peter's Atlas*, 2002; the *CIA World Factbook*, 2003   1. Part of Islam; 2. Includes Sikhs

World's Top 5 Organized Religions, by Membership

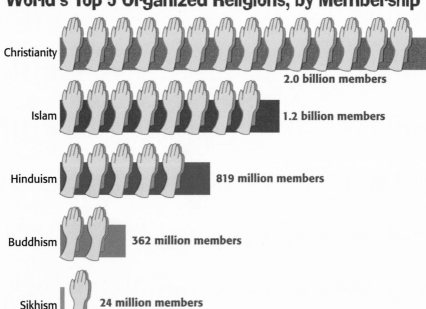

Christianity — 2.0 billion members

Islam — 1.2 billion members

Hinduism — 819 million members

Buddhism — 362 million members

Sikhism — 24 million members

Source: *2002 Encyclopedia Britannica Book of the Year*

Profile of U.S. Religious Attendence

U.S. Religious Attendees by Marital Status

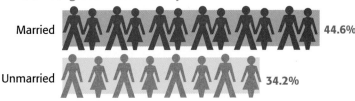

Married — 44.6%

Unmarried — 34.2%

U.S. Religious Attendees by Family Status

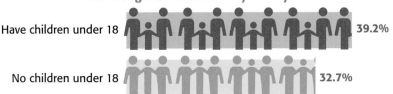

Have children under 18 — 39.2%

No children under 18 — 32.7%

Attend Religious Services on a Typical Weekend

Women — 47% Attend

Men — 26% Attend

U.S. Religious Attendees by Age

Ages 18–29 — 62% Attend

Ages 30–49 — 66% Attend

Ages 50 and over — 77% Attend

U.S. Religious Attendance by Region

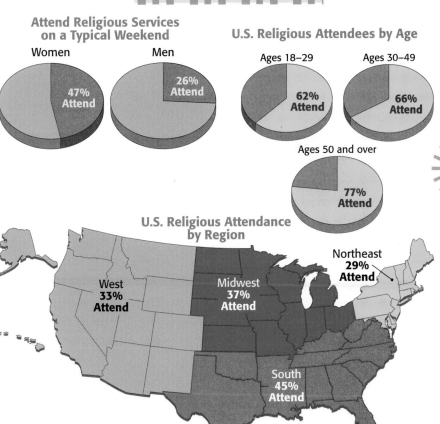

Northeast 29% Attend

West 33% Attend

Midwest 37% Attend

South 45% Attend

Source: The Gallup Organization, 2002

Christian Holy Days

Sundays: The Christian Sabbath; a day of rest and a day for prayer and spiritual observance.

Easter: Most important holy day in the Christian religion; celebration of Christ's resurrection from the dead, which gives Christians the hope of salvation and eternal life. Easter is only one day, but the full observance of the holy day spans from Septuagesima Sunday (70 days before Easter Sunday), which may fall as early as January, to Pentecost, which can occur as late as June.

Lent: 40-day period of fasting and penitence beginning on Ash Wednesday and ending on Easter Sunday, is traditionally observed by fasting, performing acts of charity, and by giving up certain pleasures and amusements. (Note that the six Sundays that fall during Lent are not considered part of the 40-day period. Thus Easter occurs 46 calendar days after Ash Wednesday.)

Ash Wednesday derives its name from the rite of burning the palms carried on the Palm Sunday of the year before and using the ashes to mark worshipers' foreheads with a cross. The ashes are a symbol of atonement and are meant to remind Christians of their mortality.

Palm Sunday: Sunday before Easter, celebrates Jesus' triumphant entry into Jerusalem, where palm branches were spread before him to honor his path.

Holy (Maundy) Thursday: Anniversary of the Last Supper. Traditional services mark three events that occurred during the week before Jesus was crucified: he washed the feet of his 12 disciples; he instituted the Eucharist (the sacrament of Holy Communion); and he was arrested and imprisoned.

Good Friday: Marks Christ's crucifixion. Observed with fasting, mourning, and penitence.

Holy Saturday: The day that anticipates the resurrection. In the Catholic and Orthodox churches, special vigils are held on Holy Saturday evening.

Easter Sunday marks the day of Christ's resurrection. Many worshipers celebrate the holy day with sunrise services, a custom believed to be inspired by the example of Mary Magdalene, who went to Christ's tomb "early, while it was yet dark."

Pentecost (literally, 50th day) is the end of the full ecclesiastical observance of Easter. It takes place on the seventh Sunday after Easter Sunday and commemorates the descent of the Holy Spirit upon the apostles.

All Saints' Day, celebrated on November 1, honors all of the Christian saints. In America many churches mark the nearest Sunday as a day to pay tribute to those who have died during the year. All Saints' Day is observed primarily by Roman Catholics.

Advent, a religious season that begins on the Sunday closest to November 30 and lasts until Christmas, both celebrates the birth of Jesus and anticipates his second coming. At one time Advent was a solemn season observed by fasting, but this is no longer the case.

Christmas: Celebration of the birth of Jesus. The exact date of his birth is unknown, but December 25 was probably chosen because it coincided with the ancient midwinter celebration that honored pagan deities. The 12 days of Christmas fall between Christmas and Epiphany (January 6), the day the Wise Men visited the Christ child.

Jewish Holy Days

Shabbat (Sabbath) is the first and most important Jewish holy day, occurring each week from sundown Friday to sundown Saturday. It is a day of rest and spiritual growth, given to men and women so they will remember the sweetness of freedom and keep it. Shabbat takes precedence over all other observances.

Rosh Hashanah (New Year), believed to be the birthday of the world, is also called the Day of Judgment and Remembrance and the day of the shofar—a ram's horn—which is blown to remind Jews of Abraham's willingness to sacrifice his son Isaac. The holiday takes place on the first and second days of Tishrei (in September or October).

Yom Kippur (Day of Atonement) ends the 10 days of repentance that Rosh Hashanah begins and takes place from sundown on the ninth day of Tishrei until sundown on the tenth. The observance begins with the recitation of the most famous passage in the Jewish liturgy—the *Kol Nidre*—which nullifies unfulfilled vows made in the past year. The entire day is spent praying and fasting.

Sukkot (Tabernacles) is a harvest festival celebrated from the fifteenth through the twenty-second of Tishrei. Sukkot also commemorates the journey of the Jewish people through the wilderness to the land of Israel. Jewish families take their meals this week in a roughly constructed *sukkah* (booth)—a reminder of an agricultural society, of an exodus, and of how precarious and fragile life can be. On Simchat Torah, the twenty-third day of Tishrei, a congregation finishes reading the last book of the Torah and immediately starts again with the first.

Hanukkah (Feast of Dedication; Festival of Lights) The importance of the eight-day feast, which begins on the twenty-fifth day of Kislev, is its commemoration of the first war in human history fought in the cause of religious freedom. The Maccabees overcame not just the military threat to Judaism but also the internal forces for the assimilation into the culture of Israel's rulers. Jews light candles for the eight nights to mark a miracle: a day's supply of oil, found in the recaptured Temple, that burned for eight days.

Purim (Feast of Lots), set on the fourteenth day of Adar, is another celebration of survival, noting events described in the Book of Esther. At Purim, Jews rejoice at Queen Esther's and her cousin Mordecai's defeat of Haman, the Persian King Ahashverosh's adviser who plotted to slaughter all the Persian Jews. Ahashverosh ruled around 400 B.C.

Pesach (Passover), beginning on the fifteenth day of Nisan and lasting seven days, commemorates the exodus of the Hebrews from Egypt in about 1300 B.C. The name Passover also recalls God's sparing (passing over) the Jewish firstborns during the plagues upon the land brought by God through Moses. The holiday is marked by eating only unleavened foods and participating in a seder, or special meal.

Shavuot (Feast of Weeks) is observed on the sixth and seventh days of Sivan. Originally an agricultural festival, Shavuot is a celebration of the revelation of the Torah at Mount Sinai, by which God established his covenant with the Jewish people.

Source: *Encyclopedia Judaica*, 1994 edition

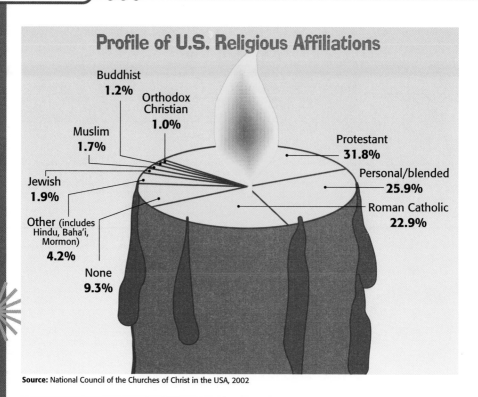

Profile of U.S. Religious Affiliations

Buddhist
1.2%

Orthodox
Christian
1.0%

Muslim
1.7%

Jewish
1.9%

Other (includes
Hindu, Baha'i,
Mormon)
4.2%

None
9.3%

Protestant
31.8%

Personal/blended
25.9%

Roman Catholic
22.9%

Source: National Council of the Churches of Christ in the USA, 2002

Calendar of Selected Christian Holy Days

Year A.D.	Ash Wednesday	Good Friday	Easter Sunday	Pentecost	Trinity Sunday	Advent
2004	Feb. 25	Apr. 9	Apr. 11	May 30	June 6	Nov. 28
2005	Feb. 9	Mar. 25	Mar. 27	May 15	May 22	Nov. 27
2006	Mar. 1	Apr. 14	Apr. 16	June 4	June 11	Dec. 3

Calendar of Jewish Holy Days, 5765–5768

The Jewish year is divided into the twelve months of Tishrei, Heshvan, Kislev, Tevet, Shevat, Adar, Nisan, Iyar, Sivan, Tammuz, Av, and Elul. The Jewish era begins at the creation (*anno mundi*, or A.M.), which is equal to 3761 B.C.E. (before the Christian era). By this formula, the Jewish year 5765 began in 2004 and ends in 2005 of the Gregorian calendar. (Tishrei, the first month of the Jewish year, falls in either September or October of the Gregorian calendar.)

Year A.M.	Rosh Hashanah	Yom Kippur	Sukkot	Hanukkah	Purim	Pesach	Shavuot
5765	Sept. 16, 2004	Sept. 25, 2004	Sept. 30, 2004	Dec. 7, 2004	Mar. 25, 2005	Apr. 24, 2005	June 13, 2005
5766	Oct. 4, 2005	Oct. 13, 2005	Oct. 18, 2005	Dec. 25, 2005	Mar. 14, 2006	Apr. 13, 2006	June 2, 2006
5767	Sept. 23, 2006	Oct. 2, 2006	Oct. 7, 2006	Dec. 15, 2006	Mar. 4, 2007	Apr. 3, 2007	May 23, 2007
5768	Sept. 13, 2007	Sept. 22, 2007	Sept. 27, 2007	Dec. 4, 2007	Mar. 21, 2008	Apr. 20, 2008	June 9, 2008

Source: Madison Jewish Community Council, 2003

Calendar of Muslim Holy Days

The Islamic calendar is broken into 12 months: Muharram, Safar, Rabi I, Rabi II, Jumada I, Jumada II, Rajab, Sha'ban, Ramadan, Shawwal, Dhu'l-Qa'dah, Dhu'l-Hijja. The calendar is based on a lunar year of 12 months, each consisting of 30 and 29 days (alternating every month), and the year is equal to 354 days.

Ramadan, the ninth month of the Islamic calendar, is the Islamic faith's holiest period. To honor the month in which the Koran was revealed, all adult Muslims of sound body and mind observe fasting—going without food, water, or even a kiss—between the hours of sunrise and sunset.

Id al-Fitr This day of feasting is celebrated at the end of Ramadan. To mark the fast's break, worshipers also attend an early morning service.

Id al-Adha The Feast of Sacrifice takes place on the tenth day of Dhu'l-Hijja, the last month of the year and the season of the haj, or pilgrimage.

Fridays At noontime Muslims attend mosques or comparable gathering places to say the congregational Friday prayer that ends the week. While Friday—Jumuah—is the holy day of the weekly Muslim calendar, it is not a sabbath comparable to Christian Sundays or Jewish Saturdays, and there are no restrictions on work.

Year A.H. (A.D.)	New Year's Day, 1 Muharram	1 Ramadan	Id al-Fitr, 1 Shawwal	Id al-Adha, 10 Dhu'l-Hijja
1425 (2004–05)	Feb. 22, 2004	Oct. 16, 2004	Nov. 14, 2004	Jan. 21, 2005
1426 (2005–06)	Feb. 10, 2005	Oct. 5, 2005	Nov. 4, 2005	Jan. 11, 2006
1427 (2006–07)	Jan. 31, 2006	Sept. 24, 2006	Oct. 24, 2006	Dec. 2, 2006

Source: Islamic Shura Council of North America, 2003

SIGNS AND SYMBOLS

Signing up to Sign

American Sign Language classes are offered in about 120 colleges and universities across the United States. Class enrollment has almost tripled in the last three years, with more than 11,000 students now participating annually.

Eyeball Attention

Scientists have discovered that black writing placed on a yellow background creates the greatest color contrast to the human eye. Because of this, the color combination is used for many traffic signs so drivers can read them easily.

Six Special Signs

The Department of Transportation uses six types of signs on major roads. Regulatory signs, such as yield signs, tell drivers to do, or not do, something. Warning signs, such as those at railroad crossings, alert drivers to possible problems. Guide signs, commonly in the form of highway markers, help drivers navigate. Motorist service signs tell drivers where food and rest areas are located. Construction signs warn drivers of work areas. Recreation signs tell drivers of places of cultural or recreational interest.

Sign of the Times

There are approximately 350,000 to 500,000 American Sign Language users in United States. Most of them use ASL as their primary language.

Stop Sign Smarts

The first official stop sign was used in Detroit, Michigan, in 1915. This sign had black letters on a white background and was printed on a sheet of metal. Big cities were using semaphores—traffic towers with "stop" and "go" signs turned by hand. The stop sign eventually replaced these.

ONE WAY

ONE WAY

STOP

DEPT OF TRANSPORTATION

Basic Signs

Fire extinguisher

Women's room

Men's room

First aid

Elevator

Information

Disabled parking

Bus

Recycle

Fallout shelter

No smoking

No admittance

No parking

Danger

Poison

Stop

Yield

Do not enter

No left turn

Falling rock

Stop ahead

Bicycle path

Traffic light ahead

Railroad crossing

Pedestrian crossing

Intersection ahead

Left turn

Right turn

Two-way traffic

Slippery when wet

American Sign Language

In the manual alphabet of the hearing impaired, the fingers of the hand are moved to positions that represent the letters of the alphabet. Whole words and ideas are also expressed in sign language.

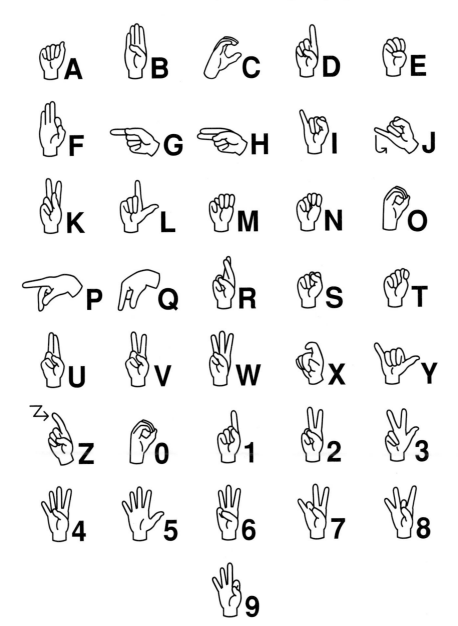

SPORTS

Just a Little Farther...

The official distance of a marathon measured exactly 26 miles until 1908. In that year, the Olympics were held in London and the royal family did not have a good view of the marathon finish line from their seats. So the race coordinators decided to move the finish line closer to the family for a better view. Since that day, a marathon has an official distance of 26 miles and 385 yards.

Golf Games Galore

About 518 million rounds of golf are played in the United States each year. On average, a golfer loses 4.5 balls per round (18 holes). In one year, U.S. golfers will use a total of 2.5 billion balls.

Major League Meals

Major League Baseball fans will eat about 26 million hot dogs in one season. Laid end to end, these summertime snacks would stretch 2,462 miles (3,962 km), or from New York's Yankee Stadium to Los Angeles's Dodger Stadium.

Superstitious Sports

Many sports have superstitions related to them. For instance, in baseball it is good luck to spit into your hand before you pick up a bat. But it's bad luck if a dog walks across the field before game time. In basketball, the last person to sink a practice basket before the game starts will score a lot of points. In football, a player who has double numbers on his uniform will have good luck.

Ring Rules

The five rings on the Olympic flag represent the five competing continents of the world—Africa, Asia, Australia, Europe, and the Americas. At least one of the rings' colors is present in each of the participating countries' flags.

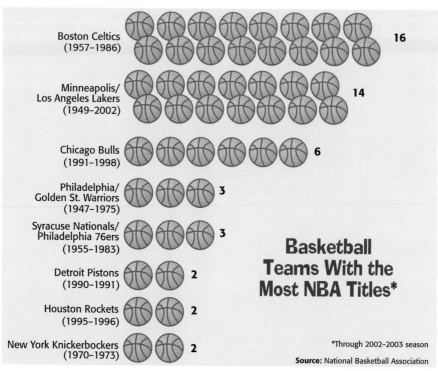

Basketball Teams With the Most NBA Titles*

Boston Celtics (1957–1986)	16
Minneapolis/Los Angeles Lakers (1949–2002)	14
Chicago Bulls (1991–1998)	6
Philadelphia/Golden St. Warriors (1947–1975)	3
Syracuse Nationals/Philadelphia 76ers (1955–1983)	3
Detroit Pistons (1990–1991)	2
Houston Rockets (1995–1996)	2
New York Knickerbockers (1970–1973)	2

*Through 2002–2003 season
Source: National Basketball Association

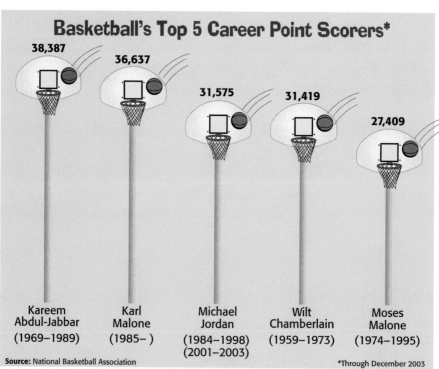

Basketball's Top 5 Career Point Scorers*

Kareem Abdul-Jabbar (1969–1989)	38,387
Karl Malone (1985–)	36,637
Michael Jordan (1984–1998) (2001–2003)	31,575
Wilt Chamberlain (1959–1973)	31,419
Moses Malone (1974–1995)	27,409

Source: National Basketball Association

*Through December 2003

Top 5 NCAA Division 1 Teams in Women's Basketball*

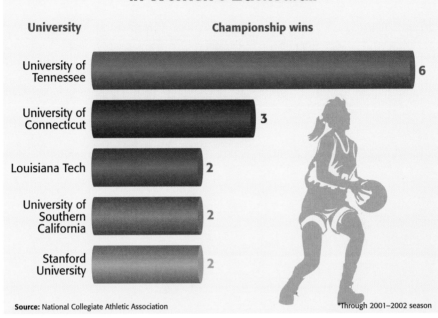

University	Championship wins
University of Tennessee	6
University of Connecticut	3
Louisiana Tech	2
University of Southern California	2
Stanford University	2

Source: National Collegiate Athletic Association

*Through 2001–2002 season

Top 5 NCAA Basketball Scoring Leaders

Pete Maravich, Louisiana State	3,667
Freeman Williams, Portland State	3,249
Lionel Simmons, LaSalle	3,217
Alphonzo Ford, Mississippi Valley	3,165
Harry Kelly, Texas Southern	3,066

Source: National Collegiate Athletic Association

Football's Top 5 Career Passers
(by total passing yards)

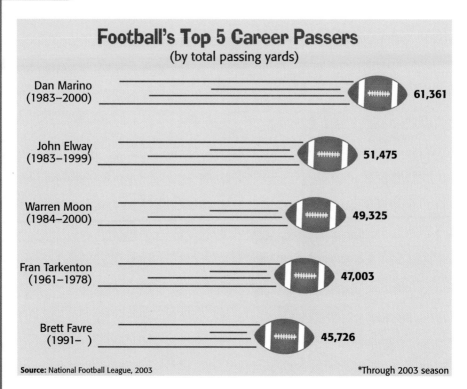

Dan Marino
(1983–2000) — 61,361

John Elway
(1983–1999) — 51,475

Warren Moon
(1984–2000) — 49,325

Fran Tarkenton
(1961–1978) — 47,003

Brett Favre
(1991–) — 45,726

Source: National Football League, 2003

*Through 2003 season

Football's Top 5 Career Touchdown Scorers
(by number of touchdowns scored)

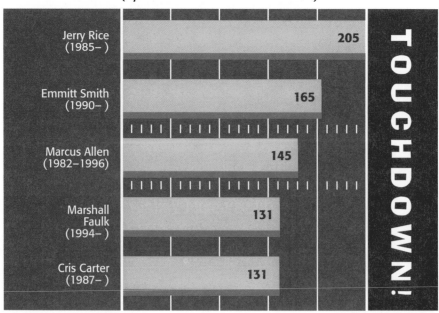

Jerry Rice
(1985–) — 205

Emmitt Smith
(1990–) — 165

Marcus Allen
(1982–1996) — 145

Marshall
Faulk
(1994–) — 131

Cris Carter
(1987–) — 131

TOUCHDOWN!

Source: National Football League, 2003

*Through 2003 season

Football's Top 5 Career Rushers*
(by number of yards rushed)

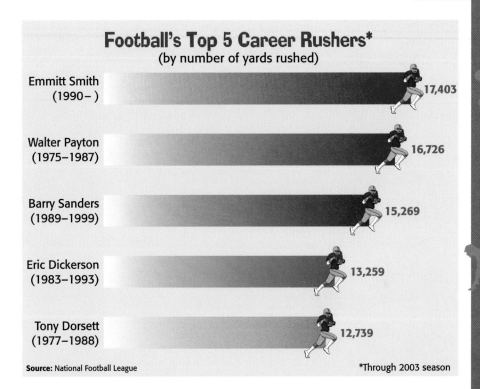

Emmitt Smith (1990–) — 17,403

Walter Payton (1975–1987) — 16,726

Barry Sanders (1989–1999) — 15,269

Eric Dickerson (1983–1993) — 13,259

Tony Dorsett (1977–1988) — 12,739

Source: National Football League

*Through 2003 season

Top 10 Universities With Most Bowl Wins*

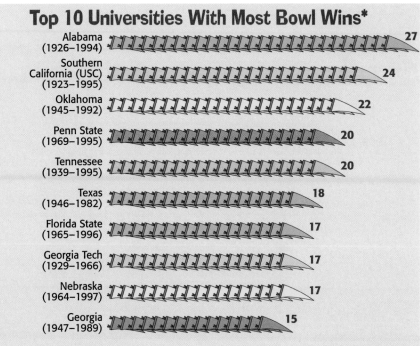

Alabama (1926–1994) — 27

Southern California (USC) (1923–1995) — 24

Oklahoma (1945–1992) — 22

Penn State (1969–1995) — 20

Tennessee (1939–1995) — 20

Texas (1946–1982) — 18

Florida State (1965–1996) — 17

Georgia Tech (1929–1966) — 17

Nebraska (1964–1997) — 17

Georgia (1947–1989) — 15

Source: National Collegiate Athletic Association

*Through 2002 season

Baseball's Top 5 World Series Winners*

New York Yankees (1923–2000) — 26

St. Louis Cardinals (1926–1982) — 9

Philadelphia/Kansas City/ Oakland Athletics (1910–1989) — 9

Brooklyn/Los Angeles Dodgers (1955–1988) — 6

New York/San Francisco Giants (1905–1954) — 5

Boston Red Sox (1903–1918) — 5

Cincinnati Reds (1919–1990) — 5

Pittsburgh Pirates (1909–1979) — 3

Source: Major League Baseball   *Through 2003 season

Baseball's Top 5 Run Scorers
(career total)

Rickey Henderson (1979–) — 2,294

Ty Cobb (1905–1928) — 2,245

Babe Ruth (1914–1935) — 2,174

Hank Aaron (1952–1976) — 2,174

Pete Rose (1963–1986) — 2,165

Source: Major League Baseball

Hockey Teams With the Most Stanley Cup Wins*

Montreal Canadiens
(1916–1993) — 24

Toronto Maple Leafs
(1932–1967) — 11

Detroit Red Wings
(1936–2002) — 10

Boston Bruins
(1929–1972) — 5

Edmonton Oilers
(1984–1990) — 5

New York Islanders
(1980–1983) — 4

New York Rangers
(1928–1994) — 4

Chicago Blackhawks
(1934–1961) — 3

Philadelphia Flyers
(1974–1975) — 2

Pittsburgh Penguins
(1991–1992) — 2

Source: National Hockey League

*Through 2003 season

Hockey's Top 5 Career Point Scorers

Player	Seasons	Goals	Assists	Total points
Wayne Gretzky (1978–1999)	20	894	1,963	2,857
Mark Messier (1979–)	25	686	1,172	1,858
Gordie Howe (1954–1980)	26	801	1,049	1,850
Marcel Dionne (1971–1990)	18	731	1,040	1,771
Ron Francis (1981–)	24	541	1,224	1,765

Source: National Hockey League

*Through 2003 season

Top 5 Most-Winning Men in Tennis*
(all-time Grand Slam singles titles)

Player/Country	Australian Open	French Open	Wimbledon	U.S. Open	Total
Pete Sampras (U.S.)	3	0	6	5	14 (1990–2002)
Roy Emerson (Australia)	6	2	2	2	12 (1961–1967)
Björn Borg (Sweden)	0	6	5	0	11 (1974–1981)
Rod Laver (Australia)	3	2	4	2	11 (1960–1969)
Bill Tilden (U.S.)	0	0	3	7	10 (1920–1930)

Source: American Tennis Professionals

*Through 2002

Top 5 Most-Winning Women in Tennis*
(all-time Grand Slam singles titles)

Player/Country	Australian Open	French Open	Wimbledon	U.S. Open	Total
Margaret Court Smith (Australia)	11	5	3	5	24 (1960–1975)
Steffi Graf (Germany)	4	6	7	5	22 (1987–1999)
Helen Wills-Moody (U.S.)	0	4	8	7	19 (1923–1938)
Chris Evert-Lloyd (U.S.)	2	7	3	6	18 (1974–1986)
Martina Navratilova (Czech./U.S.)	3	2	9	4	18 (1974–1995)

Source: American Tennis Professionals

*Through 2002

Top 6 Most-Winning Men in Golf*
(all-time wins at majors)

Player/Country		British Open	U.S. Open	Masters	PGA	Total
Jack Nicklaus (U.S.)	(1963–1986)	3	4	6	5	18
Walter Hagen (U.S.)	(1914–1929)	4	2	0	5	11
Ben Hogan (U.S.)	(1946–1953)	1	4	2	2	9
Gary Player (S. Africa)	(1959–1978)	3	1	3	2	9
Tiger Woods (U.S.)	(1997–)	1	2	3	2	8
Tom Watson (U.S.)	(1975–1983)	5	1	2	0	8

Source: Professional Golfers Association

*Through 2002

Top 5 Most-Winning Women in Golf*
(all-time wins in majors)

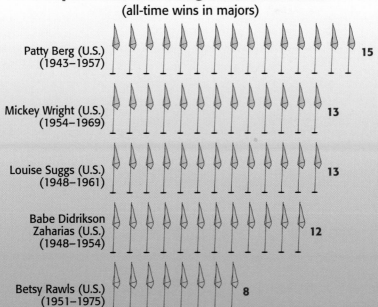

Patty Berg (U.S.) (1943–1957) — 15

Mickey Wright (U.S.) (1954–1969) — 13

Louise Suggs (U.S.) (1948–1961) — 13

Babe Didrikson Zaharias (U.S.) (1948–1954) — 12

Betsy Rawls (U.S.) (1951–1975) — 8

Source: Ladies Professional Golfers Association

*Through 2002

Top 5 Countries in the World Cup*

Country	Win	Runner-up	3rd	4th	Total
Brazil (1958–2002)	5	1	3	1	30
Germany/W. Germany (1954–2002)	3	4	2	1	29
Italy (1934–1982)	3	2	1	1	21
Argentina (1978–1986)	2	2	–	–	14
Uruguay (1930–1950)	2	–	–	2	10

*Based on 4 points for winning the tournament, 3 points for runner-up, 2 points for 3rd place, and 1 point for 4th. Includes 2002 World Cup.

Source: Fédération Internationale de Football Association (FIFA)

Top 5 Most Winning Championship Auto Racing Team Drivers*
(by races won)

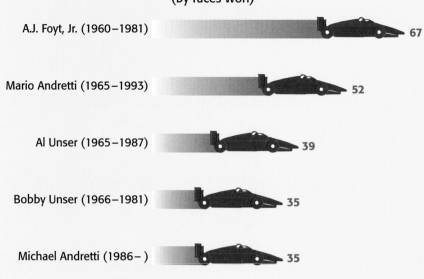

A.J. Foyt, Jr. (1960–1981) 67

Mario Andretti (1965–1993) 52

Al Unser (1965–1987) 39

Bobby Unser (1966–1981) 35

Michael Andretti (1986–) 35

Source: Championship Auto Racing Teams

*Through 2002

Top 10 College Sports in the United States

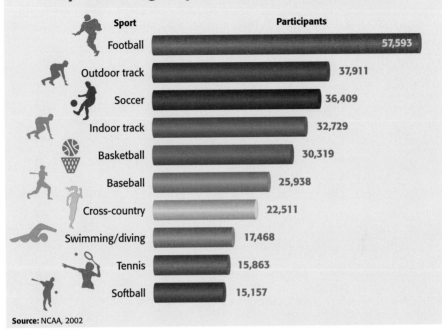

Sport	Participants
Football	57,593
Outdoor track	37,911
Soccer	36,409
Indoor track	32,729
Basketball	30,319
Baseball	25,938
Cross-country	22,511
Swimming/diving	17,468
Tennis	15,863
Softball	15,157

Source: NCAA, 2002

America's Favorite Spectator Sports
(percentage of Americans who listed these sports as their favorites)

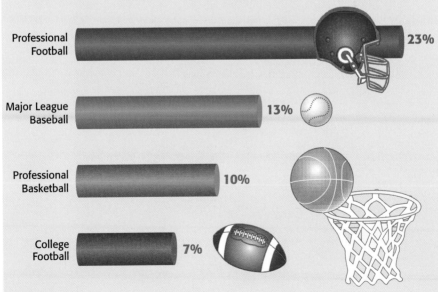

Professional Football	23%
Major League Baseball	13%
Professional Basketball	10%
College Football	7%

Source: ESPN, 2002

Winter Olympics by the Numbers

Olympiad	Year	Place	Competitors	Nations	Events
X	1968	Grenoble, France	1,158	37	35
XI	1972	Sapporo, Japan	1,006	35	35
XII	1976	Innsbruck, Austria	1,123	37	37
XIII	1980	Lake Placid, NY	1,072	37	38
XIV	1984	Sarajevo, Yugoslavia	1,274	49	39
XV	1988	Calgary, Canada	1,423	57	46
XVI	1992	Albertville, France	1,801	64	57
XVII	1994	Lillehammer, Norway	1,739	67	61
XVIII	1998	Nagano, Japan	2,302	72	68
XIX	2002	Salt Lake City, UT	2,399	77	78

Summer Olympics by the Numbers

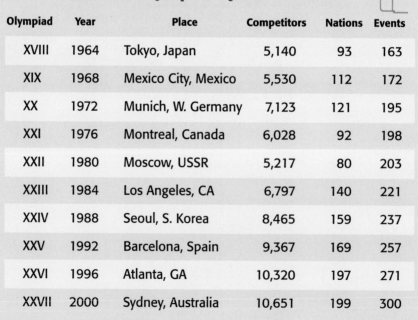

Olympiad	Year	Place	Competitors	Nations	Events
XVIII	1964	Tokyo, Japan	5,140	93	163
XIX	1968	Mexico City, Mexico	5,530	112	172
XX	1972	Munich, W. Germany	7,123	121	195
XXI	1976	Montreal, Canada	6,028	92	198
XXII	1980	Moscow, USSR	5,217	80	203
XXIII	1984	Los Angeles, CA	6,797	140	221
XXIV	1988	Seoul, S. Korea	8,465	159	237
XXV	1992	Barcelona, Spain	9,367	169	257
XXVI	1996	Atlanta, GA	10,320	197	271
XXVII	2000	Sydney, Australia	10,651	199	300

Source: International Olympic Committee

Average Number of Home Runs per Game

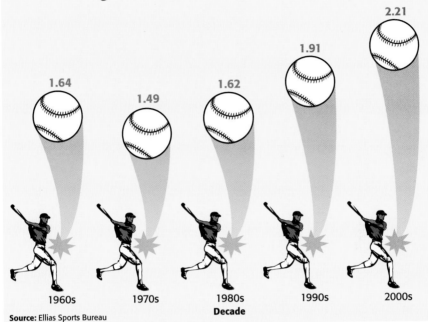

Decade	
1960s	1.64
1970s	1.49
1980s	1.62
1990s	1.91
2000s	2.21

Source: Ellias Sports Bureau

Free Time in the United States

(millions of Americans that participate
in each activity on a regular basis)

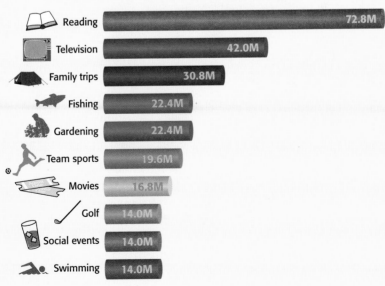

Activity	Millions
Reading	72.8M
Television	42.0M
Family trips	30.8M
Fishing	22.4M
Gardening	22.4M
Team sports	19.6M
Movies	16.8M
Golf	14.0M
Social events	14.0M
Swimming	14.0M

Source: The Harris Poll, 2002

TELEVISION AND MOVIES

Movie Moneymakers

Arnold Schwarzenegger became the world's highest-paid actor when he filmed *Terminator 3: Rise of the Machines* in 2003 for a salary of $30 million. Julia Roberts is the highest-paid female movie actor, earning $20 million for her roles in *Erin Brockovich* (2000) and *The Mexican* (2001).

Tons of TV Tape

The Museum of Television and Radio, with collections in New York City and Beverly Hills, California, has more than 100,000 programs on tape. Visitors to the museum can sit in their own private viewing areas and watch their favorite programs and commercials from the past.

Sitcom Salary Success

Sitcom actors are pulling down big salaries in Hollywood these days. For their roles in *Friends,* Jennifer Aniston, Courteney Cox Arquette, Lisa Kudrow, Matt LeBlanc, Matthew Perry, and David Schwimmer earned $1 million each for every episode in 2003. Ray Romano, star of *Everybody Loves Raymond,* earned $1.75 million per episode that same year.

That Man Makes Money!

During his impressive career, Harrison Ford has made more than 25 movies that together have earned approximately $3 billion in box office revenue. Some of his most successful movies include *Star Wars* (1977), *Raiders of the Lost Ark* (1981), and *Air Force One* (2001).

Give Someone Else a Turn!

Frasier, starring Kelsey Grammer, has won more Emmy Awards than any other television series. In 2003, *Frasier* won its 31st award to break the record previously held by *The Mary Tyler Moore Show*, with 29.

Percentage of U.S. Households With at Least One TV

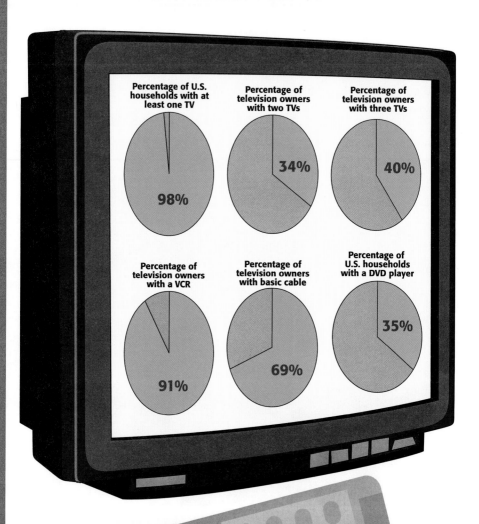

Percentage of U.S. households with at least one TV
98%

Percentage of television owners with two TVs
34%

Percentage of television owners with three TVs
40%

Percentage of television owners with a VCR
91%

Percentage of television owners with basic cable
69%

Percentage of U.S. households with a DVD player
35%

A total of 105.5 million U.S. households have at least one television.

Source: Based on data from *Statistical Abstract of the United States,* 2002; *The New York Times,* 2003

Top 5 TV-Owning Countries in the World
(Homes with a TV, in millions)

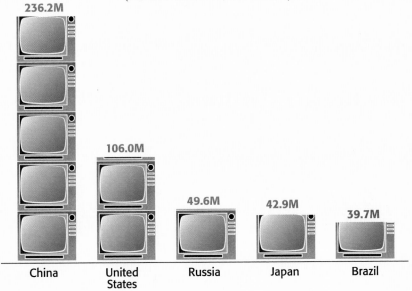

236.2M	106.0M	49.6M	42.9M	39.7M
China	United States	Russia	Japan	Brazil

Source: Based on data from *Statistical Abstract of the United States*, 2002

Top 5 U.S. "Basic" Cable Channels
(by number of subscribers)

TBS	87,000,000
The Discovery Channel	86,000,000
ESPN	85,900,000
CNN	85,600,000
USA Network	85,600,000

Source: NCTA, 2002

Top 4 U.S. Pay Cable Channels
(by number of subscribers)

67,000,000

37,000,000

25,500,000

24,500,000

| The Disney Channel | Home Box Office/Cinemax | Showtime/ The Movie Channel | Encore |

Source: NCTA, 2002

Top 5 Highest-Grossing Movies of All Time, Worldwide*
(year of release)

Titanic (1997)

$1.8 billion

Harry Potter and the Sorcerer's Stone (2001)

$975.8 million

Star Wars: Episode I— The Phantom Menace (1999)

$925.6 million

Lord of the Rings: The Two Towers (2002)

$920.4 million

Jurassic Park (1993)
$920.0 million

Source: www.boxofficemojo.com

*As of September 2003

Top 10 Highest-Grossing Movies in the U.S.*
(millions of dollars; not adjusted for inflation)

Titanic (1997) — $601.0M

Star Wars (1977) — $461.0M

E.T.: The Extra-Terrestrial (1982) — $435.1M

Star Wars: Episode 1–The Phantom Menace (1999) — $431.1M

Spider-Man (2002) — $403.7M

Jurassic Park (1993) — $357.1M

Lord of the Rings: The Two Towers (2002) — $339.8M

Finding Nemo (2003) — $339.7M

Forrest Gump (1994) — $329.7M

The Lion King (1994) — $328.5M

Source: www.boxofficemojo.com

*As of December 2003

317

Top 10 Female Actors by Total Box Office Gross
(total gross dollars, in billions, of all movies actor has appeared in)

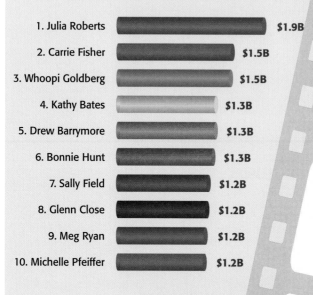

1. Julia Roberts	$1.9B
2. Carrie Fisher	$1.5B
3. Whoopi Goldberg	$1.5B
4. Kathy Bates	$1.3B
5. Drew Barrymore	$1.3B
6. Bonnie Hunt	$1.3B
7. Sally Field	$1.2B
8. Glenn Close	$1.2B
9. Meg Ryan	$1.2B
10. Michelle Pfeiffer	$1.2B

Top 10 Male Actors by Total Box Office Gross
(total gross dollars, in billions, of all movies actor has appeared in)

1. Harrison Ford	$3.2B
2. Samuel L. Jackson	$3.0B
3. Tom Hanks	$2.8B
4. Eddie Murphy	$2.4B
5. Robin Williams	$2.2B
6. Mel Gibson	$2.2B
7. Tom Cruise	$2.2B
8. Gene Hackman	$2.1B
9. Bruce Willis	$2.1B
10. Bill Paxton	$2.0B

Source: The Movie Times, 2003

Top 5 Highest-Grossing Kids' Movies of All Time, Worldwide*
(in millions)

$975.8M — Harry Potter and the Sorcerer's Stone (2001)
$869.4M — Harry Potter and the Chamber of Secrets (2002)
$789.3M — The Lion King (1994)
$772.0M — ET: The Extra-Terrestrial (1982)
$533.8M — Home Alone (1990)

Source: www.boxofficemojo.com

*As of September 2003

Top 6 Oscar-Winning Movies

Titanic (1997) — 11
Ben-Hur (1959) — 11
West Side Story (1961) — 10
Gigi (1958) — 9
The Last Emperor (1987) — 9
The English Patient (1996) — 9

Source: Academy of Motion Picture Arts and Sciences (Oscar® is a registered trademark of the Academy of Motion Picture Arts and Sciences)

Top 5 Most Expensive Movies Ever Made

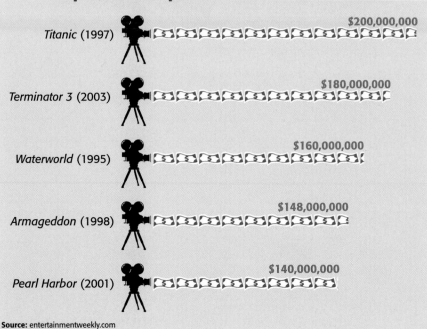

Titanic (1997) — $200,000,000

Terminator 3 (2003) — $180,000,000

Waterworld (1995) — $160,000,000

Armageddon (1998) — $148,000,000

Pearl Harbor (2001) — $140,000,000

Source: entertainmentweekly.com

Top 5 Movie-Producing Countries
(average number of movies per year)

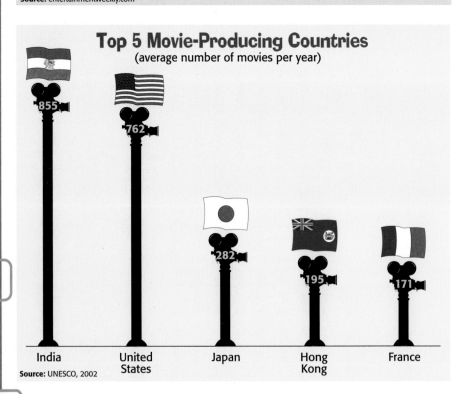

India — 855

United States — 762

Japan — 282

Hong Kong — 195

France — 171

Source: UNESCO, 2002

Top 10 Countries With the Most Box Office Revenue

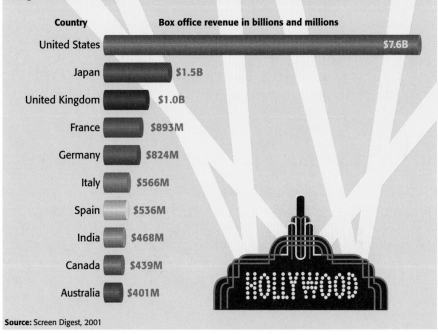

Country	Box office revenue in billions and millions
United States	$7.6B
Japan	$1.5B
United Kingdom	$1.0B
France	$893M
Germany	$824M
Italy	$566M
Spain	$536M
India	$468M
Canada	$439M
Australia	$401M

Source: Screen Digest, 2001

Top 10 U.S. Movie Studios

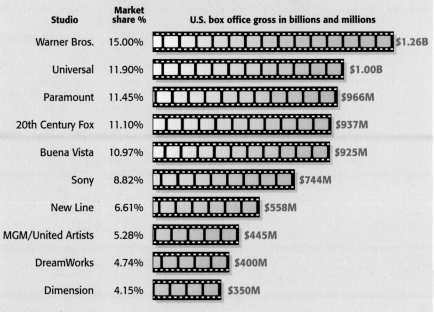

Studio	Market share %	U.S. box office gross in billions and millions
Warner Bros.	15.00%	$1.26B
Universal	11.90%	$1.00B
Paramount	11.45%	$966M
20th Century Fox	11.10%	$937M
Buena Vista	10.97%	$925M
Sony	8.82%	$744M
New Line	6.61%	$558M
MGM/United Artists	5.28%	$445M
DreamWorks	4.74%	$400M
Dimension	4.15%	$350M

Source: Screen Digest, 2002

TRANSPORTATION

The Need For Speed

The fastest passenger train in the United States is the Acela Express run by Amtrak. This train can reach a top speed of 150 mph (240 km/h) on updated tracks in Rhode Island and Massachusetts, but older transit lines between Washington, D.C. and New York limit it to a top speed of 135 mph (216 km/h).

Car Crazy

With more than 145 million automobiles, the United States has more cars than any other country. In fact, more than 30% of all the automobiles in the world are in the United States. So it's not surprising that some 90% of U.S. residents have access to a car.

Subway Stats

The MTA of New York City has the most subway stations of any subway system in the world with 490. There are 26 train lines with 6,400 train cars that run on 656 miles (1,056 km) of subway track. About 1.3 billion passengers ride on the city's subway system each year!

Train Traffic

The East Japan Railway Company carries the most train riders in the world. Approximately 16.2 million passengers board the trains every day. The trains make about 2,220 trips a day and operate on 4,684 miles (7,538 km) of track.

Boeing Basics

With all of the commercial flights in its history, the aircraft manufacturer Boeing's 747 fleet has logged more than 35 billion statute miles (56 billion km). That's enough to make 74,000 trips to the moon and back. In addition, the fleet has flown 3.6 billion people, or the equivalent of more than half of the world's population.

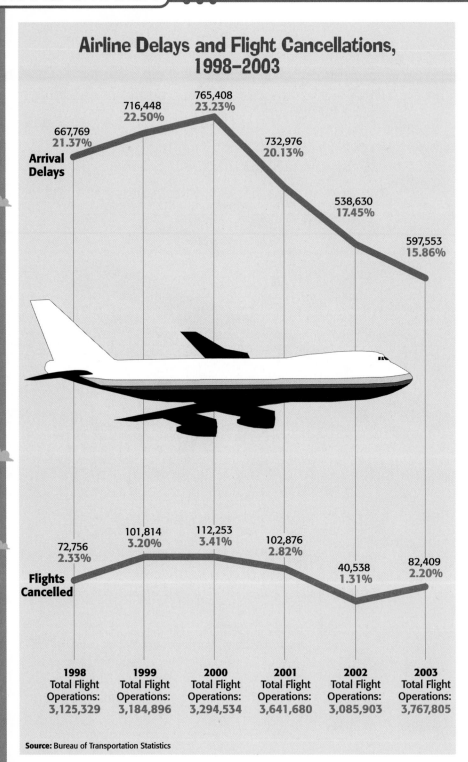

Airline Delays and Flight Cancellations, 1998–2003

Arrival Delays

667,769
21.37%

716,448
22.50%

765,408
23.23%

732,976
20.13%

538,630
17.45%

597,553
15.86%

Flights Cancelled

72,756
2.33%

101,814
3.20%

112,253
3.41%

102,876
2.82%

40,538
1.31%

82,409
2.20%

1998	**1999**	**2000**	**2001**	**2002**	**2003**
Total Flight Operations:	Total Flight Operations:	Total Flight Operations:	Total Flight Operations:	Total Flight Operations:	Total Flight Operations:
3,125,329	3,184,896	3,294,534	3,641,680	3,085,903	3,767,805

Source: Bureau of Transportation Statistics

How Americans Get to Work
(workers 16 years old and over)

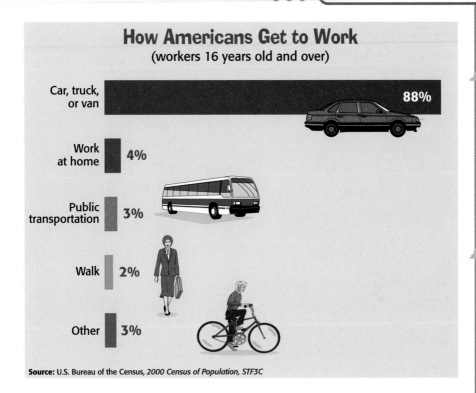

Car, truck, or van — 88%

Work at home — 4%

Public transportation — 3%

Walk — 2%

Other — 3%

Source: U.S. Bureau of the Census, *2000 Census of Population, STF3C*

Top 10 Busiest World Airports
(ranked by number of annual passengers, in millions)

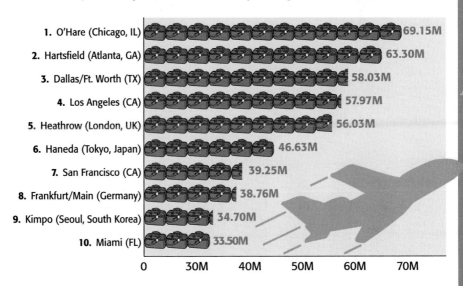

1. O'Hare (Chicago, IL) — 69.15M
2. Hartsfield (Atlanta, GA) — 63.30M
3. Dallas/Ft. Worth (TX) — 58.03M
4. Los Angeles (CA) — 57.97M
5. Heathrow (London, UK) — 56.03M
6. Haneda (Tokyo, Japan) — 46.63M
7. San Francisco (CA) — 39.25M
8. Frankfurt/Main (Germany) — 38.76M
9. Kimpo (Seoul, South Korea) — 34.70M
10. Miami (FL) — 33.50M

0   30M   40M   50M   60M   70M

Source: Airports Association Council International–North America; Air Transport Association of America, 2001

Who Is Driving in the United States?
(number and percentage of drivers by age group)

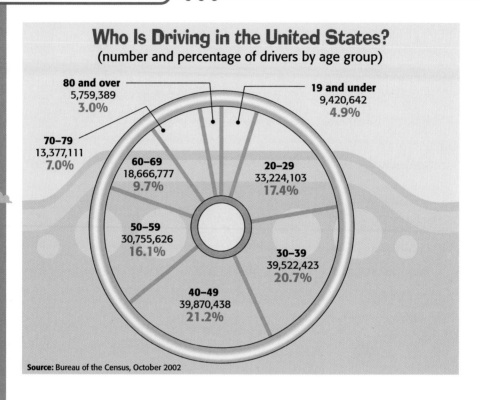

80 and over
5,759,389
3.0%

70–79
13,377,111
7.0%

60–69
18,666,777
9.7%

50–59
30,755,626
16.1%

40–49
39,870,438
21.2%

19 and under
9,420,642
4.9%

20–29
33,224,103
17.4%

30–39
39,522,423
20.7%

Source: Bureau of the Census, October 2002

Increase of U.S. Vehicle Travel, 1960–2002
(Percentage of increase in miles of vehicle travel, per vehicle)

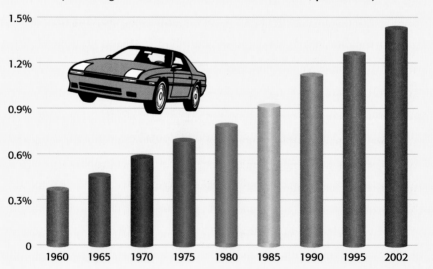

Year	1960	1965	1970	1975	1980	1985	1990	1995	2002

(Y-axis: 0, 0.3%, 0.6%, 0.9%, 1.2%, 1.5%)

Source: Federal Highway Administration, 2003

5 Best States in Safety Belt Usage, 2003
(by percentage of all passengers using safety belts)

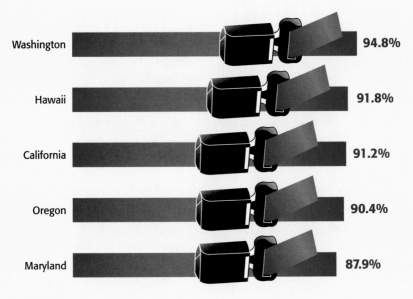

Washington	94.8%
Hawaii	91.8%
California	91.2%
Oregon	90.4%
Maryland	87.9%

5 Worst States in Safety Belt Usage, 2003
(by percentage of all passengers using safety belts)

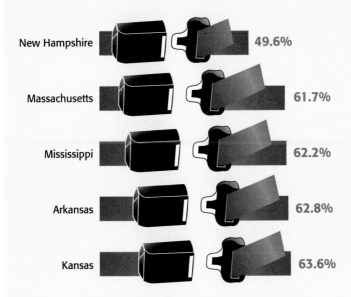

New Hampshire	49.6%
Massachusetts	61.7%
Mississippi	62.2%
Arkansas	62.8%
Kansas	63.6%

Source: U.S. Department of Transportation

327

UNITED NATIONS

No Tricks, Just Treats

Over the past 53 years, school children have raised $119 million for the underprivileged children of the world by collecting money instead of candy on Halloween. The donations go to UNICEF, the United Nations Children's Fund.

Awesome Ambassador

Jeanne Kirkpatrick was the United States' first female ambassador to the United Nations. She was appointed by President Ronald Reagan in 1981.

Countries That Contribute

The top seven financial contributors to the United Nations are the United States (25%); Japan (17.9%); Germany (9.6%); France (6.5%); Italy (5.4%); the United Kingdom (5.1%); and Russia (2.9%). Collectively, they account for more than 72% of the regular UN budget.

Headquarters History

The UN headquarters building was constructed in New York City between 1949 and 1950. The land used for the site was purchased with a donation of $8.5 million by John D. Rockefeller, Jr. UN headquarters officially opened on January 9, 1951. The land is now considered international territory.

The United Nations at a Glance

INTERNATIONAL COURT OF JUSTICE

- Principal judicial arm of UN
- Headquarters at the Peace Palace in The Hague, Netherlands
- Settles matters of international law
- Contains 15 judges, each elected to 9-year terms

GENERAL ASSEMBLY

- Main deliberative organ of UN
- Composed of members from all member states; each has one vote
- Key decisions require two-thirds majority; others require simple majority
- Meets at world headquarters in New York City

ECONOMIC AND SOCIAL COUNCIL

- Serves as central forum for discussion of international economic and social issues; formulates policies
- Conducts studies
- Coordinates activities of special agencies around the world
- Composed of 54 members, each elected for 3-year terms by the General Assembly

Includes:
UNESCO (UN Educational, Scientific, and Cultural Organization)
WHO (World Health Organization)
UNICEF (UN Children's Fund)

Source: www.un.org, 2002

Total Member States in the U.N.: 191

SECURITY COUNCIL

- 15 members; 5 permanent and 10 elected by General Assembly for 2-year terms
- Responsible for maintaining international peace and security
- Representatives of each member present at UN headquarters at all times
- Mediates and arbitrates to try to bring about peaceful resolutions to global conflicts
- Deploys peacekeeping forces
- Imposes economic and other sanctions
- Presidency of the council rotates by member countries

SECRETARIAT

- International staff in New York and around world that supports the other divisions of the UN
- Members prepare studies, organize conferences, monitor UN activity and events, interpret speeches, work with the media and in educational areas
- Staff is made up of more than 8,900 men and women from approximately 170 countries

TRUSTEESHIP COUNCIL

- Chartered to administer and oversee issues regarding UN trust territories
- Suspended operation in 1994, when last remaining trust gained independence

Contact information:
United Nations
Publications
Room 1059
New York, NY 10017
212-963-1234

Web site:
www.un.org

The 191 Member Countries of the United Nations

Afghanistan (Nov. 19, 1946)
Albania (Dec. 14, 1955)
Algeria (Oct. 8, 1962)
Andorra (July 28, 1993)
Angola (Dec. 1, 1976)
Antigua and Barbuda (Nov. 11, 1981)
Argentina (Oct. 24, 1945)
Armenia (Mar. 2, 1992)
Australia (Nov. 1, 1945)
Austria (Dec. 14, 1955)
Azerbaijan (Mar. 2, 1992)
Bahamas (Sept. 18, 1973)
Bahrain (Sept. 21, 1971)
Bangladesh (Sept. 17, 1974)
Barbados (Dec. 9, 1966)
Belarus (Oct. 24, 1945)
Belgium (Dec. 27, 1945)
Belize (Sept. 25, 1981)
Benin (Sept. 20, 1960)
Bhutan (Sept. 21, 1971)
Bolivia (Nov. 14, 1945)
Bosnia and Herzegovina (May 22, 1992)
Botswana (Oct. 17, 1966)
Brazil (Oct. 24, 1945)
Brunei Darussalam (Sept. 21, 1984)
Bulgaria (Dec. 14, 1955)
Burkina Faso (Sept. 20, 1960)
Burundi (Sept. 18, 1962)
Cambodia (Dec. 14, 1955)
Cameroon (Sept. 20, 1960)
Canada (Nov. 9, 1945)
Cape Verde (Sept. 16, 1975)
Central African Republic (Sept. 20, 1960)
Chad (Sept. 20, 1960)
Chile (Oct. 24, 1945)
China (Oct. 24, 1945)
Colombia (Nov. 5, 1945)
Comoros (Nov. 12, 1975)
Congo (Sept. 20, 1960)
Costa Rica (Nov. 2, 1945)
Côte d'Ivoire (Ivory Coast) (Sept. 20, 1960)
Croatia (May 22, 1992)
Cuba (Oct. 24, 1945)
Cyprus (Sept. 20, 1960)
Czech Republic (Jan. 19, 1993)
Democratic People's Republic of Korea
   (Sept. 17, 1991)
Democratic Republic of the Congo (Sept. 20, 1960)

Denmark (Oct. 24, 1945)
Djibouti (Sept. 20, 1977)
Dominica (Dec. 18, 1978)
Dominican Republic (Oct. 24, 1945)
Ecuador (Dec. 21, 1945)
Egypt (Oct. 24, 1945)
El Salvador (Oct. 24, 1945)
Equatorial Guinea (Nov. 12, 1968)
Eritrea (May 28, 1993)
Estonia (Sept. 17, 1991)
Ethiopia (Nov. 13, 1945)
Fiji (Oct. 13, 1970)
Finland (Dec. 14, 1955)
France (Oct. 24, 1945)
Gabon (Sept. 20, 1960)
Gambia (Sept. 21, 1965)
Georgia (July 31, 1992)
Germany (Sept. 18, 1973)
Ghana (Mar. 8, 1957)
Greece (Oct. 25, 1945)
Grenada (Sept. 17, 1974)
Guatemala (Nov. 21, 1945)
Guinea (Dec. 12, 1958)
Guinea-Bissau (Sept. 17, 1974)
Guyana (Sept. 20, 1966)
Haiti (Oct. 24, 1945)
Honduras (Dec. 17, 1945)
Hungary (Dec. 14, 1955)
Iceland (Nov. 19, 1946)
India (Oct. 30, 1945)
Indonesia (Sept. 28, 1950)
Iran (Islamic Republic of) (Oct. 24, 1945)
Iraq (Dec. 21, 1945)
Ireland (Dec. 14, 1955)
Israel (May 11, 1949)
Italy (Dec. 14, 1955)
Jamaica (Sept. 18, 1962)
Japan (Dec. 18, 1956)
Jordan (Dec. 14, 1955)
Kazakhstan (Mar. 2, 1992)
Kenya (Dec. 16, 1963)
Kiribati (Sept. 14, 1999)
Kuwait (May 14, 1963)
Kyrgyzstan (Mar. 2, 1992)
Lao People's Democratic Republic (Dec. 14, 1955)
Latvia (Sept. 17, 1991)
Lebanon (Oct. 24, 1945)
Lesotho (Oct. 17, 1966)

Source: United Nations Press Release, 2003 (www.un.org)

Liberia (Nov. 2, 1945)
Libyan Arab Jamahiriya (Dec. 14, 1955)
Liechtenstein (Sept. 18, 1990)
Lithuania (Sept. 17, 1991)
Luxembourg (Oct. 24, 1945)
Madagascar (Sept. 20, 1960)
Malawi (Dec. 1, 1964)
Malaysia (Sept. 17, 1957)
Maldives (Sept. 21, 1965)
Mali (Sept. 28, 1960)
Malta (Dec. 1, 1964)
Marshall Islands (Sept. 17, 1991)
Mauritania (Oct. 27, 1961)
Mauritius (Apr. 24, 1968)
Mexico (Nov. 7, 1945)
Micronesia (Federated States of)
   (Sept. 17, 1991)
Monaco (May 28, 1993)
Mongolia (Oct. 27, 1961)
Morocco (Nov. 12, 1956)
Mozambique (Sept. 16, 1975)
Myanmar (Apr. 19, 1948)
Namibia (Apr. 23, 1990)
Nauru (Sept. 14, 1999)
Nepal (Dec. 14, 1955)
Netherlands (Dec. 10, 1945)
New Zealand (Oct. 24, 1945)
Nicaragua (Oct. 24, 1945)
Niger (Sept. 20, 1960)
Nigeria (Oct. 7, 1960)
Norway (Nov. 27, 1945)
Oman (Oct. 7, 1971)
Pakistan (Sept. 30, 1947)
Palau (Dec. 15, 1994)
Panama (Nov. 13, 1945)
Papua New Guinea (Oct. 10, 1975)
Paraguay (Oct. 24, 1945)
Peru (Oct. 31, 1945)
Philippines (Oct. 24, 1945)
Poland (Oct. 24, 1945)
Portugal (Dec. 14, 1955)
Qatar (Sept. 21, 1971)
Republic of Korea (Sept. 17, 1991)
Republic of Moldova (Mar. 2, 1992)
Romania (Dec. 14, 1955)
Russian Federation (Oct. 24, 1945)
Rwanda (Sept. 18, 1962)
Saint Kitts and Nevis (Sept. 23, 1983)
Saint Lucia (Sept. 18, 1979)
Saint Vincent and the Grenadines (Sept. 16, 1980)

Samoa (Dec. 15, 1976)
San Marino (Mar. 2, 1992)
São Tomé and Príncipe (Sept. 16, 1975)
Saudi Arabia (Oct. 24, 1945)
Senegal (Sept. 28, 1960)
Serbia and Montenegro (Nov. 1, 2000)
Seychelles (Sept. 21, 1976)
Sierra Leone (Sept. 27, 1961)
Singapore (Sept. 21, 1965)
Slovakia (Jan. 19, 1993)
Slovenia (May 22, 1992)
Solomon Islands (Sept. 19, 1978)
Somalia (Sept. 20, 1960)
South Africa (Nov. 7, 1945)
Spain (Dec. 14, 1955)
Sri Lanka (Dec. 14, 1955)
Sudan (Nov. 12, 1956)
Suriname (Dec. 4, 1975)
Swaziland (Sept. 24, 1968)
Sweden (Nov. 19, 1946)
Switzerland (Sept. 10, 2002)
Syrian Arab Republic (Oct. 24, 1945)
Tajikistan (Mar. 2, 1992)
Thailand (Dec. 16, 1946)
The former Yugoslav Republic of Macedonia
   (Apr. 8, 1993)
Timor-Leste (East Timor) (Sept. 27, 2002)
Togo (Sept. 20, 1960)
Tonga (Sept. 14, 1999)
Trinidad and Tobago (Sept. 18, 1962)
Tunisia (Nov. 12, 1956)
Turkey (Oct. 24, 1945)
Turkmenistan (Mar. 2, 1992)
Tuvalu (Sept. 5, 1999)
Uganda (Oct. 25, 1962)
Ukraine (Oct. 24, 1945)
United Arab Emirates (Dec. 9, 1971)
United Kingdom of Great Britain and
   Northern Ireland (Oct. 24, 1945)
United Republic of Tanzania (Dec. 14, 1961)
United States of America (Oct. 24, 1945)
Uruguay (Dec. 18, 1945)
Uzbekistan (Mar. 2, 1992)
Vanuatu (Sept. 15, 1981)
Venezuela (Nov. 15, 1945)
Vietnam (Sept. 20, 1977)
Yemen (Sept. 30, 1947)
Zambia (Dec. 1, 1964)
Zimbabwe (Aug. 25, 1980)

Note: Dates in parentheses are dates of official membership.

WEATHER

Sizeable Snowflake

The largest snowflake ever to be documented measured 15 inches (38 cm) wide and 8 inches (20 cm) thick. This giant snowflake fell on January 28, 1887, in Fort Keogh, Montana. A mailman actually observed many of these giant flakes falling over an area of several miles during the same storm.

Hold on to Your Hat

Mount Washington, New Hampshire, has recorded the world's fastest wind at a speed of 231 miles per hour (371.75 km/h) on April 12, 1934. That's more than three and a half times faster than the speed limit on most highways. Mount Washington is the highest point in New Hampshire at 6,288 feet (1,918 m) and is part of the White Mountain Range.

Temperature Torture

The highest temperature ever recorded in the United States was in Death Valley, California, on July 10, 1913, with an unbearable 134°F (57°C). The lowest temperature recorded in the United States was −80°F (−62°C) in Prospect Creek, Alaska, on January 23, 1971.

Drastic Degree Drop

From January 23rd to the 24th in 1916, the temperature in Browning, Montana dropped 100°F (56°C) from 44° to −56°F (7° to −49°C). This chilly little town is located close to Glacier National Park.

Get the Umbrella, Quick!

The world's record for the greatest rainfall in one minute belongs to Unionville, Maryland. On July 4, 1956, 1.23 inches (3.1 cm) of rain fell in just 60 seconds. The U.S. record for the most rain in a 24-hour period occurred in Alvin, Texas, on July 25–26, 1979, when 43 inches (109 cm) of rain fell. That's about equal to the height of a five-year-old child!

Top 5 Driest U.S. Cities
(mean annual precipitation)

Yuma, Arizona — 2.65" (6.7 cm)

Las Vegas, Nevada — 4.19" (10.6 cm)

Bishop, California — 5.61" (14.2 cm)

Bakersfield, California — 5.72" (14.5 cm)

Phoenix, Arizona — 7.11" (18.0 cm)

Source: National Climatic Data Center

Top 5 Wettest U.S. Cities
(mean annual precipitation)

Mt. Waialeale, Hawaii — 460.0" (1,168 cm)

Mobile, Alabama — 64.6" (164 cm)

New Orleans, Louisiana — 59.7" (152 cm)

Miami, Florida — 57.5" (146 cm)

Charleston, South Carolina — 51.6" (131 cm)

Source: National Oceanic and Atmospheric Administration (NOAA)

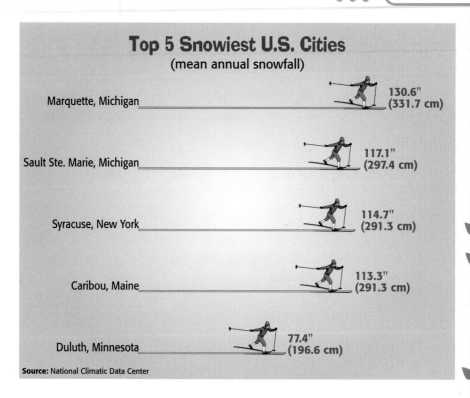

Top 5 Snowiest U.S. Cities
(mean annual snowfall)

Marquette, Michigan — 130.6" (331.7 cm)

Sault Ste. Marie, Michigan — 117.1" (297.4 cm)

Syracuse, New York — 114.7" (291.3 cm)

Caribou, Maine — 113.3" (291.3 cm)

Duluth, Minnesota — 77.4" (196.6 cm)

Source: National Climatic Data Center

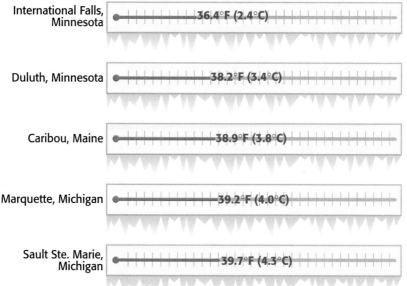

Top 5 Coldest U.S. Cities
(average annual daily low temperature)

International Falls, Minnesota — 36.4°F (2.4°C)

Duluth, Minnesota — 38.2°F (3.4°C)

Caribou, Maine — 38.9°F (3.8°C)

Marquette, Michigan — 39.2°F (4.0°C)

Sault Ste. Marie, Michigan — 39.7°F (4.3°C)

Source: National Climatic Data Center

Top 5 Hottest U.S. Cities
(average annual high temperature)

Key West, Florida — 77.7°F (25.4°C)

Miami, Florida — 75.6°F (24.2°C)

West Palm Beach, Florida — 74.6°F (23.7°C)

Fort Myers, Florida — 73.9°F (23.3°C)

Yuma, Arizona — 73.9°F (23.3°C)

Source: National Climatic Data Center

Worst U.S. Natural Disasters

Drought

1930s Many states: longest drought of the twentieth century. Peak periods were 1930, 1934, 1936, 1939, and 1940. During 1934, dry regions stretched from New York and Pennsylvania across the Great Plains to the California coast. A great "Dust Bowl" covered some 50 million acres in the south central plains during the winter of 1935–1936.

Earthquake

1906 April 18, San Francisco, CA: earthquake accompanied by fire razed more than 4 sq. mi. (10 sq. km); more than 500 dead or missing.

Flood

1889 May 31, Johnstown, PA: more than 2,200 died in a flood that caused fires, explosions, and drownings.

Hurricane

1900 August 27–September 15, Galveston, TX: more than 6,000 died from the devastating combination of high winds and a tidal wave.

Tornado

1925 March 18, Great Tri-State Tornado: Missouri, Illinois, and Indiana; 695 deaths. Eight additional tornadoes in Kentucky, Tennessee, and Alabama raised the toll to 792 dead.

Winter Storm

1888 March 11–14, East Coast: the Blizzard of 1888. Four hundred people died, and as much as 5 feet (1.6 m) of snow fell. Damage was estimated at $20 million.

Source: National Weather Service; U.S. Department of Commerce

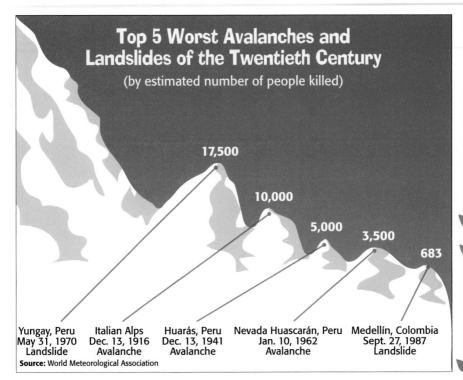

Top 5 Worst Avalanches and Landslides of the Twentieth Century
(by estimated number of people killed)

17,500

10,000

5,000

3,500

683

Yungay, Peru	Italian Alps	Huarás, Peru	Nevada Huascarán, Peru	Medellín, Colombia
May 31, 1970	Dec. 13, 1916	Dec. 13, 1941	Jan. 10, 1962	Sept. 27, 1987
Landslide	Avalanche	Avalanche	Avalanche	Landslide

Source: World Meteorological Association

Top 5 Worst Floods of the Twentieth Century
(by estimated number of people killed)

Huang He River, China
August 1931 — 3,700,000

Bangladesh
November 13, 1970 — 300,000–500,000

Henan, China
1939 — more than 200,000

Chang Jiang River, China
September 1911 — 100,000

Bengal, India
November 15–16, 1942 — 40,000

Source: U.S. State Department; United Nations

WEIGHTS AND MEASURES

A Quick Conversion

A quick way to get a rough estimate while converting Celsius temperature to Fahrenheit is to double the number and add 30. For example, if the temperature was 20° Celsius, it would be 70° Fahrenheit (20 x 2 + 30 = 70).

Differing in Degrees

Here are some examples of common temperature measurements. The average human body temperature is 98.6°F (37°C). A pot of boiling water is 212°F (100°C). A comfortable room temperature would be around 70°F (21°C). The temperature of a cool drink would be about 57°F (14°C).

Metric Meanings in Sports

Many sports competitions are international and most are measured using the metric system. How does this relate to the U.S. equivalent? Standing on a 10-meter diving platform is similar to standing on the roof of a three-story building. Competitors in a 5K race run 5 kilometers (3.1 miles)—longer than 54 football fields laid end-to-end. Female gymnasts flip and bounce on a balance beam that is only 10 centimeters (3.9 inches) wide— about the width of a paperback book.

Trading in Tens

The metric system was invented by the French Academy of Sciences at the end of the eighteenth century. They decided to base it on a decimal system that has a base of 10. This worked well because many cultures used 10 as the basis of their number systems. The new metric system made trade easier among different villages.

Weights and Measures

Converting Household Measures

From	To	Multiply by
dozens	units	12
baker's dozens	units	13
teaspoons	milliliters	4.93
teaspoons	tablespoons	0.33
tablespoons	milliliters	14.79
tablespoons	teaspoons	3
cups	liters	0.24
cups	pints	0.50
cups	quarts	0.25
pints	cups	2
pints	liters	0.47
pints	quarts	0.50
quarts	cups	4
quarts	gallons	0.25
quarts	liters	0.95
quarts	pints	2
gallons	liters	3.79
gallons	quarts	4

Simple Metric Conversion Table

To convert	To	Multiply by	To convert	To	Multiply by
centimeters	feet	0.0328	kilograms	pounds	2.205
centimeters	inches	0.3937	kilometers	feet	3,280.8
cubic centimeters	cubic inches	0.0610	kilometers	miles	0.6214
cubic feet	cubic meters	0.0283	knots	miles/hour	1.151
degrees	radians	0.0175	liters	gallons	0.2642
feet	centimeters	30.48	liters	pints	2.113
feet	meters	0.3048	meters	feet	3.281
gallons	liters	3.785	miles	kilometers	1.609
gal. water	lb. water	8.3453	ounces	grams	28.3495
grams	ounces	0.0353	pounds	kilograms	0.4536
inches	centimeters	2.54			

Length or Distance

U.S. Customary System

1 foot (ft.)	=	12 inches (in.)		
1 yard (yd.)	=	3 feet	=	36 inches
1 rod (rd)	=	5½ yards	=	16½ feet
1 furlong (fur.)	=	40 rods	=	220 yards
	=	660 feet		
1 mile (mi.)	=	8 furlongs	=	1,760 yards
	=	5,280 feet		

An international nautical mile has been defined as 6,076.1155 feet.

Common Fractions and Their Decimal Equivalents

½	.5000	³⁄₁₁	.2727
⅓	.3333	⅘	.8000
¼	.2500	⁴⁄₇	.5714
⅕	.2000	⁴⁄₉	.4444
⅙	.1667	⁴⁄₁₁	.3636
⅐	.1429	⅚	.8333
⅛	.1250	⁵⁄₇	.7143
⅑	.1111	⅝	.6250
⅒	.1000	⁵⁄₉	.5556
¹⁄₁₁	.0909	⁵⁄₁₁	.4545
¹⁄₁₂	.0833	⁵⁄₁₂	.4167
¹⁄₁₆	.0625	⁶⁄₇	.8571
¹⁄₃₂	.0313	⁶⁄₁₁	.5455
¹⁄₆₄	.0156	⅞	.8750
⅔	.6667	⁷⁄₉	.7778
⅖	.4000	⁷⁄₁₀	.7000
²⁄₇	.2857	⁷⁄₁₁	.6364
²⁄₉	.2222	⁷⁄₁₂	.5833
²⁄₁₁	.1818	⁸⁄₉	.8889
¾	.7500	⁸⁄₁₁	.7273
⅗	.6000	⁹⁄₁₀	.9000
³⁄₇	.4286	⁹⁄₁₁	.8182
⅜	.3750	¹⁰⁄₁₁	.9091
³⁄₁₀	.3000	¹¹⁄₁₂	.9167

Six Quick Ways to Measure When You Don't Have a Ruler

1. Most credit cards are 3⅜ inches by 2⅛ inches.
2. Standard business cards are printed 3½ inches wide by 2 inches long.
3. Floor tiles are usually manufactured in 12-inch by 12-inch squares.
4. U.S. paper currency is 6⅛ inches wide by 2⅝ inches long.
5. The diameter of a quarter is approximately 1 inch, and the diameter of a penny is approximately ¾ of an inch.
6. A standard sheet of paper is 8½ inches wide and 11 inches long.

Temperature Conversions

Fahrenheit		Celsius
475°	=	246.1°
450	=	232.2
425	=	218.3
400	=	204.4
375	=	190.6
350	=	176.7
325	=	162.8
300	=	148.9
275	=	135.0
250	=	121.1
225	=	107.2
212	=	100.0
110	=	43.3
105	=	40.6
100	=	37.8
95	=	35.0
90	=	32.2
85	=	29.4
80	=	26.7
75	=	23.9
70	=	21.1
65	=	18.3
60	=	15.6
55	=	12.8
50	=	10.0
45	=	7.2
40	=	4.4
35	=	1.7
32	=	0.0
30	=	−1.1
25	=	−3.9
20	=	−6.7
15	=	−9.4
10	=	−12.2
5	=	−15.0
0	=	−17.8
−5	=	−20.6
−10	=	−23.3
−15	=	−26.1
−20	=	−28.9
−25	=	−31.7
−30	=	−34.4
−35	=	−37.2
−40	=	−40.0
−45	=	−42.8

ZODIAC

Astrology 101

Astrology is an interesting mix of subjects that are studied in school. The names of the signs are from Roman and Greek mythology. The dates on which the signs are based, as well as the locations of stars, are concepts from mathematics and astronomy. And history comes into play because the practice of astrology goes back thousands of years.

Following the Signs

Approximately 25% of Americans believe that the positions of the stars and planets have an effect on people's lives. However, almost 90% of the people interviewed knew their zodiac signs; some 70% read their horoscopes daily; and 85% agreed that the description of their birth sign described their personality.

Planet-Inspired Profits

Americans' interest in astrology is growing quickly. Shoppers bought approximately 20 million books on astrology in 2002—more than four times the number that were sold just two years before.

Ancient Astrology

The original zodiac signs are thought to have originated in Mesopotamia as far back as 2000 B.C. The Greeks later picked up some of the symbols from the Babylonians and then passed them onto other ancient cultures. Some other societies that developed their own zodiac charts based on these early ideas include Egypt, China, and the Aztecs.

Plotting the Planets

The positions of the planets in the zodiac on the day you are born determines your astrological sign.

Zodiac Signs

		Planet	Element	Personality Traits
OR		Saturn	earth	serious, domineering, ambitious, blunt, loyal, persistent
Capricorn, the Goat, December 22–January 19				
OR		Uranus	air	independent, unselfish, generous, idealistic
Aquarius, the Water Bearer, January 20–February 18				
OR		Neptune	water	compassionate, sympathetic, sensitive, timid, methodical
Pisces, the Fishes, February 19–March 20				
OR		Mars	fire	independent, enthusiastic, bold, impulsive, confident
Aries, the Ram, March 21–April 19				
OR		Venus	earth	decisive, determined, stubborn, stable
Taurus, the Bull, April 20–May 20				
OR Ⅱ		Mercury	air	curious, sociable, ambitious, alert, intelligent, temperamental
Gemini, the Twins, May 21–June 21				

Source: Nightstar Astrology; zodiac_signs.htm

		Planet	Element	Personality Traits
OR		Moon	water	organized, busy, moody, sensitive, supportive
Cancer, the Crab, June 22–July 22				
OR		Sun	fire	born leader, bold, noble, generous, enthusiastic, sympathetic
Leo, the Lion, July 23–August 22				
OR		Mercury	earth	analytical, critical, intellectual, clever
Virgo, the Virgin, August 23–September 22				
OR		Venus	air	affectionate, thoughtful, sympathetic, orderly, persuasive
Libra, the Scales, September 23–October 23				
OR		Mars	water	intense, fearless, loyal, willful
Scorpio, the Scorpion, October 24–November 21				
OR		Jupiter	fire	energetic, good-natured, practical, clever
Sagittarius, the Archer, November 22–December 21				

INDEX

Photo Credits
Cover: Computer mouse: ©PhotoDisc/PictureQuest; Flag: ©Steve Allen/Brand X Pictures/ PictureQuest; Flower (pink Dahlia): ©C Squared Studios/Photodisc/PictureQuest; Frog: ©DigitalVision/PictureQuest; Globe: ©The Studio Dog/Photodisc/PictureQuest; Hand with CD: ©Photodisc Green/Getty Images; Hourglass: ©Photodisc Green/Getty Images; Lizard: ©DigitalVision/PictureQuest; Movie clapboard: ©Burke/Triolo/Brand X Pictures/PictureQuest; Soccer ball: ©C Squared Studios/Photodisc/PictureQuest; Telescope: ©Burke/Triolo/ Brand X Pictures/ PictureQuest
Interior: Pages 4–5: ©NASA/Photodisc/PictureQuest; page 13: ©DigitalVision/PictureQuest; pages 24–25: ©Ron Chapple/Photis/PictureQuest; pages 30–31: ©AP/Wide World; 40–41: ©Steve Allen/Brand X Pictures/PictureQuest; pages 48–49: ©Don Farrall/Getty Images; pages 60–61: ©Corbis Images/ PictureQuest; pages 74–75: ©Ross Durant/FoodPix/Getty Images; pages 78–79: ©Greg Ceo/Getty Images; pages 88–89: ©Monica Lau/Getty Images; page 101: ©Brian Hagiwara/Brand X Pictures/PictureQuest; pages 106–107: ©DigitalVision/PictureQuest; pages 114–115: ©C Squared Studios/Photodisc/PictureQuest; pages 124, 125: ©C Squared Studios/ Photodisc/PictureQuest; pages 132–133: ©CORBIS; pages 150–151: ©Cartesia/Photodisc Imaging/Getty Images; pages 170–171: ©CORBIS; page 183: Rubberball Productions/Getty Images; pages 198–199: ©Jeremy Woodhouse/Photodisc/Getty Images; pages 212–213: ©Photodisc Green/Getty Images; page 225: ©Photodisc Blue/Getty Images; page 233: ©Brand X Pictures/Getty Images; pages 238–239: ©Creatas/PictureQuest; ©PhotoSpin; page 251: ©CORBIS; page 260: ©Alan Bailey/RubberBall Productions/PictureQuest; page 267: ©Burke/Triolo/Brand X Pictures/PictureQuest; page 275: ©C Squared Studios/Photodisc/PictureQuest; page 283: ©AMPAS; pages 286–287: ©Thinkstock/PictureQuest; page 295: ©Image Farm/PictureQuest; pages 298–299: ©Karl Weatherly/CORBIS; pages 312–313: ©PhotoSpin and ©AP/Wide World; pages 322–323: ©Tecmap Corporation, Eric Curry/CORBIS; page 329: ©Henryk T. Kaiser/ Index Stock Imagery/PictureQuest; pages 334–335: ©AP/Wide World; page 341: ©IPS/Index Stock Imagery/PictureQuest; page 345: ©Photodisc Green/Getty Images